RELIGION AND THE
PUBLIC ORDER

RELIGION
AND THE
PUBLIC ORDER

1964

AN ANNUAL REVIEW OF CHURCH AND STATE
AND OF RELIGION, LAW, AND SOCIETY

THE INSTITUTE OF CHURCH AND STATE
VILLANOVA UNIVERSITY SCHOOL OF LAW

Edited by DONALD A. GIANNELLA

Chicago and London

THE UNIVERSITY OF CHICAGO PRESS

Library of Congress Catalog Card Number: 64–17164

THE UNIVERSITY OF CHICAGO PRESS, CHICAGO & LONDON
The University of Toronto Press, Toronto 5, Canada

CONTENTS

ARTICLES

ROBERT G. McCLOSKEY

PRINCIPLES, POWERS, AND VALUES: THE ESTABLISHMENT CLAUSE AND THE SUPREME COURT

American constitutional history has been in large part a spasmodic running debate over the behavior of the Supreme Court, but in 170 years we have made curiously little progress toward establishing the terms of this war of words, much less toward achieving concord. The justices themselves have usually felt obliged to confine their opinions to the more formalistic aspects of the matter, *i.e.*, to the historical-technical dimension rather narrowly conceived. We sometimes get hints, usually in dissenting opinions, that the justices are aware of the possible relevancy of other considerations. When Mr. Justice Frankfurter warned the judiciary against "political thickets"[1] and spoke of subjects not "meet for judicial judgment,"[2] he surely was expressing doubts about the Court's power to supervise apportionment policies, as well as about the propriety of its doing so. When Mr. Justice Field equated the Fourteenth Amendment with his own ethic of economic liberty,[3] he was telling us what values the amendment ought

---

Robert G. McCloskey is Professor of Government, Harvard University.

[1] Colegrove v. Green, 328 U.S. 549, 556 (1946).

[2] Baker v. Carr, 369 U.S. 186, 289 (1962) (dissenting opinion).

[3] Butchers' Union Slaughter-House and Live-Stock Landing Co. v. Crescent City Live-Stock Landing and Slaughter-House Co., 111 U.S. 746, 756–57 (1884).

to protect, not merely contending that it had been designed to protect them. But more often than not, such misgivings as those of Frankfurter have been either ignored by the majority or countered by ringing restatements of the doctrine of judicial supremacy, while value recommendations like those of Field have been met by appeals to history and technical legalism which, however sound, fail to touch his central point.

As for observers outside the chamber, those who endorse the majority position at a given moment are often so pleased to find the Court with them on the ramparts that they are indisposed to ask whether it really belongs there. On the other hand, those who oppose the current judicial policy are likely themselves to be so result-oriented that they contribute little to an objective appraisal of the Court's performance. And even when both disputants are able to submerge their prepossessions to some degree, the dialogue remains confused because there is no common understanding of the terms of the discussion. The result is that these recurring constitutional debates resemble an endless series of re-matches between two club-boxers who have long since stopped developing their crafts autonomously and have nothing further to learn from each other. The same generalizations are launched from either side, to be met by the same evasions and parries. Familiar old ambiguities fog the controversy, and the contestants flounder among them for a while until history calls a close and it is time to retire from the arena and await the next installment. In the exchange of assertions and counter-assertions no one can be said to have won a decision on the merits, for small attempt has been made to arrive at an understanding of what the merits are.

So it has been to a very considerable extent with the modern revival of the ancient conflict. In the last decade the Supreme Court has laid claim to a range of power that is almost unexampled in judicial history. Not even John Marshall was so bold about exerting his Court's prerogative to command the nation; and only the Court of the early 1930's seems fairly comparable in the extent of its will-to-govern. As might have been predicted, this has set the old debate going again in very much its traditional form. We see once more, on the Court and elsewhere, the exchange of time-honored generalities, the suppression of premises, and the argument at cross-purposes. The complaint that the Court has wrenched historical intent to suit its preferences is met (or rather not met) by the contention that an ethical goal has been achieved.

The reminder that the Court lacks power to cure all the Republic's social ills brings forth the counter-assertion that it is legally and ethically bound to cure this one. It is as if bridge were being played with a set of rules that permitted each player to change the trump suit at any stage. Everyone wins and everyone loses, but rational assessment of what goes on is a trifle difficult.

The Categories of Evaluation

Now of course it is not suggested here that any calculus can provide automatic answers to the problem of evaluating the Court's performance. Our ultimate assessment of that performance will depend on judgments more subtle than any articulate judgment categories, and even within each category we will always encounter imponderables. But it may be possible to push a little closer to the area where imponderables do take over, to cut away at least the unnecessary ambiguities that cloud discussion. Though rational analysis cannot resolve the problem, perhaps it can identify the channels through which an observer might move on the way to his own resolution; and that would in itself carry us a step beyond the usual clash by night.

I propose in this paper to consider the modern Court's performance with respect to the establishment of religion clause of the Constitution, to attempt an orderly and comprehensive analysis of that performance, and to conclude with an appraisal based on the analysis. This program makes it necessary to begin by being as explicit as possible about the factors that may be relevant to such an analysis and appraisal, *i.e.*, to confront at the outset the issues that are usually not confronted at all.

I suggest that our evaluation of a Supreme Court decision—or of a whole line of judicial conduct—ordinarily depends on one or more of three different judgment components: the question of what have been called above "historical-technical" standards, the question of power, and the question of value. In other words, when we criticize a judicial action we are saying that the Court has misread the Constitution, or that it has overtaxed its power capabilities, or that it has chosen the wrong ethical solution. And I further suggest that a great deal of the confusion in discussions about the Court arises from the failure to distinguish between these three factors, or to be clear about which is in mind at any given time. To be sure, the factors are related, and it is ultimately necessary to consider them in relation in order to appraise the Court comprehensively. But to treat them as identical is to confuse discussion; and to slip from one to another without notice is to make discussion impossible.

It may be necessary—though it should not be—to offer a justification of this tripartite approach to the analysis of judicial behavior. There are those who would confine all evaluation to the historical-technical category and would pronounce it illegitimate even to consider issues of power or ethics.[4] There are others so dedicated to a value-oriented assessment that they regard legalistic strictures as mere pettifoggery[5] and probably still others who would prefer to think of the Court purely in terms of its power to govern. It might be sufficient comment on such viewpoints to say that, whatever our preferences, these three different judgment criteria persist in turning up in the debates over judicial behavior; we cannot tame the subject to our own liking, however pleasant this might be. Or it might be enough to rejoin that any man is welcome to restrict himself to the analytic boundaries he prefers; only that he is then obliged in the name of reason to make it clear that he is so restricting himself and must not wander outside his chosen perspectives.

But in fact both history and common sense suggest that it is desirable to take account of each of these evaluative factors. The Court has been and must be to some extent a "courtlike" institution, trading in the orthodox legal coinage of textual analysis, precedent, and "the intent of the framers." But it has also been a value-judging agency, "a national conscience . . . a channel for moral imperatives,"[6] and this role has thrust it inescapably into the arena of political policy, where power considerations cannot be ignored. Whether it should have assumed this role, with all it entails, is an old, hard question. But that it has done so seems, after the past fifty years of scholarship, beyond serious dispute; and the pattern of the past has shaped the expectations of the present. America does expect the Court to be both courtlike and

---

4 See the discussion of "atavistic regressions to the simplicities of *Marbury* v. *Madison*, to its concept of the self-applying Constitution and the self-evident function of judicial review" in BICKEL, THE LEAST DANGEROUS BRANCH 75–78 (1962). The quoted words are at 74.

5 FRANK, MARBLE PALACE—THE SUPREME COURT IN AMERICAN LIFE *passim* (1958); Arnold, *Professor Hart's Theology*, 73 HARV. L. REV. 1298 (1960).

6 Lewis, *Supreme Court Moves Again To Exert Its Powerful Influence*, N.Y. Times, June 21, 1964, §4, p. E3.

statesmanlike, a law-finding and a value-judging agency, and the modern Court has enthusiastically endorsed that dual conception of its duty. Those who would like it otherwise are entitled to their tastes, but it would seem more useful to evaluate the Court as it is rather than a Court that never was. And since the Court we have is concerned with both the historical-technical and the ethical, and since that combination of concerns raises the issue of political power, we cannot fairly overlook any of these matters in seeking to judge how well and wisely the Court is doing its work.

Although it is necessary for the sake of clarity to recognize the separate identities of these three judgment components, however, it is also necessary to recognize, as has been intimated, that the ultimate appraisal of judicial performance depends on synthesis of the three. To put a complex matter very simply, each of the components is entitled to some weight in the evaluative process, and the final result will be a product of their cumulative force. Consider for example a hypothetical decision which is solidly based in constitutional text and precedent, which aims toward a clear ethical good, and which does not seriously tax the Court's power resources. The case for such a decision would be strong indeed. But now suppose that the historical-technical justification is more questionable. The case would be weaker, even though we might still approve the decision because of our belief in its value objective and our confidence about the Court's power to carry it off. And now suppose further that such confidence diminishes and that the ethical goal seems more cloudy and disputable: the case becomes weaker still. When we say that the Court has done well or ill, we are—or ought to be—expressing the result of such a multifactor judgment process.

It is worth emphasizing that this calculus is assumed to take place in a world where pluses and minuses are always relative. We need not consider the imaginary case in which there is *no* historical-technical argument for the Court's decision or, conversely, in which the constitutional mandate is unmistakable. No matter how dearly we prize, or bitterly deprecate, a supposedly ethical objective, we cannot ask that the Court do what is plainly forbidden or refrain from doing what is plainly commanded. Nor can we require it to essay a task that is inarguably beyond its power capacities: the Court cannot be expected to stop the tides from flowing even though it might be good to stop them and even though the Constitution clearly authorized the issuance of such a command.

To be sure there will always be critics who would denounce the Court for ruling that black is black, or for failing to rule that black is white. But they are fortunately not yet a majority, and the real questions of evaluation arise in situations where the problem is to distinguish between a plausible and a less plausible historical-technical justification, a confident or a less confident estimate of the Court's power to effect its ends, and a greater or lesser belief in the value of those ends. Let us proceed to consider the Court's establishment-clause doctrines in those terms and in that order.

THE SCHOOL RELIGION DECISIONS

The discussion will be chiefly concerned with the decisions involving religion and the public schools, *i.e.,* with the line of doctrine represented by the *Everson,*[7] *McCollum,*[8] *Zorach,*[9] *Engel,*[10] and *Schempp*[11] decisions although other cases bearing on this doctrinal development will be referred to when they seem germane. These school decisions are particularly appropriate for the kind of analysis proposed, since they constitute a fairly well circumscribed package and raise sharp questions in all three of the judgment categories delineated above.

The story of the Court's performance in this area has been told so often and chewed over so much that it is unnecessary here to do more than remind the reader of its outlines. The idea that the "no establishment" principle was applicable to the states by way of the Fourteenth Amendment was first seriously discussed by the Supreme Court in 1947, in *Everson.* Mr. Justice Black, for the majority, there held that state payment of bus fares for parochial school students was a general welfare measure, not aid to religion. But he declared, before reaching that result, that actual state aid to religion was indeed constitutionally forbidden, that no government in America "can pass laws which aid one religion, aid all religions, or prefer one religion over another."[12] This standard, literally applied, was quite enough to invalidate a religious instruction program conducted in public school buildings during school

---

7 Everson v. Board of Educ., 330 U.S. 1 (1947).

8 Illinois *ex rel.* McCollum v. Board of Educ., 333 U.S. 203 (1948).

9 Zorach v. Clauson, 343 U.S. 306 (1952).

10 Engel v. Vitale, 370 U.S. 421 (1962).

11 School Dist. of Abington Township v. Schempp, 374 U.S. 203 (1963).

12 330 U.S. at 15.

hours; and Mr. Justice Black, for the Court, invoked it to strike down such a program in *McCollum*.

His opinion, however, emphasized certain factual circumstances —that the school buildings used for religious instruction were tax-supported and that the state was in a sense lending religion the coercive power of the compulsory education laws. This emphasis gave Mr. Justice Douglas an opening (albeit a very thin one) to hold for a new majority in *Zorach* that New York's "released time" religious instruction program was distinguishable from the arrangement condemned in *McCollum*, since here tax-supported buildings were not used and no coercion appeared on the record. Though not repudiating the unequivocal *Everson* standard quoted above, he proceeded to enunciate one that seems rationally irreconcilable with it: that state *encouragement* of and *co-operation* with religion is not state *aid*, that the difference between them is a question of degree, and that the question starts from the premise that "we are a religious people."[13] At this point then the Court was armed, as so often in the past, with two quite different constitutional yardsticks: the absolutist *Everson* standard forbidding all aid, and the pragmatic, "common sense" standard of *Zorach* permitting aid so long as it can be labeled "encouragement" or "co-operation" and so long as it does not exceed some undefined degree of state-church involvement. Both standards had been endorsed by a majority of the Court; neither had been nominally repudiated by a majority. The judges could take their choice between them when the next school religion case appeared.

The next important one was *Engel*, the school prayer decision, and here the majority, now again speaking through Mr. Justice Black, seemed to have chosen in favor of the all-out *Everson* principle. Indeed the opinion suggested a certain eagerness to reconfirm that principle, whether or not the case required it. For the Court explicitly refused to rest its judgment merely on the argument that the state-prescribed prayer was coercive, insisting that the "Establishment Clause . . . does not depend upon any showing of direct governmental compulsion."[14] And the only concession to *Zorach's* relativism was a hint that patriotic ceremonies and hymns might still be allowed, even though they mention a Supreme Being, presumably on the ground that their significance is primarily secular. The wall of separation now seemed nearly im-

---

13 343 U.S. at 313.
14 370 U.S. at 430.

passable once more, and Mr. Justice Douglas filed a puckish con-
currence suggesting that observances like the supplications preceding sessions of the Supreme Court and Congress were likewise
unconstitutional government support of religion.

Yet a year later in *Schempp* the Court, though forbidding the
recitation of the Lord's Prayer and Bible reading in public schools,
again somewhat moderated the spirit, if not the actual letter, of
its doctrine. The guiding principle, said Mr. Justice Clark for
the Court, is that an enactment must have "a secular legislative
purpose and a primary effect that neither advances nor inhibits
religion."[15] This might seem to be a mere restatement of the
Everson no-aid dogma, with the additional proviso that the Court
is obliged to wrestle with the enigmatic distinction between primary and secondary effects and to tread the "quicksands"[16] of
legislative purpose, before applying the dogma. But the proviso,
precisely because of the slipperiness of those distinctions may give
the Court some leeway in judging practices that have a religious
tinge.

Mr. Justice Brennan, who joined in both the opinion and judgment, believed that the Court was still free to uphold provisions
for army chaplains, invocational prayers in legislative bodies, non-
devotional Bible study, tax exemptions for religious bodies, and
other practices which do not import the dangers which the framers
of the establishment clause feared. He even ventured "to suggest
that the public schools present a unique problem,"[17] which at least
invites the inference that the no-aid principle could be construed
less strictly outside the public school context. And Justices Goldberg and Harlan, also concurring in the Court's opinion, seemed
to say that the establishment clause applied only to practices that
have "meaningful and practical impact,"[18] *i.e., de minimis non
curat lex.*

It is true that these glosses do not appear plainly on Mr. Justice
Clark's majority opinion, but the concurring justices seemed to
believe they were compatible with it, and perhaps in some para-
logical sense they are. If so the Court can be said to have reached
in *Schempp* a position somewhere between the absolutism of

---

15 374 U.S. at 222.

16 Pollak, *Foreword: Public Prayers in Public Schools,* 77 HARV. L. REV. 62, 67
(1963).

17 374 U.S. at 294.

18 374 U.S. at 308.

Engel and the pragmatism of *Zorach*. The doctrine might be stated as follows: that government action which "advances" religion is constitutionally objectionable if it creates in a substantial form the dangers the First Amendment was designed to prevent, unless its purpose and primary effect are secular, or unless the effect of omitting the action would be to inhibit or discriminate against religion. A corollary point might be that the action will be viewed with special suspicion when it concerns the public schools, and with more latitude when only adults are involved.

The Problem of Technical Legality

Now for the moment leaving aside as far as possible considerations of judicial power and ethical preference that usually intrude at this stage, how might we evaluate in historical-technical terms this record of judicial doctrine-making? Perhaps it can be agreed that the justification of a doctrine in this sense depends on two requirements: that it be plausibly based on constitutional language, intent, or custom; and that it be coherent enough for reasoned application, yet flexible enough so that it can be adapted to future and possibly unforeseen case situations.

The threshold question is whether the Court was warranted in grafting a broad disestablishment concept onto the Fourteenth Amendment in the first place. The only faintly relevant textual basis is the word "liberty" in the due process clause; this word would justify condemning a state-church involvement that directly infringed someone's religious liberty; but in that event the free exercise clause would invalidate the practice, and there would be no need for the establishment clause at all. It requires a semantic leap to translate "liberty" into "disestablishment" when by definition the forbidden establishment need involve no restriction of the liberty of any individual.[19] As for the intent of the framers of the Fourteenth Amendment, it is hard indeed to find in the record convincing evidence that they had disestablishment in mind.[20] And even when we hurdle that difficulty we encounter

---

[19] Freund, The Supreme Court of the United States 58–59 (1961); Brown, *Quis Custodiet Ipsos Custodes?—The School Prayer Cases*, 1963 Supreme Court Rev. 1, 27; Kauper, *Schempp and Sherbert: Studies in Neutrality and Accommodation*, 1963 Religion and The Public Order 3, 9 n.17.

[20] Corwin, A Constitution of Powers in a Secular State 111–14 (1951); Fairman and Morison, *Does the Fourteenth Amendment Incorporate the Bill of Rights?* 2 Stan. L. Rev. 5 (1949).

the further one of determining whether the establishment clause of the First Amendment was itself designed to forbid anything more than government support of a particular religion in preference to others,[21] which is a far cry from the wide-ranging independent prohibition the modern Court seems agreed on.

The truth is that from neither constitutional text nor historical intent can we wring a positive mandate to the Court to outlaw non-discriminatory and non-compulsive state aid to religion, and even those who fervently endorse the broad disestablishment idea would be better off to admit this forthwith. As for precedent, since it has its effective beginning in the period under discussion, it can hardly be invoked as a basis for settling the discussion. Yet none of this is to say that the judicially arranged marriage between disestablishment and the Fourteenth Amendment is indefensible. If we ask not whether text and history require this union but whether they permit it, we get a very different answer. In the first place it is arguable that the framers of the establishment clause were aiming, not only at the direct encroachments on liberty which the free exercise clause would reach, but at the more ambiguous and indirect losses to liberty that may result from church-state involvement. The "dangers . . . the Framers feared,"[22] it might be contended, were the perversion of government to religion's ends, and the consequent development of an atmosphere of persecutions and animosities which makes a free society impossible. Thus in this indirect sense the word "liberty" in the Fourteeenth Amendment can be accommodated to the establishment clause's purpose without showing any specific threat to the freedom of a particular individual. And if such an interpretation is not precluded by examination of text and intent, the Court's license to adopt it is certified by the whole history of judicial review and the Fourteenth Amendment. From almost the first the Court has acted as if the due process clause had expressed a generalized desire that "liberty" be preserved and had authorized the judiciary to define and redefine the term as the future might seem to require; and the nation has acquiesced in this view of the matter. Surely it is too late to contend that an exercise of that function is unwarrantable, unless the new definition is plainly incompatible with the textual-historical record. A legal order that

---

21 Murray, *Law or Prepossessions?* 14 LAW & CONTEMP. PROB. 23 (1949).
22 374 U.S. at 295 (concurring opinion of Brennan, J.).

ingested substantive due process and the doctrine of the "corpora-tion as person" need not strain unduly to swallow this morsel.

There appears, however, a formidable technical difficulty when the Court proceeds from this troublesome but perhaps allowable reinterpretation of "liberty" to the next step, *i.e.*, to apply the doctrine to a concrete case. The difficulty is the problem of stand-ing. Under orthodox principles only those whose rights have been infringed by a law in some specialized measurable way can chal-lenge the law's constitutionality. A citizen, however aggrieved, cannot rest his claim merely on "a political concern which belongs to us all."[23] If a state-ordained religious practice coerces John Doe directly, his standing can be established with relative ease; but if such coercion is not present, he cannot—under orthodox principles —challenge the practice because he shares a general interest in holding government to the path of constitutional rectitude. Thus a state law "establishing" religion would be unchallengeable, ex-cept as it coerced someone specific; in which case it could be chal-lenged under the free exercise clause, and the establishment clause would be superfluous.[24] The Court's declaration that the establish-ment clause imposes an independent restriction on government must therefore—unless it is judicially meaningless—imply some re-laxation of the normal standard requirements, and indeed both *Engel* and *Schempp* confirm this, for parents were permitted to as-sert rights not based on any claim of direct coercion.

This departure from orthodoxy may strengthen the case against the policy, but it does not conclude the case. To be sure, very grave questions would be raised if this relaxation of standing requirements were universalized: if any citizen could, apart from direct personal interest, sue whenever he doubted the validity of a governmental act, the judicial system might be smothered by an avalanche of abstract questions.[25] But if we assume that the Court is merely carving out a limited exception to the usual require-ments, an exception restricted to establishment-clause issues and perhaps, even further, only to those involving the public schools, the departure is not so unsettling. It has been hinted in the past that religious liberty may be in a preferred position, even among

---

23 Coleman v. Miller, 307 U.S. 433, 464 (concurring opinion of Frankfurter, J.).

24 Brown, *supra* note 19, at 15–31.

25 *But see* Jaffe, *Standing To Secure Judicial Review: Public Actions*, 74 HARV. L. REV. 1265, 1311–12 (1961).

the "preferred freedoms."[26] If the judges so believe, then perhaps their control over the "case or controversy" standard is wide enough to license this modification of *Frothingham v. Mellon*.[27] Under the strict *Frothingham* doctrine a congressional appropriation of $1 million to support the Presbyterian church[28] could not be judicially challenged, and in such an event the Court's commitment to the no-establishment principle would bump up against its own past interpretation of the "case or controversy" barrier. A single, limited breach in that barrier is not so great an irregularity as to be insufferable. Of course it is open to argument that the breach is not warranted by the alleged threat, that the good supposedly accomplished by reaching "pure" establishment laws does not justify straining the "case or controversy" requirement. But that is another matter.

The historical-technical case for the broad no-establishment policy seems to fall then somewhere between "must" and "must not." Whether nearer the one than the other will depend on how the reader assesses the historical record and how seriously he takes the orthodox standing requirements. But surely the Court has not here wandered far from its traditional range of discretion. It was certainly not bound by constitutional imperatives to reach this result, but neither was it strongly precluded from doing so. The next question is whether the judicially prescribed standards for implementing the policy are themselves justifiable in historical-technical terms. Here the initial difficulty is that the Court has prescribed not one standard but three: the flat and almost unqualified no-aid principle of *Engel;* the pragmatic, tolerant, question-of-degree approach of *Zorach;* and the elaborate compromise between these positions that seems to emerge from the multiple opinions in *Schempp.* As with the broader question just canvassed, history provides only general guidance to one who would choose among them, or rather it sets very broad boundaries within which choice may range. It is indeed doubtful that the New York Regents' Prayer "would have sent the Pilgrims to a stern and rockbound coast"[29] or that most of the framers of either the First or Fourteenth Amendments would have been repelled by school

---

26 See Murdock v. Pennsylvania, 319 U.S. 105 (1943).

27 262 U.S. 447 (1923).

28 The hypothetical example is offered by Brown, *supra* note 19, at 17.

29 Sutherland, *Establishment According to Engel*, 76 HARV. L. REV. 25, 36 (1962).

Bible reading. Yet there is force in Mr. Justice Brennan's point in *Schempp* that "a too literal quest for the advice of the Founding Fathers" is "futile and misdirected,"[30] that the more fruitful inquiry is whether practices "threaten those consequences which the Framers deeply feared," *i.e.*, the "interdependence between religion and state which the First Amendment was designed to prevent."[31] Once we accept this not unreasonable conception of the inquiry, however, we are free to roam widely among our prepossessions in deciding what does or does not threaten those consequences. Except at the extremes, it is hard to say that the Court is either right or wrong in condemning a practice on the ground that it threatens the dangers the First Amendment was designed to prevent. The more ponderable question is whether the tests the Court has offered us to identify such practices achieve—quite apart from their historical justification—the blending of coherence and flexibility that is requisite for a viable judicial standard.

Neither the strict no-aid principle of *Everson* and *Engel* nor the relativistic non-principle of *Zorach* seems satisfactory in these terms. The first has the appearance of coherence and predictability when it is stated boldly: no-aid means *no* aid and that is that. But thus stated it is so inflexible that it could not even be adhered to in the two opinions themselves. Mr. Justice Black felt obliged to admit an exception for "the benefits of public welfare legislation"[32] in *Everson* and for "patriotic or ceremonial occasions"[33] in *Engel*, though neither exception is compatible with the no-aid standard, if that standard simply means what it says. On the other hand, the *Zorach* principle is flexible to the point of flaccidity. Although the opinion states that the First Amendment "studiously defines"[34] the specific barriers to state-church involvement, Mr. Justice Douglas provides no clue except "common sense" to help us in discovering those studious definitions. It is hard to see how *Zorach* could provide any guidance at all to future reasoned adjudication.

In *Schempp*, however, the Court seemed to move toward a delineation that might be more promising. If we consider all the opinions, we detect an attempt to identify the criteria that merit

---

[30] 374 U.S. at 237.
[31] *Id.* at 236.
[32] 330 U.S. at 16.
[33] 370 U.S. at 435 n.21.
[34] 343 U.S. at 312.

consideration in an establishment-clause case—whether the practice has "meaningful and substantial impact"; whether the law is directly, purposefully, and primarily religious or secular; whether non-action would inhibit religious freedom; whether the persons affected by the practice are adults or children. To be sure, some of these questions may be ill chosen; most of them involve a considerable element of subjectivity and require the Court to draw distinctions between more and less. But they may represent the end of the tendency to resolve the problem by absolutist statements or by sheer intuition and the beginning of an effort to canalize the judgment process by identifying the factors that are relevant to its distinctions of degree. This would be a first, important step toward rational, yet flexible, adjudication standards. The next step is to articulate the factors more explicitly and to clear up such uncertainties as those left dangling by the bare pronouncements about standing. We may chide the Court for its tardiness in embarking on this course. But better late than never.

THE PROBLEM OF POLITICAL POWER

I turn now from the historical-technical question to the question of power. The literature of law, history, and political science contains very little systematic treatment of the nature and range of Supreme Court power, which is curious considering the interest of contemporary social scientists in power analysis[35] and the special application of such analysis to subjects like local government, the presidency, and foreign affairs.[36] No doubt this is partly explained by the long survival of Hamilton's old idea that the judiciary has neither force nor will, which survival is in turn explained by reluctance to acknowledge that the Court is a governing agency, facing some of the power problems that governors always face. There is a persistent feeling that it is somehow improper to ask whether the Court has the power to do a thing, as distinguished from the question whether it has the right to do it. Lord Milner was expressing this feeling in a different connection

35 *E.g.,* LASSWELL & KAPLAN, POWER AND SOCIETY (1950); Riker, *Some Ambiguities in the Notion of Power,* 58 AM. POL. SCI. REV. 341 (1964); Simon, *Notes on the Observation and Measurement of Political Power,* 15 J. POLITICS 500 (1953).

36 *E.g.,* BANFIELD, POLITICAL INFLUENCE (1961); NEUSTADT, PRESIDENTIAL POWER: THE POLITICS OF LEADERSHIP (1960); Ash, *An Analysis of Power, With Special Reference to International Politics,* 3 WORLD POLITICS 218 (1951).

when he said in 1909, with respect to the House of Lords: "If we believe a thing to be bad, and if we have a right to prevent it, it is our duty to try to prevent it and to damn the consequences."[37]

There is reason to suspect that the justices of the Supreme Court have sometimes taken more account of consequences than Lord Milner and his American counterparts would approve. One thinks of Marshall's wariness after 1803,[38] of *Ex parte McCardle*,[39] of the "switch in time" in 1937; and of other occasions when discretion may have moderated valor. But in its official rhetoric the Court has usually felt obliged to ignore such matters, to cloak its awareness of them under euphemisms like the doctrine of political questions, or at most to utter broad generalities to the effect that no court has power to cure all the Republic's major social ills,[40] or that judicial default of duty can weaken the law's power no less than judicial rashness.[41] Such statements are unexceptionable, but they are truisms that underline the power problem rather than resolve it. These conventions of judicial discourse are, and probably ought to be, unalterable: judicial opinions that articulated a calculus of power would be ludicrous and self-defeating. But even those outside the Court, who are bound by no such conventions, have been slow to press the appraisal much further. Although there is a growing body of empirical studies that should ultimately provide raw material for a better understanding of the Court's power,[42] analytic generalizations about the subject have been few and have, naturally enough, focused more on the Court of the past than the Court of the present.[43]

---

[37] OXFORD DICTIONARY OF QUOTATIONS 339 (1962).

[38] 3 BEVERIDGE, THE LIFE OF JOHN MARSHALL 176–78 (1919).

[39] 7 Wall. 506 (1869).

[40] Reynolds v. Sims, 377 U.S. 533, 589 (dissenting opinion of Harlan, J.).

[41] Bell v. Maryland, 378 U.S. 226, 242 (concurring opinion of Douglas, J.).

[42] See, *e.g.*, MURPHY, CONGRESS AND THE COURT (1962); PELTASON, 58 LONELY MEN: SOUTHERN FEDERAL JUDGES AND SCHOOL SEGREGATION (1961); Patric, *The Impact of a Court Decision: Aftermath of the McCollum Case*, 6 J. PUB. L. 455 (1957); Sorauf, *Zorach v. Clauson: The Impact of a Supreme Court Decision*, 53 AM. POL. SCI. REV. 777 (1959); Westin, *The Supreme Court, the Populist Movement and the Campaign of 1896*, 15 J. POLITICS 3 (1953); Note, *Congressional Reversal of Supreme Court Decisions: 1945–1957*, 71 HARV. L. REV. 1324 (1958).

[43] In addition to the works cited note 42 *supra*, see PELTASON, FEDERAL COURTS IN THE POLITICAL PROCESS (1955); PRITCHETT, CONGRESS VERSUS THE SUPREME COURT 1957–60 (1961); Dahl, *Decision-Making in a Democracy: The Supreme Court as a National Policy-Maker*, 6 J. PUB. L. 279 (1957); Latham, *The Supreme Court and the Supreme People*, 16 J. POLITICS 207 (1954); Mendelson, *Judicial Review and Party Politics*, 12 VAND. L. REV. 447 (1959); Roche, *Judicial Self-Restraint*, 49 AM.

These deficiencies cannot be wholly repaired in this paper, if only because of limitations of space and time. But it does seem both possible and worthwhile to set down a few observations that may improve our perspectives on the power question and make it easier to appraise the Court's establishment-clause decisions in these terms.

To begin with, it is desirable to dissipate some of the ambiguities usually involved in a statement that the Court has, or has not, the power to get others to comply with its wish. One of these ambiguities is suggested when we inquire who those "others" are. The problem is that the Court's direct commands usually issue to a very special group of persons in a very special context, *e.g.,* to lower court judges, or, at one remove, to the litigants in a particular dispute. These are "others" over whom the Court's influence, though not unlimited,[44] is obviously considerable. If we restrict ourselves to this level in assessing Court power, the inquiry is relatively simple. But the matter attains another dimension when we consider how the Court's pronouncements affect those outside the ambit of a specific litigation, *e.g.,* the school board in a district where no case has been brought, the legislator who may be contemplating an aid-to-religion program. Common sense suggests that the Court's power to obtain this general compliance with a given policy may be less than its power to control the results of a particular case, and it is important to be clear which idea of "others" we have in mind when we make an assertion about the Court's power capabilities.

Secondly, there are certain ambiguities in the notion of "compliance." The notion seems at first blush simple enough: a command issues and the "others" commanded either do or do not obey. But a little reflection reveals that the matter is more complicated. Even within the framework of formal litigation there can be disparities between the Court's mandate, fairly interpreted, and the actual result: lower courts may respond sluggishly or use the flexibility inherent in the remand process to reinterpret the mandate; litigants may take advantage of the law's delays and complexities to postpone and evade, even though they do not ac-

POL. SCI. REV. 762 (1955); The present article went to press before the publication of MURPHY, ELEMENTS OF JUDICIAL STRATEGY (1964), which is by far the most thorough discussion to date of the Supreme Court and the power question.

44 See Murphy, *Lower Court Checks on Supreme Court Power*, 53 AM. POL. SCI. REV. 1017 (1959).

tually defy, the Court's behest.[45] Moreover, insofar as we think of the Court as seeking results beyond the formal limits of litigation, other possibilities appear. Response may take the form of enthusiastic co-operation, grudging submission, partial compliance, stubborn inaction, or defiance, and it may well simultaneously take one form in one section of the country and another elsewhere. Nor do the complications end there. So far we have been talking as if the responses to the Court's action were limited to a range between obedience and disobedience, but there is another possibility that transcends this range: political retaliation. It is quite possible to imagine a situation in which all those subject to a Court mandate might dutifully obey, but might then mount a political counterattack designed to impair the whole basis of judicial authority. An observer might say with perfect truth that the Court did possess the power to obtain compliance with the mandate, but his statement would be misleading unless it reckoned the cost of obaining the compliance; for the result of that reckoning might reveal a net power loss. Furthermore, while costs are being considered it is important to recognize that they may be cumulative. The Court may have the power to exact obedience to policy A and the prestige to withstand the resulting retaliatory backlash, but if it concurrently seeks to enforce policies B, C, and D the force of the backlash may be augmented to a point where costs become prohibitive and even policy A becomes unfeasible. At the same time, it should also be recognized that the possibility of backlash implies its own opposite; resistance and retaliation from some quarters may tend to restrict the Court's power, but support from other quarters may simultaneously tend to augment it.

Yet one who is interested in adding up *pro* and *con* forces and judging the balance between them, should bear in mind that not all potential supporters and defenders are of identical weight. Congress itself is the most dangerous foe, because of its ultimate authority over such vital matters as appellate jurisdiction. It is also, of course, an invaluable ally. The President's acquiescence or positive support is essential to the enforcement of many judicial policies. His enmity is not in itself fatal, as Franklin Roosevelt learned, but it is not to be taken lightly. History suggests that an individual state government, or even a cluster of them, is no match for the Court's prestige, unless the sympathy of Congress or the

---

[45] Note, *State Court Evasion of United States Supreme Court Mandates*, 56 YALE L. J. 574 (1947).

President can be enlisted. Other public and private forces—*e.g.*, the press, pressure groups, distinguished individuals—will vary in weight depending on the intensity of their *pro* or *con* commitments and, again, on their capacity to influence congressional or presidential attitudes.

Much of this is simply to say that the Court's power is not entirely its own, that its capability depends in part on a preponderance of friends over enemies. This lineup will, of course, vary somewhat from time to time and from issue to issue depending on whose oxen are being gored; but there are some secular trends that may have special significance for the modern Court. One of these developments is obvious enough, although its importance in this connection has not been widely remarked. Since 1937 the Court has to a considerable degree lost its most faithful historical ally: the conservative business-legal community.[46] For the first 150 years of our national existence this powerful element could usually be counted on to defend the Court in anxious moments, because the Court was recognized as the mainstay of economic rights. But for the past thirty years, the justices have been telling business that the old love affair is over, and there is reason to believe that businessmen have received the message. Whether or not they and their minions are actually hostile to the judicial power, they will no longer automatically rally to its support. Of course the modern Court, while losing old friends, has acquired new ones, but it remains to be seen if it has gained or lost—in power terms —by the exchange.

A final point is not unrelated to what has just been said. It is arguable that the modern Court stands in a novel relation to the American body politic, and that historically derived views about the range of judicial power are no longer reliable. The difference is not merely that the Old Court protected economic liberty and the New Court protects "humanistic" values like free speech, fair trial, and racial equality, although that difference is, as has been said, significant. Nor is it merely that the modern Court has more or less frankly acknowledged that it is a policy-making body, rather than the "powerless symbol of justice"[47] of historical myth, although that too may be important. There is another, less obvious, distinction that also merits attention, a difference in the nature of

---

46 BICKEL, *op. cit. supra* note 4, at 75.
47 MASON & BEANEY, THE SUPREME COURT IN A FREE SOCIETY 317 (1959).

what the historical Court and the modern Court have tried to accomplish. In a word, the Old Court was usually trying to preserve the cake of custom; the New Court has been trying to break it. To put the matter in another way, the Court of the past characteristically told people they must continue to do what they were accustomed to doing; the Court of today is more often telling them they must *not* continue their accustomed ways, but must on the contrary do something else.[48] Plainly the justices have been conceiving of themselves in the last decade as one of the chief initiative-supplying agencies in American government.[49] It seems probable that it is harder to compel people to break with their customs than it is to prevent them from doing so, and any appraisal of the modern Court's power problem should take account of this probability.

With these general considerations in mind, what can be said about the establishment-clause decisions and the question of judicial power? No very specialized knowledge is required to convince us that both the compliance problem and the backlash problem are substantial in this field. Any prohibition declared by the Court will be regarded by some as antireligious, and will awaken the spirit of piety from its usual Sunday-to-Sunday repose. Most Americans, though often secular enough in their weekday behavior, are accustomed to what Veblen called "devout observances" in public life; and they may be surprised and displeased to be told by the Court that these usages are at war with our constitutional tradition. While it is very difficult to measure accurately the impact of a Supreme Court decision, the evidence suggests that the *McCollum* rule against use of school buildings for religious instruction was frequently ignored—estimates of non-compliance

---

[48] Marshall's Court was an arguable exception to these generalizations about Courts of the past. Certainly he would have liked to shake America out of its localist preconceptions and to stimulate a bolder use of national power. But his commands to the states in such fields as the contract clause were largely negative, *i.e.*, they did not call on those affected to take affirmative action, as the modern desegregation and apportionment decisions do. And his decisions on the commerce clause and the necessary and proper clause offered the national government the opportunity to act nationally, but did not require it to do so. In fact of course, the invitation was not accepted in Marshall's lifetime.

[49] " 'Our judges are not monks or scientists,' the Chief Justice wrote in 1955, 'but participants in the living stream of our national life, steering the law between the dangers of rigidity on the one hand and formlessness on the other. . . .' As Thurman Arnold has observed, the Court under Chief Justice Warren, is becoming 'unified,' 'a Court of inspired choice and policy, . . . rather than a Court of law as we used to know it.' " MASON & BEANEY, *op. cit. supra* note 47, at 318.

ran from 15 per cent up to 40 and 50 per cent in some states."[50] I have found no comparable estimates of non-compliance with the prayer and Bible-reading prohibition, but considering the furor it aroused, we can guess that the response has been somewhat similar. As for backlash, the evidence is fresh and vivid. Within a few weeks after *Engel,* more than fifty proposals for constitutional amendments had been introduced in Congress; and the Court was denounced in journal and pulpit.[51] The *Schempp* decision produced a more mixed reaction, and influential voices were heard defending the Court and opposing the "Becker amendment," which would override both *Engel* and *Schempp.*[52] Nevertheless the House Judiciary Committee was in June, 1964, still seriously considering the Becker proposal; and the 1964 Republican platform called for an amendment permitting religious exercises in "public places" so long as they were non-coercive and not state-prescribed.[53] Congress cut the salary increase for Supreme Court justices from $7,500 to $4,500 (though other federal judges received the full $7,500 raise); and the vote was attributed to congressional resentment over the prayer decisions, among others.[54] This last event, petty in itself, illustrates what was said above about the tendency of the backlash threat to be cumulative. The prayer issue alone was probably not enough to alienate more than a minority of congressmen, but when their number was augmented by others who were disturbed about racial desegregation, apportionment, criminal procedures, or obscenity, a hostile majority could be formed. The more serious threat of the Dirksen-Mansfield amendment, to stay court action in reapportionment cases, was also felt to represent a reaction to multiple provocations.[55]

---

[50] Sorauf, *supra* note 42, at 784.

[51] Sutherland, *supra* note 29, at 50: Pollak, *W.B.R.: Some Reflections,* 71 YALE L. J. 1451, 1455–56 n.17 (1962).

[52] Spokesmen for the National Council of Churches, the Baptists, Lutherans, Presbyterians, Seventh-Day Adventists, Unitarians, and the United Church of Christ made declarations opposing the proposal. N.Y. Times, May 23, 1964, p. 22. The legal department of the National Catholic Welfare Conference advised Catholics to be "very cautious" about supporting proposals of this sort. N.Y. Times, June 23, 1964, p. 2. "223 Constitutional lawyers, including the deans of 55 law schools" petitioned Congress not to tamper with the Bill of Rights. N.Y. Herald Tribune, June 10, 1964, p. 22.

[53] 110 CONG. REC. 16025 (daily ed. July 22, 1964). There is some reason to doubt that an amendment so worded would be incompatible with present Court doctrines.

[54] N.Y. Times, Aug. 9, 1964, §4, p. 8E, col. 1.

[55] See Lewis, *Congress vs. the Court—Issue Joined on Redistricting,* N.Y. Times, Aug. 16, 1964, §4, p. E3. "What is about to be tested is whether the recent line of

Since compliance is likely to be at best only partial and the backlash threat seems substantial, a cautious judiciary might have preferred to leave the religious-establishment issue severely alone and to devote itself to more tractable and less dangerous tasks. Alternatively the Court might have confined its rulings to religious practices that involved an element of coercion, *i.e.*, an invasion of religious liberty.[56] Perhaps such a narrowing of the implications would diminish the backlash threat. But it would also, as Professor Pollak has pointed out, reduce the likelihood that the practices would be generally abandoned; for they would presumably be valid until challenged, and school boards would be "under no discernible legal obligation, as they assuredly now are, to suspend ongoing . . . programs on their own initiative."[57] In short this approach, though lessening backlash, would also lessen the incidence of compliance with the policy against public religious practices. At any rate the Court has chosen to extend its reach to situations which are not directly coercive, and the practical question is how its various doctrines in pursuance of that choice should be evaluated in power terms.

The relativist doctrine of *Zorach* might at first appear to tax the Court's power capacities the least, but appearances are notoriously deceptive. Of course this doctrine would excite little anti-judicial feeling if it were always applied permissively as in *Zorach* itself. To quote Professor Pollak again, "few major interest groups are deeply committed antagonists of official prayer."[58] But presumably a time would come when considerations of degree would lead to a restrictive application, and in such event the Court might be disarmed by its own doctrine from defending itself adequately. The trouble with a completely relativist doctrine is that it gives the community no notice of what to expect and provides the Court with no legalistic refuge from its adversaries. It is a confession that cases are decided by purely subjective judicial hunches, and it in-

---

Supreme Court decisions protecting individual liberty has offended public opinion so much that the political forces arrayed against the apportionment decision will be able to limit or overcome it. On the answer depends not only a good measure of the states' future political makeup but the great role of the Supreme Court in the American system of government." *Ibid.*, col. 8.

[56] Professor Paul Freund suggested that this would enable the Court "to put to one side all the problems of state aid on which feelings are now running high, and to limit the decision to the context of the school room." Quoted by Pollak, *supra* note 16, at 70.

[57] *Ibid.*

[58] *Id.* at 62.

vites an outraged citizen to question whether the hunches of nine men in Washington should be more binding than his own.

On the other hand, it seems possible that the strict no-aid principle of *Engel* would strain judicial power to something near the breaking point. Compliance with such an absolutist prohibition might be extremely spotty, and it is unhealthy for Court prestige that its policies be widely flouted. If the Court undertook to wipe out religious services in government hospitals and prisons, tax exemption for religious contributions, the use of "In God We Trust" on coins, chaplains' salaries for Congress and for the armed forces, and all the other tradition-encrusted "aids" to religion that honeycomb our system, the retaliatory uprising in Congress and elsewhere is easy to imagine. A Court insistent on such a standard might gravely impair its power to govern in other areas as well as this one.

The more qualified and balanced doctrine that was beginning to take shape in *Schempp* seems more viable in power terms. To be sure, the assault on the Court for its "anti-religious" rulings continues as of this writing, but this merely confirms what has already been said—that public religious practices present a tender issue which a timid Court might elect not to prod at all. Having elected otherwise, a justice might nevertheless find a moral in the contrast between the reaction to *Engel* and the reaction to *Schempp*. No doubt the difference can in part be explained by the fact that *Schempp*, unlike *Engel*, was no surprise; and that the case against such practices in the schools had been canvassed in public debate during the interval between the two holdings. It turned out that some allies could be found to mitigate the thrust of the policy's adversaries. But it is also important that the decision carefully closed only the doors it meant to close, that it spelled out some reasoned exceptions to the no-aid barrier and hinted—especially in the concurrences—that there might be more. The way seems open for the development of a moderate but meaningful doctrine based on articulated judgment factors. The advantage of this, as has been well said in another connection, is "to focus the attention of all concerned on actualities and away from the never-never land of private, and perhaps unconscious, preconceptions."[59] No such balanced explication will sway those whose preconceptions are immovable or whose anti-judicial spirit is

---

[59] Mendelson, *The First Amendment and the Judicial Process: A Reply to Mr. Frantz*, 17 VAND. L. REV. 479, 482 (1964).

chiefly grounded on opposition to the Court's policy in quite different fields. Senator Eastland is probably unpersuadable. But a doctrine like this provides the best chance of maximizing results and minimizing cost in a situation that is at best fraught with risks for the judicial power.

THE PROBLEM OF ETHICAL OBJECTIVES

Our next concern is with the normative validity of the Court's aims in this field. Disregarding for the moment the issue of historical-technical justification and the issue of power, how "good" are the policies the Court seeks to enforce—or to turn the query around, how grave are the "evils" it seeks to correct? This matter is the one most difficult to judge with any semblance of objectivity. We all know that one man's meat is often another's poison, and while this knowledge may not resign us to complete solipsism, it moderates our confidence about our own "can't helps" and even more about our ability to persuade others in the realm of ethics.

Whether or not there exists some comprehensive and infallible system for dispelling such difficulties, no attempt will be made to present one here. At some point each of us will claim the right to his own peremptory dogmas. But there are perhaps a few things that can be said to those who are willing to postpone that point while they are making up their minds about the ethic of the establishment-clause decisions.

For one thing it serves little purpose to talk as if the evil against which the decisions are aimed is a seventeenth-century theocracy or the threat of pograms or wars of religion. This is not the seventeenth century, nor even the eighteenth: America is not John Calvin's Geneva; it is in no peril from a new Inquisition or a new Pilgrimage of Grace. The state-church involvements that the decisions touch upon are much less dramatic and horrendous: marginal relief from the financial burdens of parochial school attendance, a nudging of moppets in the direction of religious instruction classes, a modest amount of classroom praying and Bible reading. This is not the stuff from which crusades and martyrs are made.

On the other hand, neither does it forward the discussion much to contend that such involvements are not noxious at all. They can, however slightly, entail results that most of us recognize as harmful. A child may feel to an extent coerced toward religiosity by a released-time program and toward a particular sectarian commitment by the classroom reading of the Lord's Prayer. He may be offended by the King James Bible, and his parents may be offended by the thought that their tax money or their government is supporting a religion they do not avow. Equally important, although a policy of judicial *laissez faire* about such matters would not expose us to religious civil war, it might affect the political process regrettably. It is arguable that religion has a special propensity to stir emotions and breed animosities when it becomes a subject of political controversy. Those ills may be precluded if the organic law simply forbids the state to enact any laws respecting religion.

A rejoinder to all this might be that laws almost always coerce or offend someone, and that most political questions are controversial by definition. Everyone endures some coercion he would like to avoid, sees his tax money used for policies that offend him, because the community has decided that the case for the policies is weightier than his objections. But of course the argument is that coercion in matters of religious belief is especially objectionable, that offenses to sensibilities are in this area especially exacerbating, that disagreement over religion is especially likely to embitter the political process and divert the community from its other common concerns. Perhaps the state can never altogether avoid these encroachments and diversions. Some of its secular policies may incidentally burden religion as in the case of conscription laws. It must then choose whether or not to relieve these burdens by providing chaplain service and granting religious exemptions, and in either event consciences will be wounded and passions aroused. The price must be paid to gain the secular end. But a religious law for a religious end can find no such external justification. It offends one religious conscience in the name of another, and unless we reject the sovereignty of religious belief, we must find this blameworthy. Nor is such a law vindicated by the contention that it employs religious means to a secular end, *i.e.,* the development of a moral citizenry which will in turn produce a just and happy society. For whatever tendency the means have to accomplish that end may be canceled by their simultaneous tendency to generate the bitterness that makes such a society difficult.

Unless they are warranted by a secular purpose or by the need to avoid burdening religious freedom, all laws and state practices aiding religion seem to some degree objectionable. This verdict, as far as it goes, applies to the school prayers and Bible reading in *Engel* and *Schempp*, and to the religious instruction programs of *McCollum*, or for that matter of *Zorach*. But having determined this (or if the reader prefers, having assumed it for the sake of the argument) we have not settled the evaluative issue. "Bad" like "good" is an adjective that can be compared. And even if we grant that these laws blemish our polity, it is hard to contend that the disfigurement is a very great one. School instruction programs and released-time programs may coerce some a little; they do not in themselves coerce many very much. The praying and Bible reading involved in *Schempp* seem even less constraining; and the compulsiveness of *Engel's* Regents' Prayer is hardly visible to the naked eye. As for the tendency of such practices to embitter and distort political discourse, that threat too, though not imaginary, seems relatively mild.

My point is not that these injuries and dangers are negligible, but that they fall rather low on the scale of evils in our imperfect world. I am of course aware that judgments like these are ultimately subjective. Even the merest hint of coercion may seem insufferable to the extremely sensitive or timid; even a trace of religiosity in public life may offend some past all bearing. But most of us would admit that there is no comparison between the wrong of the Regents' Prayer and other wrongs that currently exercise our judicial system: racial discrimination in school and polling booth; the "rationing" of criminal justice; the arbitrary censorship of art and thought—to name only three. To be sure, it can be argued that the Regents' Prayer is a first step toward more palpable outrages to come. But this only means that we must be prepared to alter our estimate of evil when alteration is called for. It does not convert the prayer requirement itself into a serious present danger.

SUMMARY AND CONCLUSIONS

As I said at the outset, the final stage in our evaluative process is to reunite the categories which have so far been, for analytic purposes, kept artificially separate; to essay some synthetic judgments based on a summary view of the historical-technical, the power, and the value questions. Taking them all into account, how well has the Court performed in the establishment-clause field? What prescriptions are indicated for handling the subject in the future?

On the basis of power and value considerations taken together, a strong case could be made for judicial avoidance of the whole issue of state aid to religion, at least for the time being. The subject seems peculiarly well calculated to generate resistance and backlash and peculiarly ill calculated to enlist adequate countervailing support. Congressmen feel that defending prayer is like defending motherhood: it wins them some votes and costs them almost none. If the evil aimed at by the Court was a great one, this expenditure of judicial power might not be excessive. But the evil in its present manifestations is fairly moderate. Even so, judicial correction of it might be warranted, if there were not other, graver wrongs simultaneously pressing for judicial attention and also taxing the power capacities of the Court. But when we take into account that there are those other wrongs, the price of dealing with this one may seem very dear. It would be unfortunate if the Court, in its zeal to wipe out public pieties, impaired its ability to cope with race discrimination, injustice to accused persons, and inhibitions on free expression, not to speak of other massive self-assigned tasks such as control of legislative apportionment, or of further threats to just government that might appear tomorrow or the next day.

How much one worries about the prospect of these impairments depends on how near one thinks the Court of today is to the limits of its practical power. Those who believe that its potential is still not strained, that it has large unexpended reserves to call on, will shrug such apprehensions off, and if their belief is correct they are right to do so. But confidence on that score is open to question in the light of modern circumstances. The Court of present times has assumed a more creative place in American government than any of its predecessors; it has undertaken to defend a galaxy of values very different from those defended by Courts of the past; it has cast off its traditional "constituency," the business community. We cannot be sure about the net effect of all this, but we should at least consider the hypothesis that this highly ambitious Court is also proportionately vulnerable.

There have been some signs that anti-judicial sentiment may develop more readily today than it has usually done in the past. One such omen was the near-enactment in 1958 of a bill which would have seriously undermined Court authority by forbidding it to strike down state laws on "federal pre-emption" grounds.[60] The pettish discrimination against the Court in the salary bill of 1964 seems to be another, and the congressional move to stay reapportionment judgments is one more. In short, evidence suggests that, although the Court has not yet passed the combustion point, it may be coming close to it. If so, the judiciary might have been better off to ignore such public religious observances as these and to husband itself for the tasks that matter more. It would not have baffled judicial ingenuity to keep the doctrinal way open for the time when a really malign establishment law might be presented. Until then the hot potato could be left alone.

Such a policy of judicial self-restraint might be best if we were back in pre-*Everson* days and could foresee the manifold judicial problems of the 1950's and 1960's. But perfect foresight cannot be expected, and the judicial clock is hard to reverse. Once the Court decided, as it did in *Everson,* to subject state aid to judicial supervision, it lost the option of complete forbearance, and the question was how best to handle the job to which it was now committed. Some insight into this matter may be achieved when we add the historical-technical dimension to the power and value factors that have just been discussed. When a Court elects to deal with a subject that may tax judicial power, it is prudent to ground itself on the firmest possible constitutional base. The firmer that base, the stronger is the Court's claim to legitimacy for its mandates; and the stronger that claim, the greater are the Court's power capacities. A solid historical-technical justification will not, as has been

---

60 See MURPHY, *op. cit. supra* note 42, at 91, 193–223; PRITCHETT, *op. cit. supra* note 43 at 35–40. Although these two scholarly volumes have treated the 1958 counterattack in considerable detail, it seems fair to say that the incident has been inadequately noticed by even the informed public. Because only one of the "anti-court" bills considered in the summer of 1958 was actually passed, Professor Pritchett is reassured about the modern Court's capacity to withstand such threats. That is one way to look at it. But the anti-pre-emption bill passed the House easily and was defeated in the Senate by only one vote. That such a mischievous measure could come so close to passage is the remarkable—and perhaps ominous—fact. The trouble is that, although we are accustomed to talk loosely about the "prestige" of the Court, we know very little about its nature or about what causes it to ebb and flow. I would suggest that when we use the term, we usually have two somewhat different things in mind: the pro-judicial opinion that derives from approval of the Court's specific recent policy trends, and the pro-judicial opinion that rests on a belief in the value of the judicial institution, quite apart from the question of how that institution is currently behaving. Obviously the first variety is less constant and dependable than the second, and it would be useful (though perhaps impossible) for purposes of prediction to know what proportion of the Court's "prestige" at any given time is to be attributed to each.

said before, mellow the wrath of a policy's really determined opponents, but it will weaken their arguments and decrease their capacity to enlist anti-judicial allies. In this field, it seems clear, the most convincing historical-technical case can be made for a holding that a state-aid program directly infringes personal liberty, for liberty is specifically named in the due process clause, and such a holding would require no distortion of orthodox standing requirements. Moreover the value served by such a holding is one most of us would regard as precious and clear-cut. With a certain regard for the principle of *de minimis,* the Court, having chosen to supervise state aid, might have been wiser to limit itself to cases challenging programs on individual freedom grounds.

To suggest that this course would have been wiser is not to contend that the argument for it is overwhelming, that there is nothing to be said for the Court's chosen policy of bringing all religious aid within immediate judicial reach. That policy strains constitutional language and intent and disrupts orthodox procedural understandings, but it is not wholly unwarrantable in view of the Courts traditional, creative attitude toward constitutional interpretation. It helps to augment the contemporary drain on judicial power resources, but it does not plainly deplete those resources disastrously. The wrongs that it aims at are not the worst that we face, but they are wrongs nonetheless. With respect to each of these evaluative categories, I think the case against the policy is somewhat stronger than the case for it, and that the cumulative appraisal falls on the negative side. Another might assess each category differently or might assign them different relative weights. As I said earlier, these three judgment components provide no ready-made answers; they provide only channels within which our personal evaluative inquiries can proceed.

At any rate the judges have not confined themselves to the boundaries here recommended and quite evidently they have no intention of doing so. The remaining inquiry then is whether the Court has performed as well as it might have even within its chosen terrain. Very little can be said for the absolutist doctrine of *Everson* and *Engel* or the indefinite relativism of *Zorach.* The strict no-aid principle, coupled with an open door on the matter of standing, and with no respect for the notion of *de minimis,* would plunge the judiciary into an endless, dangerous, and largely fruitless crusade against minor evils and would deprive constitutional law of the flexibility that is one of its primary attributes. The

Zorach doctrine, insofar as it can be called one, forsakes the juristic virtues of coherence and predictability, and leaves the Court's flanks unguarded for the future. As for the judicial oscillation between these two approaches from 1947 to 1962, this seemed to offer the worst of both worlds and can hardly be regarded as a model policy.

Since the Court feels that it must oversee state-aid practices, the *Schempp* case—in its opinions but not necessarily in its result— comes nearest to achieving a viable position. If the implications of the several opinions are followed up, we can envision a set of standards elastic enough to give the judicial process some leeway, coherent enough to provide some guidance, and discriminating enough to distinguish between real and trivial wrongs. The concept of *de minimis,* which Mr. Justice Black seemed to extinguish out of hand in *Engel,* flickered a little in *Schempp;* and this concept alone, duly applied, would spare the Court gratuitous self-inflicted wounds in the state-aid field. The implied tolerance for religious enactments designed to protect freedom of worship— *e.g.,* provisions for army chaplains—would serve the same purpose and would help maintain a sensible balance among democratic values. The intimation that there may be a constitutionally significant difference between observances affecting adults and those affecting children suggests another basis for separating bad from less bad, and for circumscribing the arena of conflict with the political branches of government.

The distinction between a law that is directly, primarily, or purposefully religious and one that is not, has its difficulties. Judicial experience in other fields with the notion of directness and with legislative motive is not reassuring. But the problem of determining whether or not a law's primary thrust is religious, though not subject to precise solution, would at least direct judicial attention toward realities and away from prepossessions.

No doubt other and better-thought-through criteria can be devised.[61] One of the recurrent lessons of judicial history is that

---

[61] Professor Kurland suggests that the concept of "neutrality" will resolve the Court's decisional problems in this field: "The freedom and separation clauses should be read as stating a single precept: that government cannot utilize religion as a standard for action or inaction because these clauses, read together as they should be, prohibit classification in terms of religion either to confer a benefit or to impose a burden." KURLAND, RELIGION AND THE LAW 112 (1961). I am inclined to agree that this principle, taken alone, would impose too rigid a standard. Konvitz, *The Constitution or Neutral Principles,* 1963 RELIGION AND THE PUBLIC ORDER 99; Sherbert v. Verner, 374 U.S. 398, 422 (dissenting opinion of Harlan, J.). But as one factor, among

the first, quick thoughts about constitutional doctrine are seldom the best, that viable standards must be evolved step by step as the complexities of a subject unfold, that unnecessarily sweeping pronouncements generate more political heat than legal light. This precept has been confirmed once more by our modern experience with the establishment-clause cases. Perhaps there is reason to hope that the Court, while expanding and articulating the latent promises of *Schempp*, will not forget it again.

---

others, in evaluating a religious law, the criterion could be viable and relevant. Professor Kauper finds that *Schempp* and *Sherbert* yield the ideas of "accommodation" and "involvement" to modify and supplement a presumption in favor of "neutrality." Kauper, *supra* note 19. Though, as he says, these terms do not in themselves carry us very far, they point toward the kind of factors that must be considered when "balancing interests in arriving at responsible judgment." *Id.* at 39.

Another commentator proposes as principles of interpretation: "(1) The function of the Constitution is to exclude calculation of religious values, be they motives for deceit, or aid, or violation of statutes. (2) The Constitution also prevents the formulating or examining of the possible private ways of acting on religious beliefs." Weiss, *Privilege, Posture and Protection: "Religion" in the Law,* 73 YALE L. J. 593, 619 (1964). The point of this paper has been that it is relatively easy to compose a formula that is coherent and internally consistent or unlikely to overstrain the Court's power to command or in accord with plausible value premises. The great difficulty is to construct one that takes account of all three of these desiderata. The variant analyses cited may all add layers to our understanding of the matter, however, and they suggest how important it is to let judgment ripen in judicial and scholarly discussion rather than to seize upon the first tidy absolute that comes to mind.

NORMAN ST. JOHN-STEVAS

BIRTH CONTROL:

MORALS, LAW, AND PUBLIC POLICY

Birth control is an explosive issue religiously, morally, and politically and is causing tensions in every part of the world, and
nowhere more so than in the United States, a pluralist society of
Protestant culture with a powerful and growing Catholic minority.
Over the last fifty years the whole center of gravity in the discussion has been in a state of continual movement. In the opening
decades of the century birth control was condemned by all Christians as being contrary to the law of God, and public opinion generally in the West was hostile to its employment. After the First
World War there came a dramatic shift in opinion outside the
Catholic Church, and birth control began to be acceptable as a
normal part of married life. Many individual Christians practiced
birth control, but it was only grudgingly accepted by the churches
in their official teaching. In 1920 the Lambeth Conference representing the world-wide Anglican Communion was forthright in its
condemnation of all forms of contraception and ten years later
still maintained that only in very limited circumstances would its
use be permissible. The position had, however, been undermined,
and under the impact of the Second World War and the increase
in world population the Church of England in company with the
major Protestant denominations gave its complete approval to the
use of contraceptives within the marriage relationship. The Roman Catholic Church continued to condemn contraception but

Norman St. John-Stevas is a barrister and Member of Parliament.

modified its attitude to birth control. "The safe period" was accepted by many theologians as providing an acceptable means of family planning, and this view has become the official teaching of the Church. Today the Catholic Church accepts family planning as a positive duty for Christian parents and has much reduced its emphasis on the virtues of producing a large family. A further revolution in Catholic thought now appears to be in progress, triggered by the invention of the birth control pill. A minority of Catholic theologians argue that its use as a method of family planning is morally acceptable; others think that its use should be confined to regularizing the safe period. The blanket condemnation of contraception by the Church is also under attack and some Catholic thinkers argue that the whole teaching on contraception needs radical revision. This is the background against which the present civil struggle in the United States over the attitude of the state to birth control and contraception has to be considered.

The present legal position in the United States on the birth control issue is anomalous in that although the use of contraceptives is (Catholics apart) generally accepted, their sale and distribution are still restricted by law. Opinion on the morality and desirability of contraception has changed, but the law has not kept pace. The birth control movement in the United States has its roots in the nineteenth century, the best-known pioneer being Dr. Charles Knowlton, a Massachusetts physician who in 1832 published anonymously a treatise on contraceptive methods with the rather odd title *Fruits of Philosophy*. He had been preceded two years earlier by Robert Dale Owen, who brought out what I believe is the first American booklet on birth control, *Moral Physiology*. Both these publications achieved wide circulation. *Moral Physiology* went through several editions within a year and by the time of the author's death in 1877 had achieved a combined circulation in England and the United States of 75,000. *Fruits of Philosophy* had a more spectacular career, achieved a far wider circulation, and was the subject of a famous British trial in 1877, when Charles Bradlaugh and Annie Besant were indicted before an English court for publishing it in Britain. The trial, which received immense publicity, did much to familiarize the public on both sides of the Atlantic with a subject which had hitherto been obscured in the murk of the underworld. Mrs. Besant used the trial as a means to spread her views on birth control and was eventually convicted by the court for publishing obscene matter. Later, however, the verdict was upset for a defect in the indictment and the trial and publicity led only to an increase in the number of books and pamphlets on birth control. In the United States a number of medical writers on birth control emerged, including A. M. Mauriceau, J. Soule, Edward Bliss Foote, and his son Edward Bond Foote. Their activities provoked a sharp Protestant reaction, and as a result Anthony Comstock was able to mount a campaign against birth control which resulted in the enactment of a statute by Congress in 1873 excluding contraceptives and contraceptive information from the mails and declaring them obscene.[1] This federal example was followed by the states, many of which passed laws banning the sale and distribution of contraceptives. These laws were not always successfully enforced, but their existence, so long as they were supported by public opinion, undoubtedly held back to some extent the advance of birth control.

In 1912 the American movement for birth control entered a new phase when Margaret Sanger, a New York nurse, started her life's work as an advocate of the cause. In 1914 she began publication of a new monthly magazine, *The Woman Rebel*, but was arrested and indicted under the Comstock law. She retired to Europe, and the following year her husband was imprisoned for a short term for handing out a copy of her work *Family Limitation*. Mrs. Sanger returned to the United States and in Brooklyn on October 16, 1916, opened the first birth control clinic in the United States. The clinic was raided and closed by the police, and Mrs. Sanger and her sister were both sentenced to thirty days' imprisonment in 1917. Undaunted by this experience, she continued her work and propaganda, basing her appeal less on the Malthusian arguments favored by Annie Besant and more on the suffering caused to women by unlimited child-bearing. In 1917 the National Birth Control League was founded and Mrs. Sanger began publication of the *Birth Control Review*. The upheaval caused by the First World War undoubtedly helped advance her cause, and she played a leading part in national and international conferences on the birth control question. In 1921 the New York birth control clinical research bureau was opened. Mrs. Sanger and her associate, Mary Ware Dennett, were well aware that the existence of hostile laws was hampering their work; they made strenuous efforts to secure their repeal but were not suc-

---

[1] 17 Stat. 598 (1873), the modern version of which may be found in 19 U.S.C.A. § 1305(a) (1960).

cessful. In 1929 their New York clinic was raided but after an abortive trial of the director and assistant was able to continue its work.

Meanwhile public opinion was changing. The gynecological section of the American Medical Association passed a motion in 1925 recommending the alteration of the law to allow physicians to give contraceptive advice, and in 1931 the Federal Council of the Churches of Christ published a report favoring birth control. Support also came from the American Neurological Association, the Eugenics Society, and the Central Conference of Rabbis. In 1937 the American Medical Association unanimously agreed to accept birth control "as an integral part of medical practice and education."

Today birth control, including contraception, is generally approved in the United States with the exception, of course, of Roman Catholics and also of Orthodox Church members. Hundreds of different types of contraceptives are in use and contraception has become big business, hundreds of millions of dollars being spent in the trade every year. Planned parenthood centers are found throughout the country, save in Connecticut and Massachusetts; and medical birth control care is provided by maternal health clinics and other child-spacing information centers. Birth control of some variety is practiced by the vast majority of married couples, methods ranging from contraceptives and the pill to *coitus interruptus* and the use of the safe period. Despite this revolution in mores the laws restricting the sale of contraceptives remain at least in theory unchanged and it is necessary to examine the legal provisions before going on to consider the problem of whether they should be further altered to take into account what really amounts to a moral revolution.

Federal law restricts the distribution of contraceptives in a number of ways. Knowingly to deposit any contraceptive in the mails or to take such articles from the mails for the purpose of distribution is a felony under federal law.[2] The ban extends to any information on where contraceptives may be obtained, and any written or printed matter telling "how or by what means conception may be prevented." A further federal felony is committed by depositing contraceptives or information on where they may be obtained with

---

[2] 18 U.S.C.A. § 1461 (1963 Supp.).

an express company or other common carrier.[3] Books on contraception are not specifically mentioned, but obscene books are included in the ban. To import contraceptive articles or obscene books is also a felony and prohibited by federal statute.[4]

Were these statutes to be strictly and literally enforced, the whole trade in contraceptives would be brought to a standstill. A number of attempts have been made to amend them by legislation, but they have not been successful.[5] They have, however, been drastically modified by judicial interpretation. The first case came in 1930 and was an action for trademark infringement by a manufacturer of prophylactics. The defense was that redress was contrary to public policy since the federal statutes were being violated in carrying out the business.[6] The point was not taken by the judge. "We conclude," said Judge Swan, "therefore that a manufacturer of drugs or instruments for medical use may in good faith sell them to druggists or other reputable dealers in medical supplies, or to jobbers for distribution to such trade."[7] He suggested without finally disposing of the point that the Criminal Code should be interpreted as requiring an intent on the part of the sender that "the article mailed or shipped by common carrier be used for illegal contraception or abortion or for indecent or immoral uses."[8] The judge's reasoning was applied in *Davis v. United States* when an intent to use the articles for illegal purposes was held necessary for a conviction under the postal and transport statutes.[9] This decision enabled manufacturers of contraceptives and others in the trade to dispatch their goods to druggists, jobbers, and physicians.

These decisions prepared the way for *United States v. One Package*[10] in 1936, when Dr. Hannah Stone was allowed to import a package of vaginal pessaries into the United States. Judge Augustus Hand conceded that the Tariff Act of 1930 exempted only

---

[3] 18 U.S.C.A. § 1462 (1963 Supp.). For either mailing contraceptives or causing them to be transported the penalties are fines of not more than $5,000 or not more than five years' imprisonment, or both, for a first offense; and fines of not more than $10,000 or ten years' imprisonment, or both, for a second offense.

[4] 19 U.S.C.A. § 1305 (1960).

[5] For a list of these attempts see SULLOWAY, BIRTH CONTROL AND CATHOLIC DOCTRINE 190 n.20 (1959).

[6] Youngs Rubber Corp. v. C. I. Lee & Co., 45 F.2d 103 (2d Cir. 1930).

[7] *Id.* at 109.

[8] *Id.* at 108.

[9] 62 F.2d 473 (6th Cir. 1933).

[10] 86 F.2d 737 (2d Cir. 1936).

those articles excepted by the Comstock Act of 1873 but went on to state that the court was satisfied "that this statute, as well as all the acts we have referred to, embraced only such articles as Congress would have denounced as immoral if it had understood all the conditions under which they were to be used. Its design, in our opinion, was not to prevent the importation, sale, or carriage by mail of things which might intelligently be employed by conscientious and competent physicians for the purpose of saving life or promoting the well being of their patients."[11] Judge Learned Hand, impatient about these verbal gymnastics, contented himself with observing that people had changed their minds about such matters in recent years, and concurred in the judgment.

As has been noted, books on contraception are specifically banned from the mails by the postal statute, but the section restricting imports mentions only "obscene" books. It is now established that a book on contraception is not per se considered obscene by the federal courts. Dismissing a charge against *Contraception* by Marie Stopes in 1931, Judge Woolsey stated: "It is a scientific book written with obvious seriousness and with great decency, and it gives information to the medical profession regarding the operation of birth control clinics and the instruction necessary to be given at such clinics to women who resort thereto." Such a book was not obscene "for the reading of it would not stir the sex impulses of any person with a normal mind."[12]

The federal statutes are thus not dead letters and have incidental significance in their bearing on other parts of the birth control controversy which will be considered later, but contraceptives intended for *bona fide* medical use or for the treatment or prevention of disease, and books and pamphlets concerning contraception which are not written in obscene language may be freely imported, transported, and mailed. In practice this means that contraceptives must be going to or coming from doctors or other professional persons, or anyone acting at their direction or under their supervision. To secure a conviction under the statutes an intention to use the materials illegally must be established by the prosecution.

Federal law on birth control is supplemented by state law, although eighteen states and the District of Columbia have no legis-

---

11 *Id.* at 739.
12 U.S. v. One Book Entitled "Contraception," 51 F.2d 525, 527–28 (S.D.N.Y. 1931).

lation on the subject. Seventeen states prohibit traffic in contraceptives but exempt doctors, pharmacists, or others operating under special license from the statutory prohibition. Five states—Connecticut, Kansas, Massachusetts, Mississippi, and Nebraska—prohibit the sale and advertising of contraceptives and make no exceptions to their restriction. Eight states have no law against contraceptives but restrict or prohibit their advertisement. In Arizona the constitutionality of a ban on advertising has been recently upheld.[13] In all, thirty states prohibit such advertising, fifteen making an exception for medical journals and textbooks. Sixteen states regulate the trade by requiring contraceptive information to be accurate and probiting the sale of articles which do not comply with certain defined standards. In some states sale of contraceptives from slot machines is forbidden. In New Jersey[14] the constitutionality of such a ban has been recently challenged in the courts but has been upheld.

Legal writers and others have put forward the view that any federal or state statute regulating birth control is unconstitutional in that they deny the individual his personal right to the pursuit of happiness and also take away the rights protected by the due process clause of the Fourteenth Amendment. Writing on this subject, Professor H. Kalven concludes: "Despite the lack of judicial success to date it would seem that the freedom of sex relations within marriage and the freedom to have children when wanted rank high among the basic personal liberties in our society and their curtailment presents a serious civil liberties issue."[15] The courts have consistently taken an opposite view. The federal courts for example have upheld the federal statutes as constitutional with an exemption for physicians and others professionally qualified. On the state level prohibition of the sale or advertising of contraceptives or the dissemination of information on birth control has consistently been held to be within the police power of individual states.[16]

It is also claimed that when the laws are strictly interpreted physicians are denied a fundamental right to advise patients on

---

[13] Planned Parenthood Comm. v. Maricopa County, 375 P.2d 719 (Ariz. 1962).

[14] Sanitary Vendors, Inc. v. Byrne, 190 A.2d 876 (N.J. 1963).

[15] Kalven, *A Special Corner of Civil Liberties,* 31 N.Y.U.L. REV. 1223, 1228–29 (1956).

[16] *E.g.,* Tileston v. Ullman, 26 A.2d 582 (Conn. 1942), *appeal dismissed,* 318 U.S. 44 (1943).

professional matters involving life and health. This argument too has been rejected by the courts. Until 1938 none of the cases had included a qualified physician as party to the proceedings, or else the statute under review contained a clause exempting physicians from its operation. In that year, however, in the *Gardner* case a statute imposing an unconditional ban was upheld by the Massachusetts courts and an appeal to the United States Supreme Court was dismissed, "for want of a substantial federal question."[17]

In Connecticut in 1957 a bill was introduced into the legislature to allow physicians to give information on contraception to married women, but it made no progress. As a result a group of nine citizens in conjunction with the Planned Parenthood Association resolved to challenge the constitutionality of existing Connecticut birth control legislation. Five of the cases came to court. It was argued that the birth control statutes infringed the basic liberties guaranteed by the Fourteenth Amendment. A physician maintained that it was essential for the fulfilling of his professional obligations that he should be able to give advice on contraception. A mother argued that the use of contraceptives was necessary to safeguard her health. The statutes were upheld in the lower court and the case then went to the supreme court of errors. The court decided that it could not overrule the interpretation laid down in previous cases that the statutes were constitutional.[18] It added that while contraception might be the safest way to safeguard a mother's health it could not ignore the fact that there was an alternative, namely abstention from sexual intercourse. "We cannot say," declared the judge, "that the legislature, in weighing the considerations for and against an exception legalizing contraceptive measures in cases such as the ones before us, could not reasonably conclude, that, despite the occasional hardship which might result, the greater good would be served by leaving the statutes as they are."[19]

The Supreme Court of the United States agreed to hear the appeal in 1960, only to dismiss it the following year.[20] Mr. Justice Frankfurter maintained that the statutes were dead letters, since

---

17 Commonwealth v. Gardner, 15 N.E.2d 222 (Mass. 1938), *appeal dismissed,* 305 U.S. 559 (1938).

18 Buxton v. Ullman, 156 A.2d 508 (Conn. 1959). Another case where a right to family planning was alleged irrespective of health was also dismissed. Trubek v. Ullman, 165 A2d. 158 (Conn. 1960), *appeal dismissed,* 363 U.S. 907 (1960).

19 156 A.2d at 514.

20 Poe v. Ullman, 367 U.S. 497 (1961).

contraceptives were freely on sale throughout Connecticut without any likelihood or threat of prosecution, and in the whole history of the legislation only one prosecution had in fact taken place. "This court," he declared, "cannot be umpire to debates concerning harmless, empty, shadows."[21] In November, 1961, the Planned Parenthood League opened a clinic in Connecticut under the auspices of Mrs. Griswold and Dr. Buxton. The clinic was closed by the police, and in January, 1962, they were fined one hundred dollars each. They appealed and the case again went to the supreme court of errors which again refused to overrule its earlier precedents.[22] Appeal has been taken to the Supreme Court of the United States to demonstrate that the statutes are not as shadowy as Mr. Justice Frankfurter made them out to be. At this writing no action on the appeal has been taken.

On the other hand, in New Jersey in May, 1959, a county judge declared New Jersey's statute banning the sale or distribution of contraceptives "without just cause" unconstitutional. He maintained that it was so vague and indefinite that it would not fairly inform a defendant of "the elements constituting a quasi-criminal infraction."[23] This judgment was overruled by the New Jersey Supreme Court, which held that the statute was intended to regulate but not prohibit sale of contraceptives and held that the prohibition of selling contraceptives by means of vending machines was permissible under the Act.[24]

The grounds of attack on birth control statutes are now widening. Although the police power may be exercised to protect public morals, it must be reasonable. With the general acceptance of birth control as a normal part of married life, the statutes can be attacked on the ground that they are "unreasonable" they are also open to attack on the grounds that they violate the separation of Church and State guaranteed by the First Amendment. Recent theological developments have left the Roman Catholic Church practically isolated among Christian denominations in condemning artificial birth control. It could therefore be contended that the birth control statutes enforce the doctrine of a particular denomina-

---

21 *Id.* at 508. For a reasonably full discussion of the constitutional issue with special reference to the Connecticut cases see Smith, *The History and Future of the Legal Battle over Birth Control*, 49 CORNELL L.Q. 275 (1964).

22 State v. Griswold, 200 A.2d 479 (Conn. 1964).

23 See New York Times, May 13, 1959, p. 27.

24 Sanitary Vendors, Inc. v. Byrne, 190 A.2d 876 (N.J. 1963).

tion at the expense of that of other religious communions. Alternatively it could and has been argued that the statutes limit religious freedom. This point has in fact been raised in Connecticut. In May, 1959, three Protestant ministers—an Episcopalian, a Lutheran, and a Methodist—asked the Superior Court for a ruling on the Connecticut statute. The ministers claimed that the law prohibiting dissemination of birth control advice deprived them of their "liberty, freedom of speech and right to freely practice their religions." They stated they were "bound by the teachings of the church and their own religious beliefs to counsel married parishioners on the use of contraceptive devices and to advise them and to counsel to use same and to give such advice in pre-marital counseling."[25] The court did not accept this plea.

The United States is not unique in attempting to control the sale of contraceptives or dissemination of birth control information by law, and the experience of other countries in this field is of some relevance. In Britain there has never been an actual statutory ban on the distribution of contraceptives as such, but in the nineteenth century contraceptive information was classified as obscenity and the sale of contraceptives came within the common-law offense of publishing obscene matter. This is no longer the case. Books are no longer considered obscene if they advocate or describe methods of birth control. "It cannot be assumed," said the Home Secretary in answer to a question in the House of Commons in 1922, "that a court would hold a book to be obscene merely because it deals with the subject referred to."[26] Sale of contraceptives is not today subject to common-law or statutory restriction save for certain bylaws which restrict the sale of contraceptives from slot machines in public places.[27] Advertisements for contraceptives are not per se considered obscene. The absence of statutory limitation has enabled the common law to adapt itself to changed social and moral views about contraception with a minimum of public controversy. The lack of legal restraint accords with prevailing English opinion on the subject summed up by the Royal Commission on Population when it stated: "Control by men and

---

25 See New York Times, May 6, 1959.

26 See ST. JOHN-STEVAS, OBSCENITY AND THE LAW 70 (1956).

27 The bylaws were suggested by the Home Secretary in a circular of Oct. 22, 1949, after public controversy over sale of contraceptives from slot machines. He circulated a model bylaw suggesting this was the appropriate remedy, since the practice was an evil only in some public places. For a discussion of what constitutes a "public place" see 144 THE JUSTICE OF THE PEACE AND LOCAL GOVERNMENT REVIEW 4 (1950).

women over the numbers of their children is one of the first conditions of their own and the community's welfare, and in our view
mechanical and chemical methods of contraception have to be accepted as part of the modern means, however imperfect, by which
it can be exercised."[28] The commission expressed the hope that
voluntary parenthood would become universal.

In a number of Catholic countries any information or sale of
contraceptives is prohibited by law. Thus in Ireland the Censorship of Publications Act forbids the sale or publication of matter
which "advocates or might reasonably be supposed to advocate the
unnatural prevention of conception."[29] The Criminal Law
(Amendment) Act of 1935 forbids the sale or importing of contraceptives. Penalties under both statutes are a fine not exceeding
£50 or imprisonment for not more than six months, or both. In
Spain, an act of January 24, 1941, forbids any form of public instruction on methods of birth control, and the exhibition or offering for sale of contraceptives. Customs regulations forbid the importing of contraceptives. Doctors are not forbidden to prescribe
contraceptives but birth control advice may not be given as part
of any public health service and there are no birth control clinics
in Spain. In Italy birth control propaganda is forbidden but the
sale of contraceptives is allowed in pharmacies. No birth control
clinics exist and contraception may not be advised by those discharging public health service duties. Birth control is also restricted by law in France but for sociological rather than religious
reasons.[30] No birth control clinics operate, nor is advice given
through public health services. Doctors may prescribe contraceptives in certain limited circumstances such as the need to avoid
danger to a mother's health from further pregnancies.

In the Western world today the divisions over contraception
and birth control reflect underlying differences in religious attitudes. Broadly speaking, Catholics are against contraception and
everyone else is for it.[31] There are three principal focuses of social
dispute: the regulation of contraception by law, the provision of

---

28 Cmd. 7695 para. 427 (1945).

29 Ireland: No. 21 of 1929.

30 By a law of July 31, 1920. Use of the mails is restricted by article 91 of the
Decree-Act of July 20, 1939. Importing of propaganda on contraceptives is restricted
by a decree of Feb. 5, 1946.

31 The Orthodox do not accept contraception but the social influence of Orthodoxy has never been marked, and for practical purposes opposition can now be
considered as coming exclusively from Catholics.

birth control facilities through public health services, and the role to be played by contraception in solving the problems raised by the increase in world population. The position is complicated by differences of emphasis and approach on the birth control issue among Catholics themselves and developments and changes in the teaching of the Church. The first Catholic attitude was a complete condemnation of all forms of birth control without exception. Family planning was an unacceptable concept and the Catholic couple was expected to welcome a large family as a sign of God's favor: if there was material need God would provide. Trust in providence, not birth regulation, was the ideal Catholic response. Little was known about the safe period as a means of birth control, and there was respectable authority for rejecting its employment as immoral in the teaching of St. Augustine and his followers.[32] St. Thomas elaborated the teaching of Augustine and articulated the orthodox Catholic view that contraception was contrary to the natural law, since it prevented the primary end of marriage, the procreation of children, a conclusion which man could reach by the use of reason. Accordingly contraception was a very grave sin and Catholic writers rammed this point home by expatiating on the evils, moral and social, which come about through the use of contraceptives. The health of the woman, it was maintained, suffered; the chances of sterility were increased; contraception increased the likelihood of contracting cancer and caused an unsatisfied sex-craving leading to overindulgence and the destruction of matrimonial harmony. Catholics also made much of the argument that contraception leads to population decline and eventual race extinction. The constant repetition of these views, the polemic approach of many Catholic authors, the somewhat superstitious reverence attached to human semen, and the puritanical approach to sexual matters of many Catholics combined to create an emotional horror of contraception leading to the conclusion that contraception constituted one of the gravest of moral and social evils.

In the period between the wars, however, the foundations were laid for a modified Catholic attitude. Of primary importance was the discovery in 1930 by two doctors working independently, Dr. Ogino of Japan and Dr. Knaus of Austria, of a reasonably reliable method of calculating the duration of the cylical period of sterility

---

32 See ON THE MORALS OF THE MANICHAEANS xviii, 65.

in women. The existence of this period had been known for centuries but until the work of these researchers no means had been available of establishing its duration. The nub of the Ogino-Knaus discoveries is that a woman's menstrual period is normally twenty-eight days and during this time ovulation occurs only once, the ovum or egg being discharged from the ovary into the Fallopian tubes. Conception can take place only when the egg is present. Thus if the date of ovulation can be accurately calculated, the commencement of the sterile period can be ascertained. The latest research based on the findings of Ogino and Knaus indicates that ovulation takes place on the fifteenth day before the onset of menstruation. In working out the infertile period allowance has to be made for the period in which male sperm can survive in the female genital tract (approximately two days) and for the life of the ovum (one day). Accordingly in the case of a woman with an absolutely regular cycle of twenty-eight days the fertile period will be five days. Allowance has to be made for the irregularities in the cycle, a variable factor in different women but constant in the same subject. Once a woman's particular cycle has been established then a formula can be worked out indicating her sterile period. Various new methods have since been developed for pinpointing the day of ovulation. These methods are on the whole reliable but not foolproof, and the question is further complicated by the fact that the cycle in individual women can be upset by emotional or other disturbance and by the anomaly of some women who have no regular cycle.

Use of the safe period as a means of family planning was at first frowned upon by many Catholic theologians, but in his encylical *Casti connubii* (1930) Pius XI left the way open for an acceptance of rhythm and today a consensus has emerged among theologians that the deliberate use of the safe period as a means of family planning is indifferent morally and its employment is licit provided there is adequate reason for its use. Pius XII made two statements to this effect in 1951.[33] The theological argument concludes that since use of the safe period involves no actual frustration of nature but merely makes use of what nature provides, it is not intrinsically immoral. If the parties resort to it for purely selfish or inadequate reasons, its employment would, however, be sinful. This development of Catholic doctrine has had a profound effect on the

---

[33] See Address to Italian Catholic Union of Midwives, Oct. 9, 1951, 43 A.A.S. 835; Address to National Congress of the Family Front, Nov. 26, 1951, 43 A.A.S. 855.

Catholic approach to the problem of birth control, since many of the social evils attributed to the use of contraceptives could equally well result from use of the rhythm method. Many polemic arguments have accordingly been abandoned and the emotional temperature has been lowered.

Since the Second World War there have been further radical developments. First of all there has been mounting dissatisfaction with the whole Augustinian-Thomist approach to the theology of marriage. Between the wars a handful of Catholic theologians challenged the emphasis on the social and procreative purposes of marriage and the underestimation of the personal factors of friendship and love between the spouses. They stressed the personal aspects of marriage, its role in increasing mutual love and perfecting the personalities of the spouses. They criticized the rigid traditional division between the "primary" and "secondary" ends of marriage as misleading and legalistic. Thus Dr. Herbert Doms in his book *The Meaning of Marriage* denied that the constitution of marriage consists in a subservience to a purpose outside the spouses themselves, for which they marry. "It consists in the constant vital ordination of husband and wife to each other until they become one. If this is so, there can no longer be sufficient reason, from this standpoint, for speaking of procreation as the primary purpose (in the sense in which St. Thomas used the phrase) and for dividing off the other purposes as secondary."[34] The meaning of marriage is the community of life between the spouses, of which the child is the fruit and visible embodiment.

This view was at the time that of a minority although it had to some extent been foreshadowed by Pius XI in his encylical on marriage, *Casti connubii*. "This mutual, interior, moulding of husband and wife," wrote the Pope, "this determined effort to perfect one another, can in a very real sense, as the Roman Catechism teaches, be said to be the chief reason and purpose of matrimony, provided matrimony be looked at not in the restricted sense as instituted for the proper conception and education of children, but more widely as a blending of life as a whole, and the mutual interchange and sharing thereof." Dr. Doms and his followers incurred a Vatican censure in 1944, but they have had a profound influence on contemporary Catholic writing on marriage and have concentrated the attention of religious writers on the hitherto

---

34 DOMS, THE MEANING OF MARRIAGE 87 (1939).

neglected "secondary" ends of marriage which now tend to be treated as of primary importance in Catholic writing on marriage. An excellent example of the new positive Catholic approach to marriage is *Love and Control,* a treatise on marriage by Cardinal Suenens, Archbishop of Brussels.

This new approach has led to speculation that the Catholic Church is likely at some date in the future to abandon her opposition to contraception, a step which would have profound social consequences, since it would at a stroke remove many of the tensions caused by birth control in contemporary pluralist societies. The likelihood of this happening must therefore be dispassionately assessed. The nub of the argument in favor of a revision of Catholic teaching on contraception is contained in a recent article published in *Cross Currents* by Professor Louis Dupré of the Jesuit University of Georgetown.[35] Professor Dupré opens the argument by asserting that there is no infallible document finally condemning contraception and excluding the matter from further discussion within the Catholic Church. He goes on to draw a distinction between the intrinsic procreative purpose in sexual activity and the individual acts, only some of which are intended by nature to result in procreation. He criticizes the treatment of individual sexual acts as isolated or absolute phenomena unrelated to the spiritual or marital life of the spouses on a number of grounds. This, maintains the professor, confuses the biological structure of nature with human nature itself, and furthermore treats human nature as though it were static instead of allowing for an inevitable development. Dupré gives support to the argument advanced by Dr. John Rock in his book *The Time Has Come* that the use of contraceptives may be justified for the benefit of living children whom it is the duty of the parents to bring up in reasonable standards of comfort and education. "Dr. Rock's argument," he writes, "seems to be basically sound, for the protection of life itself is not the only ground which justifies drastic measures. The well-being of the living is a sufficient moral ground, and this well-being can become seriously jeopardized by an undue extension of the family, or even, as psychiatrists have pointed out, by complete continence of the parents."[36] Dupré does not reach the conclusion that contraceptives are legitimate in marriage, although this is certainly a

---

35 Dupré; *A Reexamination of the Catholic Position on Birth Control,* Cross Currents, Winter, pp. 63–85 (1964).
36 *Id.* at 73.

conclusion which could be drawn from his arguments, but stops at the point of downgrading the sinfulness of contraception. "We readily admit that *ideally* the highest perfection would consist in having the marriage act with all its consequences, or in not having it at all, when those consequences cannot be accepted. But we wonder whether this ideal is always an essential perfection which man cannot commit without violating the moral law. If it is not, then we can only conclude that 'le mieux est parfois l'ennemi du bien,' and that someone should not be called immoral because he has not reached the heights of perfection."[37] A similar point is made by Archbishop Roberts, S.J., in an article in the newsletter *Search*, published in London in April, 1964, and expanded in an article on contraception and war in *Objections to Catholicism*, also published in London, in November, 1964. Archbishop Roberts throws doubts on the condemnation of Protestant missionaries in India by Catholics for offering contraceptives to mothers of large families who are struggling for survival against poverty and hunger. "He offers a contraceptive," writes the Archbishop, "not as an ideal solution but as a lesser evil than sterilization, than abortion, than the hunger of his children, than the death of his wife or the death of their married life."

Neither the Archbishop nor Professor Dupré argues that the use of a contraceptive is in accord with Catholic moral teaching, but the logical conclusion from their reasoning is that Catholic teaching needs revision. My own view is that the acceptance of contraceptives as such by the Catholic Church is highly unlikely but that the Church is moving toward a position where the employment of contraceptives by married couples in certain circumstances will not be regarded as the heinous and abominable sin it has been in the past. This pastoral modification must in the long run lead to a modification of the Catholic social and legal attitude to the sale of contraceptives and the provision of birth control information, and narrow the gulf between Catholics and Protestants that exists on the issue.

An equally important development of a scientific character which is likely to have religious and social implications is the discovery of the birth control pill. There are a variety of such pills but here I want to consider one in particular, based on the use of progestin. All women, when pregnant, secrete a natural hormone,

---

37 *Id.* at 85.

progesterone, which prevents ovulation during the pregnancy period. A synthetic substitute for this hormone, progestin, has been developed, which has the same effect of inhibiting ovulation and can be taken through the mouth. The drug has been used in a number of experiments and is now considered safe enough to be marketed. Under the name of "Enovid" it has been marketed in the United States, and the United States Federal Food and Drug Administration has stated that it is safe and effective when taken under doctor's orders.[38] Use of the pill is spreading widely in the United States and is likely to continue to do so.[39]

Early reaction to the pill among Catholic theologians especially in the United States was hostile[40] but since then there has been a rallying of support for the pill on the ground that it is not a contraceptive in the normally accepted sense of the word. The theological argument for the pill is deployed most fully in an article by Canon Janssens, a priest and professor of moral theology at the Catholic University of Louvain.[41] The argument of Canon Janssens is subtle and complex, but reduced to its basic terms it maintains the proposition that the pill is not a contraceptive since it leaves the essential, given structure of the sexual act unimpaired. Neither does it constitute sterilization (also forbidden by the Church), since the function of ovulation is merely postponed; the ova remains in the ovaries ready for future fertilization. The use of the pill is further justified by drawing a parallel between it and the use of the sterile period as a means of family planning. The use of either device to exclude children from a marriage for selfish reasons would be wrong, but the employment of either prudently for serious reasons would be lawful. The use of the pill, writes Canon Janssens, is essentially indistinguishable from periodic continence,

---

[38] "Enovid," formerly recommended for use for a maximum of two years, may now be used up to four years under the ruling. But the agency said the manufacturer must caution doctors against prescribing it for certain classes of patients—including women over 35—because of possible health hazards. It is said that women with cancer of the uterus and certain other cancers, those with liver diseases, and those with a history of blood clots in the veins or lungs probably should not be given the drug.

[39] The use of pills has been blamed for a recent slump in the U.S. birth rate. Figures show that 337,000 babies were born in the U.S. in March 1964, 6,000 fewer than in the March of 1963 and the lowest since 1955. The cost of pills has gone down to under $2.00 for a month's supply.

[40] E.g., 122 AMERICAN ECCLESIASTICAL REVIEW 225 (1950); 137 id. 50 (1957); Lynch, Fertility Control and the Moral Law, 20 LINACRE QUARTERLY 83 (1953).

[41] EPHENERIDES THEOLOGICAL LOVANIENSIS 787 (1963).

and since use of the sterile period is not regarded as sterilization, neither should using the pill.

In both England and the United States fierce debates have gone on among Catholics about the legitimacy of the use of the pill. In the United States the debate was conducted principally by means of articles in newspapers and periodicals both Catholic and non-Catholic.[42] The progress of the controversy was similar in England until a statement by Archbishop Heenan on behalf of the English hierarchy on May 7, 1964, turned it into a subject of national debate throughout the country. The English hierarchy quoted (or misquoted) a statement by the Dutch bishops of the previous year in order to condemn the pill. Far from quieting Catholics the statement made them more voluble than ever, and these dissidents received support from Rome in a statement from Father Häring, one of the leading Ecumenical Council theologians, repudiating Archbishop Heenan's views. Father Häring later denied the mode of expression attributed to him, but the substantial dissent was not retracted. Cardinal Ottaviani then intervened with an order for silence on the issue, and the Pope himself then acted, requesting all parties to the controversy to cease public utterance until the matter had been gone into by a special papal commission appointed by himself. In the autumn the matter came before the third session of the Council, when discussion of schema XIII was begun, the schema on this issue making no final pronouncement but calling for the co-operation of doctors, priests, scientists, and others in working out answers to the moral, medical, and social problems involved. During October the controversy once again flared in the Council with Archbishop Heenan demanding a more definitive statement, Cardinal Ottaviani reasserting the traditional teaching on marriage and Cardinal Suenens and Cardinal Leger of Montreal calling for an objective re-examination and restatement of the Church's marriage theology. There for the moment the controversy rests with no final position taken.[43]

A subsidiary question of considerable importance is whether use of a similar pill to stabilize a woman's menstrual cycle would be acceptable to Catholic teaching. There is growing agreement

---

42 For a reasonably full documentation of the controversy on both sides of the Atlantic see *The Pill*, edited by Leo Pyle (1964).

43 For an account of the Council proceedings, see The Times of London, October and November, 1964, especially on this point, October 23, 1964, and October 30, 1964.

that such a pill would in fact be legitimate, but such a pill has not as yet been perfected. The likelihood that research in this direction will be successful within a short period of time is considerable and if in fact achieved would provide a way out of the present controversies acceptable to all parties. Married couples would be required to abstain from intercourse for only a few days a month, which would impose no great psychological or emotional strain and would probably be beneficial to their health. Pinpointing the day of ovulation would make the "safe period" by far the safest means of birth regulation and most people would prefer, on aesthetic and psychological, let alone moral, grounds, to use such a method of family planning rather than a contraceptive.

I have gone into these developments at some length because they have direct bearing on the question of what role the state should play in regulating birth control. The first question to be answered is whether Catholic theology requires that contraception be banned by law. The fact that Catholic theologians teach that it is contrary to natural law does not mean that it should be banned by positive law, since all contraventions of natural law are not fit subjects for legislation. Fornication, adultery, and lying, for example, are contrary to natural law, but civil sanctions are not advocated for such offenses. A breach of natural law must be a fit subject for legislation and injure the common good substantially before it is forbidden by law. The law must be capable of enforcement and equitable in its incidence. Finally if it would cause greater evils than those intended to be avoided, it should not be resorted to.

The banning of the *use* of a contraceptive by law as in Connecticut fulfills none of these criteria. Using a contraceptive is essentially a private act, and though it may be argued that it has harmful social consequences, it is impossible to isolate any particular act and demonstrate that harmful consequences flow from it. In practice such a law is unenforceable, and the attempt to enforce it would involve an intolerable interference in the private lives of individuals.

Banning the sale of contraceptives and the dissemination of birth control information, on the other hand, is a possible subject for legislation, since these are public acts, capable of regulation by law. Certainly such laws are difficult to enforce but their effect would be far from nugatory, given a climate of moral opinion which approved their content. Thus in a predominantly Catholic country like Ireland such a law is not unreasonable. It is true that minorities in countries like Ireland are denied access to contraceptives (at least in theory) by the law. It is argued that while to allow the sale of contraceptives in no way diminishes the rights of Catholics since they are under no compulsion to use them, a prohibitory law adversely affects the rights of Protestants and others. This is true in one sense, but on the other hand a society which allows complete freedom in the sale and advertising of contraceptives exerts a strong pressure on its members to use them or at least makes it more difficult for them to abstain from doing so. The fact is that if religion is more than a purely personal and private exercise, if it sets out to provide a *Weltanschauung*, then it is bound to have social effects which may diminish the freedom of those who reject the faith. One cannot expect a society in which the vast majority of its inhabitants condemn contraception as a moral and social evil to allow its unfettered spread in the name of a doctrine of abstract rights. It is only because moral opinion in Britain and the United States accepts contraception as more or less a good that it is largely uncontrolled.

In a pluralist society divided on religious grounds the situation is very different, and in such societies where there is no agreement on a particular moral issue, it is better taken out of the public domain and left to be decided by the private conscience. Such a conclusion is justified both on a priori and pragmatic grounds. Laws embodying moral precepts are only enforceable if they are supported by a corresponding moral consensus in the community. The Volstead Act should have made that plain enough. A law forbidding the sale of contraceptives would be effective only if the great majority of citizens believed their use to be wrongful and even under those conditions would face enforcement difficulties. The laws of Connecticut and Massachusetts on birth control, for example, are not in fact enforceable and save for the exclusion of birth control clinics are without effect. Even so the presence of clinics over the state line does much to neutralize their exclusion from the states themselves. Catholics, then, in campaigning for the maintenance of such laws, gain little for public morality. They do, however, increase the fear of Catholicism in the minds of non-Catholics and increase the likelihood that the Protestant view of the Church will not be that of a religious body but of a political power structure.

Why then do Catholics fight so strongly for the maintenance

of these virtual dead letters on the statute book? One reason is the emotional revulsion with which many Catholics regard contraception, but this, as I have pointed out is a diminishing factor. Another reason is sociological. In Connecticut and Massachusetts the statutes have become flags or symbols around which a numerical majority with a minority mentality, a legacy of the past, can rally. Finally there is a more rational motivation. As long as the statutes making contraception formally illegal remain, it is easier for Catholics to resist pressure to extend contraception in other spheres, such as giving contraceptive advice as part of state health services. It is in this sphere that the real social struggle is taking place in the United States today and the position must be examined further.

The giving of contraceptive advice in tax-supported hospitals or as part of public health services is accepted in some states and a subject of bitter contest in others. In a number of southern states for example, where Catholics are few, such advice is freely given, and a similar practice is followed in other regions, but in many municipally financed hospitals in the North, West, Midwest, and East it is forbidden. Recently the struggle has centered on proposals in certain states to include birth control advice as part of relief programs for the poor and indigent. The form the struggle has taken has varied in different states as has the result, but there is a basically similar pattern.

The state of New York provides a good illustration of how the power struggle is being fought out. The issue came to a head in 1958 in New York City where for many years city hospitals had followed an unwritten rule that advice on birth control should not be given. In July, 1958, a Protestant physician employed at Kings County Hospital announced that he was going to fit a Protestant patient with a contraceptive diaphragm but was forbidden to do so by the New York City commissioner of hospitals. A public controversy followed with Protestants and Jews demanding that the ban be lifted in the interests of accepted therapy and preventive medicine and the Roman Catholic chancery office stating: "It would be extremely unfortunate if our hospitals and medical faculties, aimed for the preservation of life should be perverted to seek for the prevention of life." In September, 1958, the full hospital commission reversed the ban. The board ordered that municipal hospitals "should provide such medical advice, preventive measures and devices for female patients under their care whose life and health in the opinion of the medical staff may be jeopardized by pregnancy and who wish to avail themselves of such health services." A certificate of medical necessity signed by two physicians must be issued, the consent of the patient and that of her husband obtained if possible, and the board recommends that she confer with her spiritual adviser. Physicians, nurses, and other hospital employees with religious or moral objections to contraceptive procedures are excused from participation. Later in the same month the New York Department of Welfare adopted a similar policy.[44]

This policy is similar in many ways to that adopted in Britain under the National Health Service, where advice on birth control can be given but only in certain circumstances. The Ministry of Health allows contraceptive advice to be given in maternal and child welfare clinics to those married women for whom a pregnancy would be detrimental to health. Many medical officers refer patients outside this category to the voluntary birth control clinics, which are found in many areas. Local authorities may themselves with the approval of the minister open contraceptive clinics and give advice to nursing mothers requiring it on medical grounds. They may also contribute to voluntary organizations providing such advice. Many clinics of the family planning association are conducted on the premises of the local authority or regional hospital boards. General practitioners in the service are not forbidden to provide contraceptive advice for their patients. They may not charge for advice given on medical grounds but may do so when no medical reason exists for limitation of pregnancies. Contraceptive appliances are not obtainable on national health service prescriptions, but if a patient needs them on medical grounds and cannot afford to pay for them, payment may be authorized by a local medical officer or hospital consultant.[45]

The controversy broke out afresh in New York in January, 1964, when it was announced that a birth control service would be made available to recipients of state relief. On one side it was argued that this was a reasonable way of limiting the expenses incurred by the state, on the other that Catholics might well be influenced to go against their consciences and employ contraceptives. The

---

44 For an account of this incident see New York Times, Sept. 17, 18, 23, 1958.

45 On Nov. 23, 1964, the Minister of Health was asked in the Commons to make more extensive services for contraception, birth control advice, etc., available under the Health Service. He replied that he was considering what more needs to be done. 702 Hansard 906–15.

birth control advice was to be given only for medical reasons and only to married women who were living with their husbands. At the time of this writing, however, the state welfare board is considering extension of birth control services to all heads of families on welfare. Despite inclusion of unmarried women, there is strong support for the proposal.

In 1963 a similar controversy had broken out in Chicago. Cook County has an especially heavy financial burden to bear, with 165,000 adults and children on relief costing about $96 million a year to the taxpayer. The relief recipients have a birth rate of 37 per 1,000, twice the normal birth rate in Chicago. The rule for welfare workers before the dispute broke out was that they were not to mention the subject of birth control unless it was first raised by the aid recipient, after which they were authorized to refer them to their clergy or to private physicians but not to the Planned Parenthood Association. The state authorities could pay the doctor's fee but were forbidden to pay for the supply of any contraceptive devices. In September, 1962, a legislative committee voted to instruct the Illinois Public Aid Commission to make family planning information available to those receiving aid who requested it and the chairman of the commission then went one better and issued instructions that any doctor's fees and charges for appliances should be met out of public funds. After a storm of controversy both orders were rescinded on advice by the Attorney General on the ground that they called for aid to single men and unmarried women in violation of the state's public policy. The position at present is that birth control advice, etc., can be paid for out of public funds but is restricted to married women on relief living with their husbands. A special commission is going into the whole question and is to report in 1965. Disputes of the same kind have taken place recently in California, Wisconsin, and Colorado, where attempts have been made to provide birth control services for those on relief at the cost of the state. None of the proposals has been successful. The latest scene of a dispute has been the District of Columbia, where in March, 1964, an appropriation of $25,000 was made to distribute birth control information and devices at health department clinics. This action was vigorously denounced by the Catholic archdiocese of Washington despite a provision for instruction on the rhythm method of birth control, and the Archbishop then set up his own clinic.[46]

---

[46] The facts about these controversies have been taken from NCWC press releases.

The rival arguments in all these clashes have been basically the same. On the one hand, Catholics claim that since their money is being used to finance public institutions, practices which they consider immoral should not be allowed; on the other, Protestants maintain that no religious body should be allowed to impose on others restrictions which it sets up for its own members. Catholics reply that this is not the point: they object to birth control policies being formally made the policy of welfare departments, since this is publicly endorsing and promoting a course of conduct which they as part of the taxpaying public cannot accept as moral. A further argument put forward is that by providing contraceptive advice at public expense to single people and wives living apart from their husbands immoral behavior is more likely to occur because fears of pregnancy are removed. Finally, it is claimed that proffering such advice to the indigent makes them second-class citizens, an argument met by the counterargument that the poor need this sort of help more than the self-supporting citizen and that it offers them one of the best chances of improving their position.

The theoretical arguments put forward by the contending parties in the birth control struggle are not in fact reconcilable and a compromise has to be sought on the practical level. A strong case exists for the abandonment by Catholics of efforts to secure or preserve a total legislative ban on contraceptives. Efforts to preserve public morality would be more constructive if confined to measures commanding general support, such as the banning of sales of contraceptives from slot machines or the restriction of sales to adults. In the case of tax-supported hospitals and relief services it is unrealistic of Catholics to argue that no birth control advice at all should be given because Catholics are taxpayers. There are a great number of projects undertaken by government with which individual citizens may disagree, but this does not give them a right to withhold taxes or to dictate policies. Money paid in general taxation cannot be tracked down as having been appropriated in any particular way. In a society where family planning is accepted by all and the dispute is about means, a clear line of principle is hard to draw. Once the safe period was accepted by Catholics as a means of family planning, the battle to exclude contraceptive advice from hospital and welfare services was lost. The distinction between use of the sterile period and use of a contraceptive may or may not be a valid one, but it is not one which is apparent to the ordinary citizen and not a distinction on which social policies can successfully be based in a pluralistic society. With the development of the pill and its acceptance by some Catholic theologians as a legitimate means of family planning, the Catholic position has been further undermined. It can hardly be seriously suggested that in a non-religious hospital birth control advice involving pills and the sterile period should be given and advice on contraceptives denied when use of the latter is accepted by the majority of the citizens as normal and moral. In the services for the indigent the distinction between asking for advice on contraception and being offered it may sound valid enough in theory but cannot be of great significance in practice.

A compromise is all that can be hoped for, but some are better than others, and the one originally evolved in New York might well prove generally acceptable with certain modifications. It is suggested then that in tax supported hospitals and welfare services birth control aid and advice should be available to any married woman whose life or health might be threatened by pregnancy. This would meet most practical difficulties without making population control an official policy. Any doctor or employee with religious or moral objections to contraceptive procedures should be excused from participation. Single women should not be given birth control advice unless there is evidence that they are contemplating marriage in the immediate future. In Catholic hospitals different conditions exist, and here it is reasonable that birth control advice should be restricted to the type accepted by Catholic ethics. It is also reasonable to require Catholic doctors as a condition of employment not to take part in the activities of organizations such as the Planned Parenthood League, since such participation could give rise to confusion and scandal, but this restriction should not apply to non-Catholics. To attempt to extend hospital jurisdiction to private practice or to activities carried on outside the hospital in a personal capacity would be a grave infringement of individual liberty. It also shows a confusion in practical aims. A Catholic hospital is not primarily an academy of morals but a hospital existing to give the best medical treatment available to its patients. If conditions such as that forbidding Protestant doctors to prescribe contraceptives outside the hospital were generally imposed, it would materially restrict the talent on which the hospital could draw.

A final source of conflict between Catholics and Protestants concerns the policy of the United States on world population problems. This is not the place to go into figures about the world population explosion, over which there is much dispute, but whatever view one takes of the statistics, it is clear that the increase in world population, especially in the poorer, underdeveloped countries, mainly because of declining death rates, is one of the gravest problems facing the contemporary world. World food shortages and shortage of capital in the underdeveloped countries can be met only by a concerted program of trade and aid by the richer countries. Family planning policies have a part to play but in reality they are a palliative, not a real solution to the problem of world poverty.

The United Nations has adopted a policy of neutrality on the issue of contraception. Attempts to secure adoption of a worldwide family planning program have failed because of the opposition of Catholic and Communist countries. One of the agreed-upon principles of co-operative action among different countries established at the 1954 World Population Conference was to respect different ethical and religious values and to promote mutual understanding. This attitude of Catholic countries has been criticized but is not in fact unreasonable. The United Nations is not a superstate whose majority decisions are binding on all members but an agency for co-operation between equal partners. If delegate countries take radically different stands on birth control, the only possible line for the United Nations to follow is neutrality. At the same time, advice and the services of experts are available to individual states on request. If the pill or some variant of it were to prove acceptable to Catholics, then the conflict regarding Catholic countries at any rate would largely cease.

In 1959 the United States attitude to world population control became a national issue. In July the Draper Committee appointed to study the foreign aid program submitted its third interim report to the President. With the report went a covering letter stating that the committee recommended that, when requested by aid-receiving nations, the United States should help them to formulate programs "to deal with the problem of rapid population growth and should support research leading to better understanding of this problem." Mr. Draper agreed with reporters that this reference included the provision of birth control information by the United States but added hopefully that the point should not be unduly stressed. In September the issue was raised again when the Senate Foreign Relations Committee published a report by the Stanford Research Center recommending that the United States study the possibility of backing large-scale foreign tests of birth control devices.

In November came a statement from the Roman Catholic bishops of the United States announcing that they would fight any attempt to use foreign aid funds to promote "artificial birth prevention programs." They stated that the logical answer to world hunger problems was not to decrease the number of people but to increase the food supply. James A. Pike, the Protestant Episcopal Bishop of California, condemned the statement and asked whether it was binding on candidates for public office. The reference was clearly to the late President Kennedy, one of the aspirants for the Democratic nomination in 1960, who replied that he thought such policies would be mistaken, since they would be interpreted as discriminatory. The United States had never urged them either at home or in Western Europe. If faced with a bill embodying such a program Kennedy stated he would judge the measure by whether "it would be in the interests of the United States." If it became law, he would uphold it.

In December, 1962, a specific statement of government policy on the issue was made by Richard N. Gardner, Deputy Assistant Secretary of State for International Organization Affairs, at a meeting of the Economic Committee of the United Nations General Assembly, a position outlined again in New York in May, 1963. "While the United States," said Mr. Gardner, "will not advocate any specific family planning policy to any other country, we can help other countries, upon request, to find potential sources of information and assistance on ways and means of dealing with population problems. The provision of materials for this purpose can best be done by those governments whose citizens are not divided on this question, by private foundations, and by business firms."[47]

An attempt was made in the Senate in 1963 to depart from this approach when a section was written into the Foreign Aid Bill by the Senate Foreign Relations Committee to provide for the spending of United States funds "to conduct research into problems of controlling population growth and to provide technical and other assistance to cooperating countries in carrying out programs of

---

[47] NCWC News Service, Dec. 12, 1963.

population control." Senator Fulbright, sponsor of the amendment, was challenged by Monsignor Tanner, secretary of the National Catholic Welfare Conference, who declared in a letter to the Senator that "for the Federal Government to adopt a policy approving the promotion of artificial contraception is to infringe upon the freedom of conscience of many of its citizens. . . . It is not the business of government to enter into this question."[48] As a result the section was eliminated from the bill by the Senate-House conferees and the House version of the bill limited the provision to research on population problems making no reference to birth control. In fact federal agencies are providing $5.2 million for research on reproduction, and Catholics, far from opposing this, have welcomed government sponsorship. Monsignor John Knott, director of the Family Life Bureau in Washington, has pointed out that it will benefit thousands of sterile couples and may prevent the malformation of hundreds of thousands of babies in the future. "The fact," he added, "that such information could be used for what we, as Catholics, would consider immoral purposes should not prevent us from supporting those who are seeking the truth. . . . Ignorance is more to be feared than truth or even its misuse."

The United States policy of fostering research on reproduction but not committing itself to promoting contraception as such was reiterated by Mr. Adlai Stevenson, United States ambassador to the United Nations, in a speech in New York in October, 1963. "The United Nations," he said. "already possesses authority to lend technical assistance in all aspects of population problems. Quite apart from legal authority, however, there is no reason for the United Nations to supply particular birth control devices which are repugnant to many of its members. The limited resources of the United Nations are insufficient for this purpose. What is more important, such materials are already available from certain governments and through private channels. The less developed countries are perfectly capable of securing these materials without special provision for technical assistance or external financing." Mr. Stevenson added that the United Nations should be equipped to "advise countries upon request, on how to transmit information on family planning consistent with the cultural and religious values of their people—so that individual parents

48 *Ibid.*

will have free access to the growing fund of knowledge in this field."[49]

The present policy of the United States government, given the difference of opinion among member states of the United Nations on contraception and the division of opinion within the United States, is reasonable. To devote the funds of the foreign aid program to the spreading of contraception would be to commit the nation to a policy positively favoring such practices, a commitment not made when facilities for obtaining birth control information are simply made available as part of domestic hospital and welfare services. Nevertheless the United States policy of neutrality on the issue of birth control is under attack, as is the similar policy pursued by the United Nations, and the controversy is likely to continue into the future.

[49] NCWC News Service, Oct. 17, 1963.

THEODORE POWELL

SHARED TIME, 1964:
A TURNING POINT?

Not every revolution begins with explosions or with the cries and alarums of street rioting. Sometimes great changes occur with no more noise than is made by the shifting of the ocean current at the turn of the tide. During 1964, the sea of public debate over public and parochial education was not quiet. There was the familiar clash and roar of the waves of argument from opposing sides. Few took notice of a significant shift in the tides of contention—a shift that might turn previously opposing forces so that one day they will become confluent streams.

This confluence, this general agreement, was not achieved in 1964, but the turning may have occurred; this may have been the beginning of a revolution in public education policy.

SHARED TIME AND CURRENT EDUCATIONAL PROBLEMS

The crises in parochial and public education during 1964 were not, of course, unheralded events. The problems being pressed to a resolution were tied to a long history, a long and unhappy history of conflict between the two systems of education. And, as might be expected, the problems faced by educators in one system were related to the problems to be resolved in the other.

Theodore Powell is Consultant to the Connecticut State Department of Education.

The financial and administrative difficulties of Catholic schools propounded by Mary Perkins Ryan[1] sent shock waves through the pages of many Catholic periodicals. Mrs. Ryan protested that it was not her intention to "make a case" against Catholic education but, in her words, to initiate:

> . . . a reasonable discussion of what I believe to be a most urgent question: in the present situation of the Church and our society, might it not be better to concentrate the educational effort of the Church on the *religious* formation of *all* Catholics, adults as well as children, rather than to continue to expend such a large proportion of our human and material resources on providing religious education and general education under Catholic auspices to approximately half of our young people, to the neglect of the religious formation of adults, of young people not in Catholic schools, and even of the young people in these schools?[2]

In short, Mrs. Ryan seemed to be asking, "What is the most effective way for the Catholic Church if it is to fulfill its main educational mission—to form a people acceptable to God—to expend its educational effort?"

Not all her critics accepted Mrs. Ryan's statement of her intent. Her book was taken by some as an indictment of the Catholic schools and a proposal to abandon them in favor of some other use of the Church's budget for education. Such an interpretation, especially when made by those engaged in Catholic elementary and secondary education, did not stir much enthusiasm. One telling refutation was offered by a diocesan superintendent to an education conference at the University of Notre Dame. "If we are to economize by redirecting our educational expenditures," he suggested, "would it not be wiser, since the cost per student is so very much greater in higher education, to start by abandoning Catholic colleges and universities?" (The roof did not fall in, but this visitor was almost certain that the floor trembled.)

In addition to the debate over the financial problems of Catholic school operation, Mrs. Ryan's book raised questions of curriculum and school organization. She deplored the "siege mentality" produced by conditions of an earlier age but still governing

---

1 RYAN, ARE PAROCHIAL SCHOOLS THE ANSWER? CATHOLIC EDUCATION IN THE LIGHT OF THE COUNCIL (1964).

2 New City, Mar. 15, 1964, p. 9.

the schools today; she questioned uninspired and mechanical
teaching methods which neither conveyed the Church's approach
to modern human problems nor imparted to children the true
spirit of prayer; and she regretted the fostering of "a kind of
socio-religious segregation" which tended to cut off parents of
Catholic school children from their fellow citizens' concern with
public school interests. Needless to say, these comments provoked
as much contention as the questioning of the use of the Church's
educational budget.

While Mrs. Ryan's book aroused the strongest response, there
were others involved in Catholic education who offered similar
criticism and called for similar reappraisal. The elimination of
Catholic textbooks was suggested by Brother DePaul, librarian
and teacher at Louisville's St. Xavier High School.[3] Such textbooks
had been needed when Catholic education was "defensive and
apologetic." With the Catholic school now "a vital, dynamic and
established part of the American educational system, only unfortunate misunderstandings can result from insisting on the use
of special textbooks," he said.

In similar vein, a report of a research team advised that Catholic schools, which once were principally devoted to protecting the
faith of the Catholic immigrant, should now emphasize the teaching of the expanded values of American Catholicism.[4] The study,
conducted by a Catholic priest, a Protestant, and an agnostic,
found that Catholic schools were effective in orienting children to
symbolic matters. But in civic behavior, a Catholic education
seemed to make little difference. The report urged emphasis on
such values as intellectual and civic competence, love of a meaningful liturgy, and an understanding of interracial and international justice.

The keynote for the growing chorus of pleas for reappraisal of
the Catholic school may have been sounded at the beginning of
the year by the issue of *Commonweal* featuring a collection of
articles by Catholics and other writers entitled "Federal Aid and
Catholic Schools."[5] The articles were prefaced by an editorial
quoting from an estimate of Catholic education by Father Denis
Geaney, O.S.A.:

---

[3] U.S. Catholic, May 1964.
[4] Rossi *et al., The Social Effects of Catholic Education,* reported in Education,
U.S.A., Oct. 29, 1964.
[5] Jan. 31, 1964.

There is nothing sacred about the Catholic school system in the United States. The system is not of divine origin. On the contrary, it is a response to a Protestant-oriented culture. It is the product of the genius of the great episcopal minds of the past century, and the generosity and hard work of the priests and laity. It might be that the best service we could render the Church today would be to stop singing the paeans of praise for the men and deeds of by-gone days and ask ourselves if the premises of the bishops of 1884 are valid in the drastically changed world of 1963.[6]

The drastic changes were specified in the introductory article by *Commonweal*'s associate editor Daniel Callahan:

Today Catholics are coming to see, by and large, that the old ideal of every Catholic child in a Catholic school is impossibly utopian. . . . Faced with a growing shortage of priests, nuns and brothers, the Catholic schools have been forced to rely increasingly on lay teachers. This means, not surprisingly, increased expenses. A booming Catholic population has necessitated a vast and rapid building program—not to increase the percentage of children in Catholic schools, but just to stay even. . . . The schools themselves, to cap the story, require facilities and equipment hardly dreamed of even a few decades ago. Still more expenses.[7]

The truth of this description of the financial and staffing difficulties was illustrated by the changed organization of Catholic schools in many places. To adjust facilities and staff to the increased enrollment, many dioceses decided to eliminate kindergarten or first-grade classes. This action was taken in communities including such major cities as Washington, Cincinnati, St. Louis, Kansas City, Cleveland, Spokane, Green Bay, Columbus, and Fargo.

Monsignor Carl Ryan, superintendent of schools for the archdiocese of Cincinnati, explained the problem he faced: "In 1950 there were 961 sisters and 129 lay teachers in the archdiocese. In 1963 there were 1,026 sisters and 867 lay teachers. In other words, during this period the increase of sisters was 65, that of lay teachers 738." It was no simple matter to find the lay teachers willing to work for salaries about $1,500 less than those offered by public

---

6 *Id.* at 500.
7 *Id.* at 501–2.

schools. With the elimination of the first grade, Monsignor Ryan hoped to increase salaries of both lay teachers and sisters.

A similar description of the problems of a Catholic school administrator were stated by Reverend Oscar Winninghoff, explaining the closing of the first four grades of St. Aloysius School in West Allis, Wisconsin, a suburb of Milwaukee. A survey of Catholic parents whose children were not attending the Catholic school revealed the main reasons to be that classes were "overcrowded," "understaffed," and "not enough personal attention" was given to the pupils.

The decisions to close parochial schools in Cincinnati and West Allis were cause for concern both to Catholic parents and to public school authorities. In Cincinnati Paul C. Mecklenborg, president of Ohio Citizens for Educational Freedom, contended that "through economic pressure, the state is forcing parents to send their children to the state schools." At stake, he contended, was the very survival of the independent schools.

Wendell Pearce, Cincinnati's public school superintendent, had to plan for an additional 3,014 first-grade pupils in September. In the nineteen-county area of the archdiocese there was a total of 10,000 additional children who would be going to public instead of Catholic schools. Since the plans of the archdiocese were announced in March, public school officials had several months to make preparations. The increased enrollment meant additional problems of staffing and classroom space for public school superintendents to solve. Pearce, noting that relations between the two systems over the years had been excellent, commented that "the archdiocesan school board has been thoughtful and has good reasons for its decision to discontinue the first grade."

In West Allis, Father Winninghoff sought a resolution of his problem of overcrowding by proposing a shared-time program to the public school board. His plan, which is discussed in more detail later, was judged unacceptable by the public school board. The superintendent of schools was instructed to report on the additional needs of the system in order to absorb the parochial school pupils.

The same problems—limited funds, inadequate facilities, shortage of staff—were forcing a number of Catholic school administrators in 1964 to consider reorganizing their educational systems. Public school authorities, prepared for increased enrollments, were making the necessary extraordinary arrangements to accommodate additional pupils from Catholic schools where certain grades were closed.

Although the needs were met, at least on a temporary basis, it seemed clear that debate would continue for some time among Catholic educators and parents about the future organization of Catholic education. A public school educator may enjoy the detached role of observer of that family argument. However, if he is wise he will avoid involvement, knowing full well what is likely to happen to the friend or neighbor who intervenes in a family argument. Also, it should be immediately apparent to him that the public school system inevitably will be affected by the decisions reached by his fellow educators in the Catholic school system.

In 1964, as in earlier years, public school educators and other public officials discussed, debated, and declaimed about the financing and the organization of public education. Congress passed the Higher Education Facilities Act, continued federal aid to public education in areas where federal military personnel are located in large numbers, and appropriated funds for a variety of programs collected in the anti-poverty legislation. All this was federal aid to education. But the proposal for general aid to elementary and secondary education was lost once more. A major factor in the defeat of that legislation was the division over limiting aid to public schools only. Out of the long-time conflict over public aid for religious schools had grown wide interest in shared time as the most promising solution for this ancient dilemma.

For many years—in some places as long as forty years—shared-time programs have been operating successfully. Catholic school pupils have attended a neighboring public school for a few hours a week to take instruction in home economics, industrial arts, or other subjects. In the search for accommodation of public and parochial school differences, there was strong interest in the early 1960's in shared time. New programs were initiated in school districts in Michigan and Pennsylvania. Discussions of shared time were frequent in sectarian journals and at educational meetings.[8]

---

[8] The possibility of using shared time as the basis for federal aid to education that would win the support of a wide range of educational and religious leaders, was presented by this writer at the annual meeting of the American Association of School Administrators, February 20, 1962. Specifically, a federal aid to education law can be drafted so that the administration of educational services is under public authority and solely for non-religious instruction; but the aid should be contingent upon such instruction being available to all children, even though they may be regularly enrolled in a non-public school for other instruction. See also, *Shared*

Finally, a bill was drafted by the staff of the Committee on Education of the House of Representatives and introduced by Chairman Adam Clayton Powell.

THE HEARINGS ON H.R. 6074

The excitement which may occur during any official proceeding is seldom adequately conveyed in the documentary record. The United States government publication with its drab, tan cover, laconically titled, "Shared Time Education," gives no suggestion in its appearance of the drama that was played out in a committee hearing room in Washington in late February and March, 1964.[9]

For assistance to, and evaluation of, shared-time projects, there would be appropriated $5 million annually for three years. Under the administration of the United States Commissioner of Education, grants would be made to shared-time projects which, "in his judgment, hold the greatest promise of making a substantial contribution to the solution of problems incident to the effective utilization of public secondary school facilities and personnel. . . ."

In his opening statement Committee Chairman Adam Clayton Powell stated a major theme of the hearings that were to follow in declaring:

> . . . a credo which serves as a basis for my thinking regarding education. In short, I believe in the principle that every American has the right to as much education as he can use; that the education received must be limited only by the individual's aptitudes and abilities, and nothing else; that no artificial restrictions must ever be placed on the right of any American to seek that full education.

Before the proposal was drafted, the staff of the House Committee on Education corresponded and held discussions with members of religious and education groups who had been advocating or exploring the possibilities of shared time. The results of the

Time and Federal Aid: A Solution to the Cold War in Education, New City, May 16, 1963, Chicago. (Reprint of an address delivered to the 1963 convention of the American Association of School Administrators.)

9 *Hearings on H.R. 6074 before the Ad Hoc Subcommittee on Study of Shared Time Education of the House Committee on Education and Labor*, 88th Cong. 2d Sess. (1964).

staff inquiries were not conclusive but did suggest that the shared-time idea was worthy of careful study by the committee. For Chairman Powell the idea of shared time was appealing, "since it simply put at the disposal of all students, public facilities which would enhance their learning experiences. It provided an opportunity whereby the public schools might be available for students attending parochial schools and yet safeguarded [against] any fear of instruction in religion taking place in public-supported institutions." Despite his favorable remarks, Congressman Powell described the prime purpose of the bill as "an opportunity to think together. . . ." He was not wedded to this particular proposal.

In the testimony of almost all the witnesses there was reflected the opinion that there was a need to know more about shared time and that this bill was a step in the right direction. Although some witnesses offered opposition or qualifications, the general tenor of the testimony was favorable. Catholic school officials, public school administrators, staff members of Protestant organizations, and even the general counsel for the vigorously "separationist" Protestants and Other Americans United for Separation of Church and State (POAU) had encouraging words to offer in support of the proposal.

Pressed for specific answers on the relation of shared time to a program of general federal aid to elementary and secondary education, witnesses from the several different groups gave the familiar answers. The National Council of Churches, Dr. Harry Stearns told the committee, would probably support H.R. 6074 "as long as no interpretation seems possible which would channel public funds to the support of any church or church body or would permit control of any public school by a church or its agents." Such a statement might seem to carry a hint of the old Protestant fear of Catholic influence. But Dr. Stearns made it very clear that he had hopes of moving beyond ancient impasses. A lifetime in public school work had convinced him of its importance to a free democratic society. But "the right of Government to control the child" he did not regard as absolute. As a result of conversations among Catholic and Protestant leadership in a search for "common ground," there seemed to be a consensus. The term "shared time" expressed the feeling "that the child's time is primarily that of his parents for guidance and direction, and that, therefore, we seek the opportunity for a broader sharing of the time of the child as it is presently preempted by the public school."

In similar fashion, George R. La Noue, research associate, Department of Religious Liberty, National Council of Churches, advanced his view that the Constitution ruled out "all direct grants or contributions to parochial schools, but it clearly permits the States to structure their public schools and other public services to be of benefit to all students, including those attending parochial schools." Describing the difficulties of financing Catholic schools in the face or rising costs, La Noue commented, "No responsible citizen can be indifferent to giving parochial schools" some consideration, "however much he may object to any particular demand."

After listing the advantages in a shared-time arrangement for Catholics, Protestants, and Jews—each faith having more opportunity to improve its religious education—and after discussing the benefit for the public schools ("shared time would give the whole community a stake in the budget and the quality of the public schools"), La Noue concluded: "We call our era in cultural terms: pluralistic; and in religious terms: ecumenical. Shared time is an educational system that reflects both pluralism and ecumenicity without fragmenting our common educational effort in the public schools."

Warm support for shared time was also present in the testimony of Monsignor Frederick G. Hochwalt, director of the Department of Education of the National Catholic Welfare Conference (NCWC). Questioning by committee members brought out the continuing commitment of NCWC to the inclusion of Catholic schools in any program of general federal aid to elementary and secondary education. No position had been taken on shared time by NCWC and passage of this bill would not change the conference's position on the question of federal aid. For himself, Monsignor Hochwalt favored passage of the shared-time proposal in order to encourage experimentation and learn more about various means of administering such programs.

The sharpest conflict with the views of Stearns, La Noue, and Hochwalt was provided by the strict "separationist" Leo Pfeffer and, paradoxically, by representatives of the Citizens for Educational Freedom (CEF), the group most prominently identified with favoring government aid for private schools.

Dr. Pfeffer, general counsel for the American Jewish Congress, first stated his group's opposition to shared time: The dangers outweighed the favorable aspects. Further, spokesmen for the Catholic Church had made it plain that this was not a compromise that would eliminate their opposition to federal aid limited to public education. If the shared-time bill were included as part of an overall program of federal aid to public elementary and secondary schools, Dr. Pfeffer thought it would be "a justifiable risk." A shared-time aid bill, by itself, might contribute to making the public school into "one gigantic gymnasium and manual training shop," Dr. Pfeffer feared, "and the meaningful, worthwhile, important values of public education will disappear from it." A second apprehension was the possibility of intensifying religious segregation through the grouping of parochial school children as a class in the public school. If each parochial school child came to the public school as an individual, if the public school avoided segregating the parochial school pupils, Dr. Pfeffer said, the program would be constitutional and desirable. He did not believe, however, that this could happen.

These views on the segregating effect of shared time were supported by the testimony of Mrs. Kay Beard, of Inkster, Michigan, a member of CEF. One of Mrs. Beard's children took part in the shared-time program offered at Cherry Hill School to seventh- and eighth-grade pupils of St. Norbert School. She objected that the two hundred children had to walk an extra two miles each day and to cross a high-speed roadway with heavy traffic. It was confusing for her daughter to have the school day divided between God-centered education with firm discipline and education which was not God-centered and which employed a more permissive discipline. Further, the purpose of the shared-time experiment of uniting the community by bringing the children together in school was not served, since the parochial school children, because of scheduling difficulties, were kept in segregated classes.

In her opposition to shared time, Mrs. Beard was joined by Dr. Mark Murphy, president of CEF, and Reverend John P. Clelland, a Presbyterian minister, member of CEF, and executive secretary of Westminister Theological Seminary.

In contrast, Franklin C. Salisbury, general counsel for POAU, avoided any expression of opposition to shared time. Indeed, his careful, generally objective description of shared-time practices concluded:

> The attitude of our organization is one of watchful waiting. As more facts are garnered from increasing experiments with shared time, we shall have a better basis from which to generalize observations. Basically, we still feel the most desirable

(and absolutely constitutional) solution would be for those nonpublic groups ambitious to conduct schools for their young people to do so at their own expense. But aware of the present financial problems of the parochial and independent schools, we are studying the various experiments in shared time to see if they will develop answers consistent with the needs of education and the freedom secured by church-state separation.

Catholics who had long viewed the POAU as a revival of the nineteenth-century Know Nothing movement may have been astounded by this expression of concern for the plight of nonpublic schools. But there was a spirit present during the shared-time hearings quite different from that of most other discussions of public policy affecting the interests of church and state in education. Congressman John Brademas of Indiana expressed his gratification that representatives of different points of view "have all spoken in tones of such moderation and restraint and with such awareness of the problems and points of view of other groups."

Study and experimentation were the principal purposes of the limited proposal set forth in H.R. 6074. There could be little question of the need for more knowledge about shared time. Conference discussions, articles, and the demonstrated congressional interest had raised the issue to a position of national importance. Witnesses and committee members had stated during the hearings on the shared-time bill that it was appropriate there be federal encouragement of experimentation with such programs.

Despite the lack of actual federal encouragement or assistance, some school districts were starting shared-time programs. In some other districts requests were being made to public school boards by Catholic parents or Catholic school administrators. Responses to these requests in 1964 were mixed. In some cases the results were negative or negligible; in others there were encouraging demonstrations that public school and Catholic school authorities could join in amicable, constructive analysis of the education problems of the community and agree upon a proper division of responsibility and function. Differences existed and would continue, to be sure, but there were signs in some places of a new spirit, a greater willingness to communicate. Methods and rules were being developed which offered hope that shared time might introduce a new era in American education.

Reports from several communities in 1964 illustrated the variety of political and administrative difficulties of arranging a shared-time program and the means of surmounting them.

THE NATIONAL EDUCATION ASSOCIATION SURVEY OF SHARED-TIME PRACTICES

A major contribution to the growing discussion of shared time was a research report prepared by the National Education Association (NEA).[10] The tentative nature of the report expressed in its subtitle was made explicit in the introduction.

> If shared time is widely adopted, it could measurably ease the non-public schools' critical shortage of facilities, funds, and teachers, but it could also create enormous problems for both public and nonpublic schools as well as drastically change their character.
>
> Shared time is being watched with mixed emotions. Some persons are optimistic and hopeful; others are cautious and doubtful.

No official policy on shared time, said the report, had been adopted by NEA, nor had other major education groups, such as the American Association of School Administrators, the National Catholic Welfare Conference, or the National Catholic Education Association, taken any official stand.

If the title and introduction were tentative, the substance of the report was impressive: In thirty-five states, one or more school systems were operating a shared-time program in 1964. The median age of shared-time programs for those school systems reporting was ten years. About 20 per cent of the programs were more than twenty years old. In the two years preceding the study, there had been a 25 per cent increase in the number of systems offering shared-time programs.

The limited nature of these statistics was carefully spelled out by the authors. A postal card inquiry had been sent to 12,366 school districts each enrolling three hundred or more pupils. Superintendents in 280 school districts reported they were operating a shared-time program. In addition, 111 superintendents reported that such a program was being considered. While thirty-

---

[10] Lambert *et al.*, Shared Time Programs: An Exploratory Study (N.E.A. 1964).

five states reported operating one or more shared-time programs, almost three-quarters of these programs (134 out of 183) were in six states (Illinois, Michigan, Minnesota, Ohio, Pennsylvania, and Wisconsin).

The subjects most frequently offered in shared-time programs were industrial arts, vocational training, and home economics. Less frequently offered were instrumental music, physical education, physics, chemistry, driver training, foreign languages, general science, and advanced mathematics. A scattering of programs offered business and clerical subjects. In one or two school systems, shared-time programs provided instruction in dramatics, social studies, economics, world history, art, or English. Significantly, the report pointed out that the subjects most frequently offered were those which were more expensive to conduct or for which qualified teachers were scarce.

Synthesizing the administrative arrangements for shared-time programs revealed by the study, the report stated:

> Arrangements between public and nonpublic schools are usually informal, unwritten, and are based on a year-to-year agreement. Policies on procedure and everyday problems are discussed and decided over the telephone or in a conference between the two principals.
>
> In almost all programs described, it is the nonpublic school that fits its schedule to that of the public schools. The subjects provided are determined by the request and the availability of space, personnel, and time in the public schools.
>
> Usually a large block of time is put aside in the morning or in the afternoon to receive parochial school pupils. Depending on their number and the availability of sections of any one course in the public schools, parochial school pupils are either placed in a class by themselves or added to a regular class.
>
> In the majority of cases, the participating schools are within a reasonable distance of each other; many are in the same block or only one or two blocks apart. Sometimes the nonpublic-school pupils are transported to and from the public schools: sometimes they are picked up by bus in the morning along with the regular public school pupils. Some programs leave transportation to the parochial school or to the pupils themselves.
>
> School systems may receive some State aid for part-time pupils, but most superintendents reported no aid.

While emphasizing the limited nature of the study in the introduction of the report, the authors pointed to the better than 90 per cent return of a follow-up questionnaire sent to the 280 school systems which had replied to the initial postal card inquiry and commented that this justified "a considerable degree of confidence in the findings as to the type of programs offered by the systems identified."

LOCAL EXPERIMENTS

From those states with a large number of school systems offering shared-time programs, there came during 1964 encouraging comments and optimistic predictions. From Michigan, Pennsylvania, and other areas with a number of long-established shared-time programs, such encouragement was to be expected and perhaps even discounted. The future of shared time might be better predicted by the experience of those communities where attempts were being made to start such programs. A random selection suggests how varied were the approaches used and the results achieved.

EAST HARTFORD AND SOUTH BEND

In Connecticut and Indiana, where there had been experience with shared time, all that was requested of the public school authorities was permission for the parochial school students to attend courses currently being offered in a neighboring public school.

In East Hartford, Connecticut, a shared-time program was undertaken. Seventh- and eighth-grade students from the Catholic school went to the neighboring public school once a week for two hours of instruction in industrial arts or home economics. This arrangement was similar to practices followed in Hartford, New Haven, Bridgeport, and other Connecticut cities for many years.

In South Bend, Indiana, public school authorities responded favorably to a request by Reverend John A. Vrabely, superintendent of St. Joseph's High School. A very limited shared-time program was initiated for three students who could not obtain the courses they wished in the parochial school. Two of the students went to a public high school for a course in physics and one for a course in advanced biology.

WEST ALLIS

In some other communities, more ambitious requests were made less successfully. In March, 1964, Reverend Oscar Winninghoff, pastor of St. Aloysius Church, asked the West Allis–West Milwaukee school board for a shared-time program. He proposed that a public school be built across the street from the parish school. The pupils at St. Aloysius could then receive instruction in secular subjects during half-day sessions at the public school. The site proposed was owned by the parish, and Father Winninghoff was willing to sell it to the school board. The system envisioned by the pastor would permit a reduction in the size of classes in his school, some of which included as many as sixty pupils. Catholics and non-Catholic pupils at the proposed school, the priest suggested, could make use of the athletic facilities for physical education classes.

In front of an audience of about 150 the school board decided against Father Winninghoff's proposal by a vote of nine to one. It could not have been an easy decision for the board. They knew that the alternative to the rejected proposal was acceptance into the public schools of some 600 children from the Catholic school. To reduce class size, Father Winninghoff would have to close out the first four grades in his parish school. The public school board, however, held to its neighborhood school policy because of a major defect in the system proposed. There were, within the parish boundaries, five public schools. Pupils at St. Aloysius transferring to the public schools, according to school board rule, would be assigned to the one in their district. The effect of the system requested by Father Winninghoff would have been a public school constructed to serve as the secular annex to the Catholic school. The school board could not agree. They directed the superintendent to prepare for absorbing into the public school system the additional 600 pupils.

BENNINGTON

A different approach to the problems of shared-time administration was followed in a Vermont school district which was planning to build a new public high school. A lengthy resolution spelling out the procedures and principles of the plan was adopted by the boards of both the Mount Anthony Union School and the Bennington Catholic High School.

After discussions between representatives of both groups, it was agreed that the proper basis for the proposed shared-time program was for the public school board "to assume full responsibility for instruction in certain specific areas of the curriculum." The areas were listed in the resolution. The new public high school would be designed so that any student residing in the Union School District and attending the Bennington Catholic High School could enroll for public school courses in mechanical drawing, industrial arts, homemaking, physics, biology, advanced business and remedial instruction, and a modern foreign language.

Some administrative safeguards were made explicit: (1) Shared-time courses would be in the public high school and on the same basis as instruction offered to regularly enrolled students. (2) Students from the two schools, as far as administratively feasible, would take shared-time courses together. (3) Administrators of the public and Catholic high schools were directed to co-operate to assure that shared-time students would have received adequate prerequisite training. (4) Transportation of the shared-time students between the two schools would be the responsibility of the Catholic high school. (5) The two boards agreed to meet annually to discuss areas of common interest and explore expansion of the shared-time programs. (6) Consultations would be held between public and Catholic school officials about course content, "but the final and sole authority" would rest with the Union School Board and its administration. (7) No tuition would be charged shared-time students who were residents of the Union School District, but non-residents would be required to pay tuition.

The resolution ended with the declaration that the purpose of the shared-time program was "better education for all the children of our community, and to that end the members of both boards pledge their mutual good-will. . . ."

The proposed regulations made plain the distinction between the responsibility of the public school and the Catholic school. They also revealed the intelligent concern of members of both boards for the observance of legal restrictions and for extension of public school services as far as reasonably possible. But the establishment of this proposed shared-time program depended on the construction of the new public high school. At a referendum in

May, on the bond issue to construct the new high school, the voters of the Union School District voted against the proposed school.

MAYWOOD

In Maywood, a suburban community of 13,000 in northern New Jersey, the question of shared time became an intense public issue for many months in 1964. The parochial school, Our Lady Queen of Peace, and the public school, Maywood Junior High, are side by side. In 1963, a group of parents of parochial school pupils had formed a nine-man committee to consider shared time. After discussion, and agreement, among parents of the 144 seventh- and eighth-grade students at the Catholic school, the committee proposed that the Catholic school pupils be permitted to enroll in science and physical education courses at the public school. Facilities for these subjects were limited or non-existent in the Catholic school.

A request made by the committee in April was denied. School board president Harold V. Petrillo explained that the board's refusal was based on the lack of sufficient time, space, and staff in the public school. Unwilling to accept this rejection, the committee requested a meeting with the school board. After a closed-door session with the committee in June, the board six weeks later announced through its attorney that the request was once more rejected.

The committee then appealed for public support of their position through news stories, an advertisement, and letters to residents of Maywood. Pressed again by the committee to reconsider, the school board met in August. By vote of seven to two, the board adopted a resolution opposing the concept of shared time or part-time enrollment. It was agreed, however, that a study would be made by the administrators of the public and parochial schools to determine the feasibility of shared time in Maywood. "We may be opposed to the principle of shared time," Petrillo said, "but we are in favor of school children and if hardship exists involving school children, and it is in our power to remedy it, we want to try."

The school board, which found it advisable to conduct the discussions of the shared-time proposals in private sessions, was apprehensive about the development of strong feeling and sharp division in the community. After the action of the board in August, Petrillo was reported as favoring as little public attention as possible to the issue. Newspaper photographers were refused permission to take pictures of the new gymnasium and science facilities at the public junior high school because "it might stir things up."

Despite these precautions, the town of Maywood was paying attention and sharp divisions were expressed over the issue. Opponents of the shared-time proposal were critical of its possible disruptive influence and raised questions about the shortage of staff and the effect on state aid. The Catholic parents responded with familiar arguments in favor of aid for parochial schools and referred to the potential saving of tax funds for education.

The feasibility argument was made most persuasively, perhaps, by a teaching sister at Our Lady Queen of Peace School: "Our children are situated closer to that gymnasium than many of the students at Maywood Junior High. It would be such a waste for us to spend money simply to duplicate what is already available."

As another school year began, the parents' committee on shared time had not succeeded in removing the invisible barrier.

CHICAGO

Despite long months of preparation, a request for a shared-time program in Chicago by the archdiocesan superintendent of schools, Monsignor William E. McManus, provoked vigorous objections by a numer of religious, civic, and educational groups.

At a public hearing before the Chicago Board of Education, on March 12, 1964, about forty groups were represented. Principal spokesmen supporting the request were Monsignor McManus and Hugh Bowler, who represented about 1,200 Catholic parents residing in the area to be served by the Kinzie Public High School, which was under construction. The Catholic parents, Bowler said, hope to have their children study science, mathematics, modern languages, technical and vocational courses, business courses, and physical education at the new public high school. Subjects related to religion, such as social studies, English, art, and music, they preferred to have their children study in a parochial school.

Bowler added that the parents wanted their children to have the advantage of mingling in a common school with non-Catholic neighbors.

In response to a question from school board chairman Clair M. Roddewig, Monsignor McManus said that the proposed shared-time experiment accorded with "a new mood in the Catholic church that calls for as much union with others as possible." The Catholic school superintendent also reported that competent attorneys advised him there were no constitutional barriers to the plan and, under Illinois statutes, payment of state aid was permitted on a prorated basis.

Strong opposition to the proposal came from Reverend Robert L. Bond, executive secretary of the Chicago Disciples Union. Noting that a majority of the school board members were Catholic and that Mayor Richard Daley, who had made a public statement in support of shared time, was also Catholic, Mr. Bond suggested that "the circumstances attending the proposal have all the appearances of a denominational power play."

Opposition to shared time because of the effect it would have on the public school program was presented by representatives of the Citizens' Schools Committee, the Chicago PTA, and the midwest office of POAU. Several other groups based their opposition to school board action on procedural objections. The Chicago branch of the American Civil Liberties Union, the American Jewish Congress, the Anti-Defamation League of B'Nai B'rith, and the American Jewish Committee all contended that formal approval of a shared-time program by the board of education was premature. No detailed information had been presented to the school board or to the public. Apart from general objections that might be made against shared time, neither the board members nor the public had any real knowledge of exactly what was being proposed other than a brief memorandum to the board of education from the general superintendent of schools, Benjamin C. Willis.

The strongest criticism of the lack of public information from the superintendent's office was made by Byron S. Miller speaking for the Illinois Division of the American Civil Liberties Union (ACLU). Board approval of an experimental program was being requested with the meager information that it would be offered at the new Kinzie High School for five years beginning September, 1964, and involve 1,500 students for one-half to two-thirds of the school day. The details of this program would be the subject of further study and report. To ask the public to comment on the merits of a proposal with so little information presented was, said Mr. Miller, "a mockery of the democratic process of public hearings."

Mr. Miller's objections went further. "As matters now stand," he declared, "we most emphatically do not feel that the shared time question has been honestly presented or accounted for by the [public] school administration." Recalling that more than two years earlier Monsignor McManus had reported to the newspapers his discussions with Superintendent Willis and his hopes for developing a shared-time program at the new public high school, Mr. Miller stated that the school administration during this period responded to inquiries that "no shared time program was under consideration." As late as October 1, 1963, Superintendent Willis wrote the ACLU that "no report has been prepared nor is there one in progress at the present time on this subject." Yet, on November 13, 1963, Mr. Miller declared, the superintendent gave an oral report to the school board that contained about as much information as was included in the written proposal submitted as the basis for the public hearing. It now appeared that despite these denials of any plans for shared time the new Kinzie School was under construction with provision being made for 1,500 extra students for sciences, foreign languages, vocational subjects, and physical education. The implication of the superintendent's recommendation to the board for a shared-time program, Mr. Miller asserted, was that provision had been made in the new high school, not only for extra classrooms but also for extra laboratories, language booths, workshops, and gymnasiums.

The ACLU had no "blanket opinions" on shared time, said Mr. Miller, but did have "grave reservations" about the possible effect on the public school system. Still, recognizing the arguments in favor of proposal, his organization, Mr. Miller said, "would be happy to give careful consideration to a specific program fairly presented."

These and similar arguments may have had their influence on the deliberations of the school board. Six weeks after the public hearing, a four-year experimental shared-time program was approved by the Chicago Board of Education. By a seven to three vote, the board authorized the program to begin, not in 1964 as recommended by Superintendent Willis, but in September, 1965.

In apparent response to some of the objections or questions presented at the public hearing, the resolution contained several provisos: (1) Part-time students would be under the "exclusive supervision and control of the board of education and its general superintendent." (2) No student would be accepted for enrollment except on written request of his parent or guardian. (Board chairman Roddewig noted that the agreement was between the school board and the parent, not with the Roman Catholic school system.) (3) Superintendent Willis was directed to request various private schools having students in the Kinzie School attendance area to co-operate in the shared-time experiment. (4) On or about August 1, Superintendent Willis was to present recommended rules for the shared-time program. (5) The superintendent was to evaluate the program periodically. (6) If the program was found to be detrimental to the public school system, it would be discontinued. Although the program was obviously designed in the interests of Catholic school children, it was possible that some students of Lutheran schools or other private schools could participate if their parents should request.

The year's delay in starting the shared-time program, Monsignor McManus commented, "was a good thing because all parties now have sixteen months in a relaxed atmosphere to decide what is best educationally for the children." The delay, however, and the details of the program required by the school board's resolution were not sufficient to win the support of all of these who had opposed shared time at the public hearing. Members of some of the Protestant groups and the Citizens' Schools Committee organized a Committee on Shared Time. Following the school board's approval of the experimental program, the Committee on Shared Time announced that a court suit would be filed to test its constitutionality. This action had been anticipated by the school board, for in adopting the resolution it had promised to "cooperate to the maximum extent for an early hearing, disposition, and determination of any issues raised in such a test case."

CONCLUSION

The year which began with the promising accord expressed in the hearings on the shared-time bill seemed to close with memories of discord echoing from the failure of local attempts to

initiate programs. Looking at the results in West Allis, Bennington, Maywood, and Chicago, could anyone conclude that a revolution was in process? Local attempts were being made to effect
change in public-parochial school relations. But the four cases reported here resulted only in frustration, litigation, or defeat.

In spite of these results, however, it would be superficial to conclude that no changes occurred. In the attempts to establish
shared-time programs, there is evident at least one great change, at
least one sign of revolution. Catholics who once were popularly regarded as against public education are now pressing for admission of their children into public schools. Those who once were
critical of parochial schools and Catholic isolationism are now
trying to raise barriers against a mixing of Catholic and public
school pupils. Neither side, of course, would fully agree with these
simple statements of its position, yet it is clear that the introduction of shared time is compelling many on either side of this
ancient debate to reconsider their positions.

In the quiet of the hearing room of the House Committee on
Education in Washington, there were recurring queries for the
specifics of shared-time operations. In the turbulence of local debate where decisions had to be made, those specifics were being developed. Proper methods of administration were being refined.
Sound principles were winning wider understanding.

If this growth of understanding was to continue there would be
need for greater receptivity among public school administrators,
school board members, and organizations taking a special interest
in public education. Such an appeal had been made to the Chicago
School Board by Earl Kalp, educational director for the National
Conference of Christians and Jews. Speaking in support of experi-
menting with a shared-time program, he said that all non-public
schools of whatever religious affiliation should be able to propose,
discuss, and plan shared-time experiments with the public schools.
Similar views had been expressed by national leaders of Protestant
organizations and by the United States Commissioner of Education. This endorsement by national leaders did not guarantee, of
course, that local Protestant church groups or public school officials would not offer resistance to requests for shared-time programs.

If the spirit that infused the hearing room, impressing congressmen and witnesses, should continue to spread its warmth, local
shared-time experiments would flower. For the basis of this new

spirit seems to be a sense not necessarily of common cause but of a general recognition at least of the responsibility each citizen should feel for the educational opportunities available to all children.

In 1964 it was possible to predict growing debate over shared time, increasing attempts to initiate local programs, and new national attention as another shared-time bill was debated again in Congress. It was possible also to forecast more requests for legal opinions and the pursuit of a decision on shared time through the courts. Another year might go by without a complete answer in either the political or judicial contests. But in the closing weeks of 1964, it did seem clear that future debates over public-parochial school relations would focus increasingly on shared time. The nature of those debates, therefore, would be very different from the bitter contests the nation and communities had known in the past. If, in fact, these changes occurred, it might be possible in some future year to say that 1964 was the turning point.

WILBER G. KATZ

NOTE ON THE CONSTITUTIONALITY
OF SHARED TIME

This note will deal briefly with the constitutionality of arrangements for part-time enrollment in public schools of students also
enrolled in private schools, usually schools conducted under religious auspices. "Shared time" is the term popularly used for such
dual enrollment. A wide variety of arrangements may be envisioned involving various degrees of joint planning and administration of such programs by public and private administrators. It is possible that in some dual enrollment plans the degree
and kind of co-operation between public and ecclesiastical officials would be of such a nature that the public authorities would
be involved in promoting religious interests in violation of the
establishment clause of the Fourteenth Amendment. Our main
concern will be with the constitutionality of programs involving
a minimal degree of joint planning, and then only of a kind related
to scheduling and similar matters having no religious connotation
whatever. With regard to such programs—and it is reasonable to
expect that most dual enrollment programs could be tailored to
involve a minimum of joint planning—the constitutional question
narrows down to whether they aid religion improperly by relieving
church-related schools of the burden of providing a complete
curriculum.

In many states this question raises two issues: one relating to the

Wilber G. Katz is Professor of Law at the University of Wisconsin and a former
Dean of the Law School of the University of Chicago.

state constitution, the other to the Fourteenth Amendment's in-
corporation of the establishment clause. There are practically no
authoritative rulings on either aspect of this question, although
the Attorneys General and other legal officers of several states have
delivered opinions on some aspects of it. This note will summarize
the few state rulings and opinions on this question after briefly
presenting the author's conclusion on the validity of dual enrollment programs under the establishment clause of the Federal
Constitution.

Constitutionality of Dual Enrollment under the Establishment Clause

The Supreme Court decisions concerning "released time"
programs are the cases that might seem to bear on the constitutional
status of dual enrollment, but they are not at all in point. "Released time" refers to arrangements for the excusing of public
school students for religious instruction. In *McCollum*[1] the Court
held unconstitutional a program where the religious instruction
was given in the public school buildings, but in *Zorach*[2] it sustained a program held off the school premises. Some of the justices
and commentators thought that the location of the instruction
should make no difference and that both types of programs are invalid because the keeping of the non-participating students in
school operates to promote enrollment in the religion classes. As
Mr. Justice Jackson put it, the public school "serves as a temporary
jail for the pupil who will not go to church." Shared-time programs
raise no such problems.

Those questioning the constitutionality of shared time could
very well start from the principle of strict separation enunciated
in *Everson*[3] and its corollary that the state may not give any aid
to religion. But the recent decisions in *Schempp*[4] and *Sherbert*[5]
have made it clear that the constitutional separation of church
and state is not absolute and that the requirement of the "no establishment" clause is government neutrality with respect to religion.
The test of neutrality was stated in the *Schempp* case as follows:

---

1 McCollum v. Board of Educ., 333 U.S. 203 (1948).
2 Zorach v. Clauson, 343 U.S. 306 (1952).
3 Everson v. Board of Educ., 330 U.S. 1, 15 (1947).
4 School Dist. of Abington Township v. Schempp, 374 U.S. 203 (1963).
5 Sherbert v. Verner, 374 U.S. 398 (1963).

. . . what are the purpose and the primary effect of the enactment? If either is the advancement or inhibition of religion then the enactment exceeds the scope of legislative power as circumscribed by the Constitution. That is to say that to withstand the strictures of the Establishment Clause there must be a secular legislative purpose and a primary effect that neither advances nor inhibits religion.[6]

In applying this test, how shall we characterize the purpose and primary effect of action authorizing shared time? We may say, of course, that the purpose and effect are the extension of public school instruction and that this is obviously a secular purpose. Or it may be said that a secular purpose is behind the choice of courses ordinarily proposed for the public school part of the shared-time programs. Sciences, mathematics, and foreign languages are frequently suggested as appropriate courses for all to take in the public schools. The National Defense Education Act of 1958 singled out these subjects as areas in which it is in the national interest to have as fully trained a citizenry as possible.

But this is not the whole story. There is also a purpose to accommodate the public school arrangements to the needs of students attending church-related schools. Professor Kurland is of the opinion that this purpose is the motivating factor behind shared-time programs. He argues that in fact such programs exist "solely for the purpose of maintaining parochial school systems" and should therefore be held to violate the policy of neutrality.[7] He goes on to say, "To my mind, only a shirking of duty or a revived stringency in the requirement of standing to sue can save the various shared time programs from judicial negation."[8] It is interesting to contrast this position with Kurland's declaration in the same essay that "making tuition payments available to students who choose to attend parochial schools, when such payments are made to students attending other schools, should be held unobjectionable."[9] Professor Kurland's view of neutrality, set forth in his book *Religion and the Law*, simply requires that "religion may not be used as a basis for classification for purposes of governmental action."[10] Thus

---

[6] 374 U.S. at 222.

[7] Kurland, Religion and Education: Some Constitutional Issues Past and Present (unpublished address 1963).

[8] *Ibid.*

[9] *Ibid.*

[10] KURLAND, RELIGION AND THE LAW 18 (1961).

this principle prevents governmental action that either advances or inhibits religion only if the action is specifically directed to this end.

This principle of neutrality should be contrasted with one in which specific government action is examined in the context of the total program of governmental regulation in an area to determine whether on balance the state is advancing religion. It is no violation of neutrality for the government to express its concern for religious freedom by measures which merely neutralize what would otherwise be restrictive effects of government action.[11] Provision for voluntary worship in the armed forces is constitutional, not because government policy may properly favor religion, but because the government is not required to exercise its military powers in a manner restrictive of religious freedom. Affirmative government action to maintain religious freedom in these instances serves the secular purpose of promoting a constitutional right, the free exercise of religion.

There is every indication that the Supreme Court has adopted this broader view of neutrality, which permits the government to accommodate its programs so as not to interfere unnecessarily with voluntary religious pursuits.[12] In *Sherbert v. Verner*[13] the Court held that a Sabbatarian could not be required to accept Saturday work contrary to her religious scruples in order to obtain unemployment compensation from the state. In answer to the charge that exemption from the Saturday work requirement for religious reasons was an aid to religion that fostered establishment, Mr. Justice Brennan relied on the neutrality principle.[14] The Court is apparently disposed to apply this broader concept of neutrality in the area of Sunday closing as well. Although exemption from the Sunday closing laws for Sabbatarians is not required by the Constitution, it is permitted.[15] Here the Court is giving the states the option to protect freedom of religion beyond the degree assured by the Constitution.

---

11 For an extended discussion of this concept of neutrality see KATZ, RELIGION AND AMERICAN CONSTITUTIONS (1964); see also Katz *Freedom of Religion and State Neutrality,* 20 U. CHI. L. REV. 426 (1953).

12 For an extended discussion of the concept of neutrality in the light of the recent Supreme Court decisions, see Kauper, *Schempp and Sherbert: Studies in Neutrality and Accommodation,* 1963 RELIGION AND THE PUBLIC ORDER 3.

13 374 U.S. 398 (1963).

14 *Id.* at 409.

15 Braunfeld v. Brown, 366 U.S. 599 (1961); Arlan's Department Store v. Kentucky, 371 U.S. 218 (1962).

It is clear that the Court in these areas has rejected a narrow concept of neutrality which forbids religious classification as the basis for governmental action. Both the exemptions from the Sunday closing laws and from the Saturday work requirement of the unemployment compensation programs are limited to members of specified religious groups. Therefore, even if one accepts Kurland's proposition that shared time programs are adopted for the purpose of complementing parochial, which is to say, religious, school systems, it does not follow that they are unconstitutional as long as they are adopted for the purpose of promoting neutrality.

It is the author's opinion that shared-time programs should be viewed as furthering the principle of neutrality. The state has mobilized its resources in the field of education to ensure that all citizens are instructed in the various fields of secular learning. The principle of neutrality would permit the state, in arranging its educational programs, to take into account the desires of those parents who for religious reasons wish to educate their children in private schools as far as the humanities and social sciences are concerned. When the state provides the parents of such children with education in the physical sciences and related fields of learning, this is certainly governmental action with a secular purpose and effect. Considered by itself, such a program of instruction would be unquestionably constitutional. If the state then goes on to permit simultaneous enrollment in parochial schools for other courses, even though they could be taken in the public school at the option of the student, this would be no more than the accommodation of the desires of the parents.

Thus dual enrollment is designed not to promote religious schools but to maintain the individual's freedom of religion as unlimited as possible in an area of government activity and regulation. Here, as in the case of Sunday laws and in legislating for the armed services, it serves a proper secular purpose to make affirmative provision to promote religious freedom. The advantage accruing to religious institutions is not a primary effect but is incidental to the valid secular purpose.

STATE RULINGS ON CONSTITUTIONALITY

A number of state constitutions have provisions prohibiting the use of public funds for the support of sectarian schools or purposes. Some of these provisions are interpreted more strictly than the First Amendment's prohibition against establishment. For in-

stance, whereas public provision of bus transportation for parochial school students is permitted under the establishment clause,[16]
it is held to violate constitutional provisions of several states.[17]

Most of the states in which the constitutionality of shared time
has been raised either in court cases or official opinions are those
having such constitutional provisions forbidding use of public
funds for sectarian purposes. The rulings have centered on the
issue of state law for the most part, although occasionally a conclusion is offered with regard to the federal question.

COURT OPINIONS

There is one decision in Pennsylvania squarely sustaining
the admission of parochial students to a public school manual
training program.[18] The statute authorizing the program provided
that "no pupil shall be refused admission . . . by reason of the
fact that his elementary or academic education is being . . . received in a school other than a public school." This statute was
attacked as violating a clause of the state constitution providing
that "no money received for the support of the public schools of
the commonwealth shall be . . . used for the support of any sectarian school." The state supreme court dismissed this contention
without discussion. It affirmed a ruling that compelled the local
school district to admit a parochial school student to manual training classes in the public school. The lower court had said:

> It is difficult to understand how, with any appearance of
> reason, it can be contended that the Act of 1911, when it
> provides . . . that certain educational institutions shall [be]
> open, not only to regular pupils of public schools, but to other
> persons residing in the school district, violates either of these
> sections [*i.e.,* the constitutional provision quoted above and
> another directed against appropriations to "corporations,
> institutions or individuals"]. If it were to be held that it did,
> it would be necessary to hold, also, that no pupil, although
> qualified by his studies in a private sectarian school teaching
> substantially the same branches as are taught in the public
> high school, could enter such school. But the manual training
> school, by admitting to its course properly qualified pupils
> from the St. John's parish school, would no more become a
> part of the said St. John's parish school or appropriate money

16 Everson v. Board of Educ. 330 U.S. 1 (1947).
17 *E.g.,* State *ex rel.* Reynolds v. Nusbaum, 115 N.W.2d 761 (Wis. 1962).
18 Commonwealth *ex. rel.* v. School Dist. of Altoona, 241 Pa. St. 224 (1913).

or lend credit to it than does the high school, to which, for years past, the pupils of the St. John's parish school have been admitted without question. It must, therefore, be held that the said act is not obnoxious to the provisions of either of these sections of the constitution.[19]

There is also a dictum concerning dual enrollment in the Wisconsin case holding that extension of public bus transportation benefits to parochial school students violates the state constitutional provision: ". . . nor shall any money be drawn from the treasury for the benefit of religious societies, or religious or theological seminaries." The court said:

> . . . it has been brought to our attention that pupils of certain parochial schools attend manual training and domestic science classes in the public schools. These parochial schools benefit in that they are saved the expense of providing the specialized equipment required for such courses, and of securing teachers trained to teach the same. However, let us assume but not decide that permitting children, who satisfy the age and residence requirements, to secure part of their education in the public schools, even though at the same time they may be in attendance at parochial schools, does not violate sec. 18, art. I [of the] Wisconsin constitution. On this hypothesis it might be argued that permitting parochial school children to take advantage of transportation by public school bus, is a use of public school facilities equivalent to attendance at manual training and domestic science classes in the public schools. However, the essential difference, from a constitutional standpoint, is that riding school buses is not an educational objective of the state in itself, but merely an instrumentality to bring the pupils to the public schools where they will secure a public education. Under ch. 648, parochial school children are not to be transported to the public schools for the purpose of receiving any public instruction; rather, such transportation is merely a convenience to assist them in attending a parochial school.[20]

LEGAL OPINIONS

Opinions by state officials on the question have been about evenly divided. Officials in California, Iowa, and New York have ruled that dual enrollment programs violate constitutional restrictions:

---

[19] Commonwealth *ex. rel.* Wehrle v. Plummer, 21 Pa. Dist. 182, 185–86 (1911).
[20] State *ex rel.* Reynolds v. Nusbaum 115 N.W.2d 761, 766–67 (Wis. 1962).

California.—The Attorney General has ruled that pupils attending a full-time parochial school may be admitted to special classes conducted in public schools.[21] He added, however, the following caution:

> Education Code section 12154 requires that in order to be exempted from full time attendance in a public school, the child must attend a private school which "shall offer instruction in the several branches of study required to be taught in the public schools of the State." Thus, if a public school board determines to permit a student who is in full time attendance at a private school to attend one or more public school classes, it is cautioned that such classes may not be established in order to provide instruction that the private school itself is required to provide by the provisions of section 12154. For to do so would in effect constitute providing public funds to support a school "not under the exclusive control of the officers of the public schools" in contravention of the provision of California Constitution article IX, section 8.

Iowa.—The Attorney General, referring to a state constitutional provision similar to the First Amendment, ruled that the establishment of a "part time partial high school for the accommodation of three classes of the parochial school . . . cannot be accomplished under the Constitution and laws of Iowa."[22]

New York.—The director of the Law Division of the Education Department has ruled:

> This is to advise you that the State Constitution, Article XI, Section 4, expressly and clearly prohibits the use of public moneys, State or local, which in any way, directly or indirectly, aid any denominationally controlled institution of learning or in which denominational tenets are taught.
>
> The shared time concept . . . has the basic purpose of increasing facilities for religious education.
>
> Consequently, this procedure would be in violation of the State Constitution. Incidentally, we also believe that the same is contrary to the First Amendment to the Federal Constitution for the same reason.[23]

---

21 Opinion No. 61/237, March 9, 1962.

22 Letter from the Attorney General of Iowa to the Superintendent of Public Instruction, May 17, 1939.

23 Letter from the director of the Law Division of the Education Department of New York State to Louis R. Critelli, Sept. 3, 1962.

Officials in Illinois, Ohio, and Oregon have ruled that dual enrollment programs do not violate constitutional restrictions:

Illinois.—The legal adviser to the Superintendent of Public Instruction has given an opinion including the following:

> The Constitution of 1870 provides in Article VIII, Section 1 that, "The General Assembly shall provide a thorough and efficient system of free schools, whereby all children of this State may receive a good common school education."
>
> Further, at Section 3, "Neither the General Assembly nor any . . . school district . . . shall ever . . . pay from any public fund whatever, anything in aid of any church . . . or to help support or sustain any school . . . controlled by any church or sectarian denomination. . . ."
>
> In line with the above constitutional provisions and with the apparent weight of authority in this country, we have come to the conclusion that the shared time program is legal insofar as boards of education are required to receive resident pupils of the district on a special enrollment in courses which the parochial or other private school may not offer its pupils.[24]

Ohio.—The Attorney General has ruled:

> It is believed that a board of education can properly permit a resident child of school age to attend only particular classes in a school. . . . The fact that he is also enrolled in another school, public or non-public, and is attending classes therein during a part of the school day, does not, in itself, appear to disqualify the child from enrolling in a public school for a particular course of instruction; and it is not believed that such dual enrollment would be unlawful even if one school attended is maintained by a church. . . .[25]

Oregon.—The Attorney General has ruled, in reply to a question concerning classes in foreign languages, arts and crafts, and related subjects:

> . . . it is our opinion that . . . resident pupils attending a parochial school are entitled to enroll in the public schools to attend select classes offered by the public schools which are not available in the parochial schools.[26]

---

[24] Letter from the legal adviser to the Superintendent of Public Instruction of Illinois to Superintendent Benjamin C. Willis, Mar. 9, 1964.

[25] Letter from the Attorney General of Ohio to the Superintendent of Public Instruction, May 14, 1962.

[26] Letter from the Attorney General of Oregon to the Superintendent of Public Instruction, Sept. 16, 1963.

In Wisconsin the Attorney General on October 27, 1964, released a long-awaited opinion which did not come to any firm conclusion. He said: ". . . it would be presumptuous of me, at this
juncture, to state flatly that in my opinion the exercise of such
power [to authorize a shared-time program] would be constitutional or unconstitutional."[27] But he declared also:

> Ours is a pluralistic society, drawing much of its vast strength
> from that fact. If a Wisconsin child, whose attendance at a
> private school is one of the evidences of the pluralistic charac-
> ter of our society, may by part-time attendance at a public
> school receive there certain valuable schooling, some of it
> unavailable in his private school, then he has been benefitted
> [sic] by such schooling, and our state and nation have bene-
> fitted [sic] as well. The founding fathers of Wisconsin, who
> held education for all children of this state in the highest
> regard, could only take comfort and pride in such a result.

Of some relevance is an opinion of the Utah Attorney General
construing a driver training statute to preclude a special charge to
parochial school students.[28]

In view of the division of legal opinion one cannot say with
certainty that shared-time programs are permissible in states
having specific constitutional prohibitions against the expenditure
of public funds for sectarian purposes. However, in view of the
fact that the expenditure of public funds in shared-time programs
goes directly to the support of secular education in the public
schools, and in view of the previously suggested analysis that the
benefits incidentally derived by religious institutions are consistent
with the principle of neutrality, it would not be at all difficult
to justify such programs in these states.

CONSTITUTIONAL RIGHT TO DUAL ENROLLMENT

It is sometimes argued not only that it is constitutional for
public bodies to authorize shared time but that citizens patronizing
parochial schools have a right to such arrangements. This argument has the support of one official opinion which seems to me
highly questionable. In an Illinois opinion already noted above,

27 Letter from the Attorney General of Wisconsin to the Superintendent of
Public Instruction, Oct. 27, 1964.
28 Letter from the Attorney General of Utah to the Superintendent of Public
Instruction, Oct. 30, 1963.

the legal adviser to the Superintendent of Public Instruction ruled that boards of education "are required to receive resident pupils of the district on a special enrollment in courses which the parochial or other private school may not offer its pupils." He based this ruling on the state constitution, which requires the legislature in general terms to provide a system of free schools "whereby all children of [the] State may receive a good common school education."

It seems to me highly unlikely that a court would interpret any such general constitutional provision as making shared time mandatory. In view of the many administrative problems entailed by shared-time programs, it is essential that public school authorities have wide discretion. It is almost unthinkable that the many questions of feasibility of shared time will be decided by the courts as questions of constitutional law.

Sherbert v. Verner,[29] the unemployment compensation case, is the one decision which might be cited as supporting a constitutional right to shared time. This was a surprising decision in view of the earlier *Braunfeld*[30] case holding that a state need not provide an exemption for Sabbatarians from its Sunday closing law. In my opinion, if the shared-time question were litigated, it is almost certain that this Sunday law precedent (rather than the unemployment compensation case) would be followed and shared time held permissible, but not required.

To be sure, there are statutes in some states giving parochial school pupils a right to enroll in special classes in public schools, for example, classes in manual training and driver education. But it is unlikely that any state, however hospitable to shared time, will attempt to spell out in a statute the circumstances under which such arrangements can feasibly be made.

---

29 374 U.S. 398 (1963).
30 Braunfeld v. Brown, 366 U.S. 599 (1961).

ARTHUR GILBERT

RELIGIOUS FREEDOM AND SOCIAL CHANGE IN A PLURALISTIC SOCIETY: A HISTORICAL REVIEW

An examination of American history reveals that social change in the relationship among America's religious groups has rarely been achieved without some degree of violence. Protestant dissenters, Roman Catholics, Jehovah's Witnesses, Jews, each in turn have suffered physical assault because they challenged the prevailing definitions of the church-state relationship and insisted on a redefinition of religious freedom. Yet because of the unique structure of our democratic institutions, such change partakes of an *evolutionary* rather than a *revolutionary* character. Recourse has been available through the legislature and constitutional convention; or, failing in these, minority groups have found the courts of the United States to be a bulwark of basic human rights, balancing political power so that justice might be pursued unfettered by mob passions. Finally, in the most recent period of American history there has emerged the phenomenon of dialogue between faith communities, suggesting to some the possibility that interreligious conflicts may also be resolved through understanding accommodations. It is instructive, therefore, to assess the methods by which the emerging pluralism of America has been dealt with and the religious and civil rights of minority groups have been extended,

Arthur Gilbert is Staff Consultant and Director of the Project on Religious Freedom and Public Affairs, National Conference of Christians and Jews.

to consider mainly what in the past is still meaningful and will shed light on how to handle contemporary interreligious conflicts as we shape the future.

In the earliest period of American history religious groups generally established the same patterns of church-state union that had prevailed in Europe. This earliest period is marked by widespread conflict and intolerance as each church used the powers of the state to enforce church law and to stifle dissent. Pluralism in creed or practice was considered scandalous.

With the adoption of the First Amendment to the Constitution of the United States a process was set in motion which set limits on the church-state establishments within the states by means of legislative enactment and state constitutional conventions. Provisions guaranteeing religious freedom were written into the law and a greater toleration for religious pluralism became evident. Nevertheless, since Protestants were such a predominant majority in the population, elements of quasi-Protestant or Christian establishment remained encrusted in various areas of the law of the land.

The first most decisive challenge to the Protestant hegemony derived from the huge Catholic immigration to this country in the first half of the nineteenth century. Not everywhere were Catholics successful in their attack on the status quo arrangements, but frequently they were able to find state judiciaries more responsive to their needs than the local or state legislatures. By testing their rights through the courts Catholics stimulated the judiciary to a new recognition of its role in the shaping of the American democratic heritage.

Not until the cases brought by the Jehovah's Witnesses in the 1930's, however, did the Supreme Court of the United States assume an active role by asserting its authority over infringements of religious liberty within the states. Because the Court played this active role and thus shared in a way in the traditional functions of the legislature, Jews, members of the Ethical Culture Society, and atheists today have been able to find decisive support in their contention that freedom *for* religion requires also freedom *from* any form of state-sanctioned or -supported religion—even if it be of the non-denominational, non-Christian religion-in-general stripe.

Since World War II much of the fear and suspicion that blocked free communication among America's religious groups has been overcome and dialogue has emerged. At the same time, members of the Supreme Court confess that there is "no simple and clear measure which by precise application can readily and invariably demark the permissible from the impermissible"[1] in defining the "wholesome neutrality" required of the state if religious freedom is to be maintained. Thus, there are religious and civic leaders who are hopeful now that dialogue itself will produce such a degree of trust among America's religious communities that new patterns of relationship will develop without the tensions evoked by utilization of either political power or litigation.

What remains clear, of course, is that religious liberty is not a gift handed down from one generation to another. It has had to be achieved through conflict, and in every generation it has been redefined and stated anew. This essay will attempt a brief review of that history with particular emphasis on the methods of achieving social change employed in each period.

The Period of Church-State Establishment

The earliest immigrants to America had themselves experienced intolerance in Europe. They sought the haven of these shores in order to worship God without fear. But each group in turn used the powers of the magistrate to support its own dispensation. Dissenters had only the freedom to enter the wilderness and carve out their own enclave, as did Roger Williams. Only when religious pluralism had become unmanageable and the violence perpetrated on dissenters had become unconscionable did a few bold clergy and courageous legislators insist on disestablishing the church and broadening the legislative provisions providing freedom of conscience.

Thus, while religion was a prime motivating factor in immigration to this country and in the founding of the colonies, the earliest charters called for the establishment of the church and made no provision for disbelievers. The grant to Sir Walter Raleigh, for example, contained an express proviso that laws of the new colony "should not be against the true Christian faith, now professed in the Church of England."[2] When in 1624 the charter of Virginia passed into the hands of the King of England, Puritans

---

1 School Dist. of Abington Township v. Schempp, 374 U.S. 203, 306 (1963) (Goldberg, J., concurring).
2 Noted in Thomas Jefferson's Biography begun in 1821, quoted in Cousins, In God We Trust 118 (1958).

were displaced and Anglican clergy alone were permitted to officiate in the colony. All believers and disbelievers alike were taxed to provide the Anglican clergy with "a fixed salary . . . a glebe house and land."[3]

On their part the Puritans in Plymouth Colony and Massachusetts earned the rebuke of King Charles II for their cruel persecution of Anglicans; and when at last they relaxed their rigid church-state establishment they discriminated against Catholics, granting by charter in 1691 "liberty of conscience to all Christians except Papists."[4] Until the Revolutionary War nearly every American colony had strict laws outlawing "Papists." The law of the Province of New York in 1700 ordered perpetual imprisonment of Catholic priests performing religious rites or teaching Catholic doctrine.[5] In 1704, Maryland law prohibited Catholic priests from baptizing children, and in 1716 the state ordered severe punishment for public officials who attended Catholic Mass.[6]

Even in those colonies where an effort was made to legislate some degree of toleration, the restrictions on religious freedom as measured by contemporary American standards would be considered abhorrent. In April, 1649, for example, under the regime of a Protestant governor appointed by the Catholic Lord of Baltimore, the Maryland Assembly passed a Toleration Act. It confessed that the enforcing of the conscience in matters of religion had frequently "fallen out to be of dangerous consequence." Nevertheless, it included penalties for the violation of the Sabbath. Those who denied the Holy Trinity or the Godhead of any of the Three Persons were to be punished with death and the confiscation of lands and goods.[7]

Similarly, Roger Williams, who had proclaimed that his Rhode Island colony "might be for a shelter for persons distressed of conscience," offered no enthusiastic welcome to Quakers and overtly discouraged Catholics, although Jews were permitted to enter his colony in large numbers.[8]

William Penn's colony of Pennsylvania, by its Great Law of 1682, insured that no man could be molested or prejudiced for his

---

3 COUSINS, *op. cit. supra* note 2, at 118.
4 See SWEET, THE STORY OF RELIGION IN AMERICA 76 (1950).
5 See BRICKMAN & LEHRER, RELIGION, GOVERNMENT AND EDUCATION 253 (1961).
6 *Id.* at 253.
7 See SWEET, *op. cit. supra* note 4, at 80.
8 *Id.* at 99.

or her conscientious persuasion or practice. In time, however, under pressure from England, first Catholics and then only Jews were excluded from holding public office.[9] A belief in "a future state of reward and punishment" was also required.[10] An act passed in 1700 enjoined all citizens to attend church on Sunday or prove that they had been at home reading the scriptures.

As late as the Revolutionary War, there were established churches in at least nine of the thirteen original colonies and multiple establishments in four others.

Federal Disestablishment

The first most successful effort to disestablish the church from the state resulted from the Revolutionary War. Not by evolution but rather by the fire of revolutionary passion, therefore, America was set on its course of church-state separation.

Sentiment against the Church of England had inevitably accompanied the war against English political domination. Isaac Backus, aggressive leader of New England Baptists in that harsh period, for example, explained that Baptists joined the Revolutionary War because "the worst treatment received by Baptists came from the same principles and persons that the American war did . . . and finally because the deliverance of America might regain for Baptists their invaded rights."[11] Hostility for the established English church was so marked that membership in the church dropped immediately and severely with its disestablishment after the war. It took thirty years for the church to regain any part of its earlier prestige and standing in the community.

It was exactly such anger at the Anglican church's use of coercion to compel fidelity to its creed and to obtain financial support for its clergy that stimulated Thomas Jefferson's and James Madison's efforts to enact a bill for religious freedom in Virginia; and its eventual adoption there paved the way for the constitutional amendment included in the Bill of Rights adopted in Philadelphia.

Virginia's Declaration of Rights of 1776 was the first legislative pronouncement that freedom of conscience was an inherent right of the individual. "That religion, or the duty which we owe our

---

9 See Thompson, *The Development in History of the Principle of Separation of Church and State* in Wood, Thompson & Miller, Church and State 71 (1958).

10 Pa. Const. art. 9 § 4 (1790).

11 Quoted in Sweet, *op. cit. supra* note 4, at 183.

Creator, and the manner of discharging it, can be directed only by reason and conviction, not by force or violence, and therefore all men are equally entitled to the free exercise of religion, according to the dictates of their conscience. . . ."[12] The effort to have this declaration condemn the existing Episcopal establishment, however, failed to muster enough votes and it took almost ten years before the convictions of the pronouncement could be translated into law. The decisive turning point was reached in 1784–85 when Patrick Henry introduced a bill containing a provision for support of teachers of the Christian religion. Designed to revive the tithes suspended for almost twelve years, the bill would have required all persons to contribute annually for the support of some Christian church or communion. Henry defended his proposal not as an aid to religion but as a service to the state. The preamble of the bill said, "The general diffusion of Christian knowledge has a natural tendency to correct the morals of men, restrain their vices and preserve the peace of the society. . . ." It was expected that Protestant dissidents would support the bill, since they were also included in its benefits.

James Madison's *Remonstrance* effectively killed Patrick Henry's bill. "Who does not see," Madison asked, "that the same authority which can establish Christianity, in exclusion of all other Religions, may establish with the same ease any particular sect of Christians, in exclusion of all other Sects?"[13] Madison had no quarrel concerning the size of the proposed tax or that it would be given to all equally; the issue for him was the power of the state to impose *any* such tax for aid to religious education. "Religion is wholly exempt from its [the state's] cognizance," he asserted.

Similarly, Thomas Jefferson argued, ". . . even forcing him [a man] to support this or that teacher of his own religious persuasion, is depriving him of the comfortable liberty of giving his contributions to the particular pastors whose morals he would make his pattern. . . ."[14] Yet despite such arguments in favor of freedom from taxation for the support of religion, both Madison and Jefferson lent their weight to legislation that provided state sanction for religious morality in general. Madison and Jefferson sup-

---

12 Quoted in KONVITZ, FUNDAMENTAL LIBERTIES OF A FREE PEOPLE at 21 (1957).

13 The text of *Memorial and Remonstrance* is quoted in COUSINS, *op. cit. supra* note 2, at 308–14.

14 COUSINS, *op. cit. supra* note 2, at 126.

ported a Bill for Punishing Disturbers of Religious Worship and
Sabbath Breakers. Jefferson's motion put teeth into a Bill for Appointing Days of Public Fasting and Thanksgiving. Ministers who
failed to preach a sermon suited to these state-appointed occasions
could be fined, according to Jefferson's amendments, up to $50.
Jefferson recommended non-sectarian instruction in the proof of
God's existence within the system of higher public education.[15]

The adoption of the Federal Constitution in 1789 and the Bill
of Rights in 1791 stimulated a reconsideration in all the states of
their obligations to protect freedom of religion for all men. The
Constitution, however, restricted only the federal government
from the establishment of religion. It had no binding power over
the states; and although disestablishment had come quickly in the
southernmost colonies under Anglican influence, the separation
principle was only slowly achieved in the states with a Congregational establishment.

Massachusetts, for example, in 1779 in the midst of the Revolution, adopted a constitution that provided that towns be required
"to make suitable provision at their own expense for the public
worship of God." Not until 1833 did Massachusetts complete its
disestablishment.[16]

In Connecticut, as late as 1816, the larger denominations
sought support for a pluralistic establishment. They favored a bill
for support of literature and religion. On a graduated scale, the
bill provided sums for Yale, Episcopalians, Baptists, and Metho-
dists. After a sharp two-year controversy, the measure was lost in
the legislature by the small margin of ten votes out of two hundred cast.[17]

In 1784, New Hampshire adopted a provision in its constitution authorizing "public support of Protestant teachers of piety,
religion and morality . . . as morality and piety rightly guaranteed on evangelical principles will give the best and greatest
security to the government. . . ." In 1792, New Hampshire's
constitutional convention reaffirmed religious restrictions that had
been written into the franchise. Baptists and Universalists were
soon thereafter granted toleration, but, as late as 1850, Catholic
emancipation was overwhelmingly defeated. Even in 1868 this

---

15 See HEALEY, JEFFERSON ON RELIGION IN PUBLIC EDUCATION 250–53 (1962).

16 See SWEET, op. cit. supra note 4, at 190.

17 LITTELL, FROM STATE CHURCH TO PLURALISM 27–28 (1962).

restriction was upheld in the state courts.[18] The dissenting judge insisted that "practical construction shows that the Protestant test is anti-Catholic and nothing else."[19] The word "Protestant" was maintained in the New Hampshire Bill of Rights until 1902, when it was changed to "Christian." It provided: "Every denomination of Christian [persuasion] . . . shall be equally under the protection of the law although guaranteeing that no subordination of any one sect or denomination to another shall ever be established." In 1912 this symbolic Christian establishment was still retained by a voters' referendum in spite of strong denunciations of implied discrimination against Jews.[20]

Although the federal government had no control over the establishment of religion in the original states, it did exercise its power when new states applied for membership in the Union. The Ordinances of 1787 passed by Congress for the government of the Northwest Territory guaranteed specifically that "no person deeming himself in a peaceable and orderly manner shall ever be molested on account of his mode of worship or religious sentiment. . . ." It also provided that "religion, morality and knowledge being necessary to good government and the happiness of mankind, schools and the means of education shall forever be encouraged."[21] It was presumed, evidently, that schools would teach morality based on generally accepted non-sectarian (Protestant) principles. Thus, while Congress prevented any establishment of religion in these new states (eventually Ohio, Indiana, Illinois, and Michigan), it nevertheless gave expression to an American policy of friendliness toward religion, acknowledging religion as a constructive ingredient in the shaping of public morality.

In 1790, Congress provided that the Southwest Territory also be administered under the same provisions.[22] An issue arose over the situation in Texas. When Texas had belonged to Mexico, the Roman Catholic Church was established by law and non-Catholics were restricted. The legislature of the new state renegotiated the property rights of the Catholic Church, and the Texas Declaration of Rights guaranteed religious freedom for all. Catholics sued in court to maintain the privilege of state support of the clergy on

---

18 Hale v. Everett, 53 N.H. 9 (1868).
19 *Id.* at 171.
20 LITTELL, *op. cit. supra* note 17, at 28.
21 Act of Aug. 7, 1789, ch. 8, 1 Stat. 51 arts. I, III.
22 Act of May 26, 1790, ch. 8, 1 Stat. 123.

the ground that the practice had been sanctioned by the "previous system." The state court denied the claim, indicating that the Catholic Church had properly been "reduced . . . from the high level of being the only national church to a level of equality with other denominations of religion." In light of this important change, added the court, "it could not for a moment be contended that assessments and contributions could be levied for the purpose of erecting church edifices and the support of ecclesiastics."[23]

The constitutions of those states formed after the Civil War were required by the federal government to provide an irrevocable ordinance that "perfect toleration of religious sentiment shall be secured and no inhabitant of said state shall ever be molested in person or property on account of his or her mode of religious worship."[24] The constitutions of Arizona, Idaho, Nevada, New Mexico, North Dakota, Utah, Washington, and Wyoming originally contained this provision. Colorado, Montana, and Oklahoma also accepted this ordinance in separate documents attached to their constitutions.

It is evident that the federal influence assured an ever broader definition of the meaning of the separation between church and state as new states were added to the Union, and thus the constitutions of the western states were more restrictive in language than those of the original colonies. Utah alone, however, specified an absolute separation of church and state. Its constitution of 1895 declared: "There shall be no union of church and state nor shall any church dominate the state or interfere with its functions."[25] This forceful language reflected in part a reaction to the control Mormons had been exercising over the life of the territory.

During the Jackson era, an unsuccessful effort was made in Congress to pass a tax in support of religion. After the Civil War, proposals were made to put the name of God in the Federal Constitution and to designate Christianity as the official religion of the country. Both of these proposals were turned aside and the new American experiment in church-state separation was affirmed as good for religion and society.[26]

---

23 Blair v. Odin, 3 Tex. 288 (1848).
24 See Zollman, *Religious Liberty in American Law*, in 2 SELECTED ESSAYS ON CONSTITUTIONAL LAW 1108–12 (Amer. Assoc. Law Schls. 1938).
25 UTAH CONST. art. 1 § 4 (1895).
26 See Thompson *supra* note 9, at 97.

From 1776 to 1880, all states except two had adopted new constitutions; all guaranteed religious liberty. Religious qualifications for holding public office, however, were retained. Arkansas, Maryland, Mississippi, North Carolina, Pennsylvania, South Carolina, Tennessee, and Texas disqualified atheists. Pennsylvania and Tennessee required from their public officials a belief in the afterlife. The emerging public schools instituted devotional exercises of the Protestant liturgy and taught history from the perspective of New England Protestantism in an effort "to promote sound religion." In most states of the United States, Protestant conceptions of individual morality were, without question, established as the law of the land.[27]

The first significant battles to enlarge the meaning of religious freedom and to guarantee the separation of church and state, as this review indicates, were fought out in the legislature; and since the population of America was overwhelmingly Protestant, these were conflicts among Protestants. The Catholic and Jewish populations were minuscule and were completely at the mercy and dependent on the good will of Protestant legislatures. Redress of injustice by appeal to the Supreme Court was impossible, since the guarantees of religious liberty in the Federal Constitution were not yet applicable to the states.

On the other hand, the federal influence was felt as new states entered the Union and the pioneer territories provided a haven for religious diversity. They were, by far, a more fertile soil for religious experimentalism. It is no accident that the Midwest became headquarters for German-speaking Reform Jews, Lutherans, and American-born Holiness and Pentecostal sects.

RELIGIOUS BIGOTRY—HINDRANCE TO RELIGIOUS EQUALITY

The American Jewish historian Rabbi Bertram Korn points out that the struggle of the Jew for religious freedom in America was aided by well-motivated *individuals*, including Christians such as Roger Williams in Rhode Island and the Scotch Presbyterian Thomas Kennedy in Maryland, not by the opinion or action of *organized religious bodies* or of their official spokesmen. The general impulse to extend equal recognition to different creeds was

---

[27] See Miller, *The Development in Constitutional Law of the Principles of Religious Liberty and the Separation of Church and State,* in WOOD, THOMPSON & MILLER, *op. cit. supra* note 9, at 86 ff.

the contribution of laymen who were frequently secularists, i.e., those who were unaffiliated with religion or who were involved in positions of civil power where they acted in terms of their public responsibility rather than in accordance with the requirements of church dogma. Each advance in the area of religious freedom was actually made in a non-religious context, through the courts or the legislature. "Had there been no courts of law or legislatures or constitutional conventions," asserts Rabbi Korn, "the ideal of religious liberty would not have been established as a realistic standard of behavior."[28]

Rabbi Korn recalls, for example, that when in 1858 for the first time Congress invited a rabbi to deliver the invocation, spokesmen for organized religion viewed the incident with horror. A Roman Catholic paper in Baltimore objected to any prayer in Congress which was not addressed to God through Jesus. A Baptist parson, William Brownlaw of Tennessee, denounced the legislators who had consented to this prayer by "a Rabbi of the Hebrew denomination, the people who killed Christ." An Episcopal journal said, ". . . it was with extreme sorrow and enormous disgust that we read the announcement . . . that Congressmen put forward as their official representative and mouthpiece before God . . . a minister who denies the Son of God. . . ."[29]

In 1861, Congress passed a Volunteer Bill establishing that every chaplain must be "a regularly ordained minister of some Christian denomination." This was the first piece of legislation ever passed by Congress that discriminated against Jews. After a year of petitions, the law was changed. Many individual Christians supported President Lincoln in an effort to repair the injustice but no official organized Christian body raised its voice in support of the right of rabbis to serve as chaplains, although many official voices were raised in protest. A YMCA meeting in Washington, called to consider the religious welfare of the Armed Forces, was quoted as insisting that even if Jewish soldiers were segregated into all-Jewish regiments, the leaders of the YMCA would still not be willing to approve the appointment of rabbis as chaplains. The periodical of the Cincinnati Presbyterian Church rejected the idea of Jewish chaplains with this strong editorial statement:

---

28 Korn, *Religious Freedom in America: The Viewpoint of American Jewish History*, Cross Currents, Winter 1963, p. 35.
29 *Id.* at 36.

Our government has already gone at great length in this respect in appointing Roman Catholic and Universalist Chaplains to the Army. . . . these denominations at least call
themselves Christians and profess to honor the laws of Jesus,
howevermuch they really dishonor Him. . . . yet should this
bill become a law, which God forbid that it should, the government in effect says that one might despise and reject the
Saviour of men and thus trample underfoot the Son of
God. . . .[30]

Despite these occasional outbreaks of religious bigotry, the
significant point is that from the period of the adoption of the
Federal Constitution until the deluge of Catholic immigration
the legislative process itself was sufficient to extend religious freedom and to encompass within its concern the small group of Jews,
Catholics, and dissenters in this country.

The situation changed markedly with the Irish immigration
into America. The good will of Protestant America was challenged by a forthright claim on the part of the Catholics for a
new definition of religious liberty and a new pattern of arrangements between church and state; and the good will was found
somewhat wanting.

CATHOLICS EXERCISE THE RIGHT TO LITIGATE FOR JUSTICE

Although it would be improper to suggest that Catholics
acted in the public order with a preconceived strategy, a pattern
of action does emerge. At first, through reasonable requests to
proper administrative channels, Catholics sought redress for
grievances. Failing in that, they attempted to turn to legislative
action and in one case organized politically for such purposes.
But, still very much in the minority, Catholics in general found
themselves blocked and outvoted and so they resorted at last to
the use of the court. Violence and harsh feeling accompanied
their action at every step of the way.

When the public schools of the United States were first instituted, Protestants generally insisted that their religious school
systems be included within the public school funds, and in most

---

[30] See KORN, AMERICAN JEWRY AND THE CIVIL WAR 56–97 (1951) for the entire
story of the chaplaincy struggle.

cases such requests were honored. The Common School Act of 1795, for example, provided funds for New York's denominational charity school. When in 1825 the Public School Society in New York City refused to share its funds with church-related schools, the Protestants acquiesced but not the Catholic Church under Bishop Hughes. What rankled the mind of the Bishop was his conviction that the Public School Society itself was "a completely Protestant organization that taught Protestant Christianity." Its charter allowed it to teach in the schools "the sublime truth of religion and morality contained in the Holy Scriptures."[31]

In 1840, Bishop Hughes brought the conflict to a head by appearing on behalf of the Catholic schools before the corporation of the city. He requested that the seven Catholic schools be permitted to share in the public school funds. The matter was denied. Catholics thereupon took the case to the state legislature where the petition was again defeated, although the lower house supported their demands. Reported nationally, this case fired the passions of the emerging Nativist movement. The Catholic victory in the New York lower house provided an ominous portent of the power of this "alien" and "foreign-dominated" church.

In bold reaction to the extremism of those Protestants who had organized an anti-Catholic political party in New York, a strictly Catholic ticket appeared for the first time. Its chief purpose was the attainment of public funds for the church schools. The anti-Catholic Know-Nothing party aligned with the Whigs suffered serious defeat at the polls, and the Democrats, with Catholic support, were victorious. Catholics did not support their own Catholic party. The response to hatred was not, in the good judgment of most Catholics, political segregation. In January, 1842, Governor Seward, redressing at least one injustice in the Protestant-Catholic relationship, signed a bill ending sectarian control of the Public School Society and created a non-sectarian public school system.[32]

During this period, Catholics throughout the country found the judiciary more sensitive to their rights than the legislature, and they made use of litigation increasingly as a means of achieving social change. The court, more than the legislature, was sheltered from the whirlwinds of prejudice then circulating the country. The court balanced the power of minorities and majorities;

---

31 See O'NEILL, CATHOLICS IN CONTROVERSY 82 (1954).
32 See BRICKMAN & LEHRER, *op. cit. supra* note 5, at 257.

and justice was a determining factor rather than the cries of the mob.

The earliest cases challenging Protestant rituals and devotional exercises in the public schools of the United States were brought by Catholic parents.[33] As the Vicar General of the Roman Catholic Diocese of New York explained in 1840: "The Holy Scriptures are read in the schools every day. . . . The Catholic Church tells her children that they must be taught religion by authority. . . . The Sects say: 'Read the bible; judge for yourself. . . .' The Protestant principle is therefore acted upon, slily inculcated and the schools are Sectarian."[34]

It was not without suffering that Catholics pressed their claims. In Boston one hundred Catholic children were expelled from Elliott School for refusal to participate in Protestant religious exercises and one Catholic child was severely flogged.[35] In Philadelphia riots erupted for three days over this issue, leaving dead and wounded.[36] In Maine, where the first Bible-reading case was argued in 1854, the church school was burned and the priests run out of town.[37] The case was lost in Maine[38] and a similar case was lost in Massachusetts in 1859,[39] but Catholic litigants were successful in Ohio in 1872[40] and in Wisconsin in 1890.[41] The language of the Wisconsin decision foreshadowed the recent prayer and Bible-reading decisions of the Supreme Court.

When it came to obtaining public funds to support parochial education, Catholics did not find the courts as ready to support their claims as in cases involving Protestant impositions in the

---

[33] Reviewing this history, Mr. Justice Brennan in the *Schempp* case points out, "The earliest . . . decisions declined to review the propriety of actions taken by school authorities, so long as these actions were within the purview of the administrators' powers. Thus, where the local school board *required* religious exercises, the courts would not enjoin them; and where, as at least in one case, the school officials *forbade* devotional practices, the court refused on similar grounds to overrule that decision." 374 U.S. at 274–75. In the last quarter of the nineteenth century, however, the courts began to question the constitutionality of public school exercises and in a half-dozen states found the compulsory religious exercises in violation of state constitutions.

[34] New York Freeman's Journal, July 11, 1840, p. 12.

[35] See O'NEILL, *op. cit. supra* note 31, at 80.

[36] *Id.* at 80–82.

[37] BRICKMAN & LEHRER, *op. cit. supra* note 5, at 257.

[38] Donahoe v. Richards, 38 Me. 376 (1854).

[39] Commonwealth v. Cooke, 7 AM. L. REV. 417 (1859).

[40] Board of Educ. v. Minor, 23 Ohio St. 211 (1873).

[41] State *ex. rel.* Weiss v. Dist. School Bd. of Edgarton, 76 Wisc. 177 (1890).

public schools. Of necessity such claims must first be established
in the legislative bodies. But even when this was achieved, the
courts at first struck down such support as unconstitutional, regardless whether the legislature restricted the aid to fringe benefits
such as aid for the secular education of inmates of Catholic orphan-
ages, free textbooks, and bus transportation. In 1848 the New York
court ruled that an orphanage school under Catholic auspices was
not "a common school,"[42] but in 1907 the court reversed itself.[43]
In 1922 a New York court ruled that furnishing textbooks was "an
aid or a maintenance of a school of learning . . ."[44] and therefore
was prohibited by the state constitution under a provision forbidding public aid to sectarian schools. This provision was also interpreted as forbidding the use of public funds for transportation of
pupils to sectarian schools.[45] Eventually, however, Catholics became strong enough in New York to achieve at least limited constitutional change. New York now provides free bus transportation
for parochial school children, a specific exemption from the constitutional provision prohibiting the use of public funds for sectarian schools, which otherwise remains unchanged.

    In recent years the courts have tended to recognize Catholic
claims. Victories in the state courts of Louisiana[46] and Mississippi[47]
upheld laws that provided Catholic children with free textbooks,
and in New Jersey[48] with free bus transportation, as the "child-
benefit theory" gained recognition. Catholics now have a right to
believe that their request for a share of the public funds and services provided to all school children need not come in conflict
with constitutional prohibitions. Recognizing, of course, that
some state constitutions may be more restrictive than the Federal
Constitution, Catholics in recent years have had to seek revision
of state constitutions. Such is the case at present in Wisconsin
where an effort is being made by constitutional amendment to
reverse a 1961 state supreme court decision providing that bus
transportation to parochial school students violated the state constitution.

---

42 People v. Board of Educ. 13 Barb. 400 (N.Y. 1951).
43 Sargeant v. Board of Educ. 69 N.E. 722 (N.Y. 1904).
44 Smith v. Donahue, 195 N.Y.S. 715 (App. Div. 1922).
45 Judd v. Board of Educ., 15 N.E. 2d 576 (N.Y. 1938).
46 Cochran v. Board of Educ., 281 U.S. 370 (1930).
47 Chance v. State Textbook Board, 190 Miss. 452 (1941).
48 Everson v. Board of Educ. 330 U.S. 1 (1947).

THE ERA OF THE SUPREME COURT

The Jehovah's Witnesses have been a small group whose size precluded any expectation that by legislative action they could achieve consideration of their minority rights. Instead, they depended upon the courts to achieve justice, creating for themselves a magnificent legal department. With the help of the American Civil Liberties Union, the Jehovah's Witnesses provided the Supreme Court opportunity to clarify in a substantial way the meaning of the First Amendment.[49] As did the Catholics before them, however, the Jehovah's Witnesses had to endure the hostility and outrages of "patriotic" Americans.

Believing that God (Jehovah) alone is the proper object of their devotion, the Jehovah's Witnesses refuse to salute any flag. During the 1930's, children of the Jehovah's Witnesses refused to engage in flag-salute exercises on the opening of the school day. Some two thousand of them were summarily expelled from public schools in thirty-one states. Local authorities in several states attempted to brand the children "delinquent" by virtue of their expulsion and to remove the children from their parents. More than 800 incidents of violence were perpetrated against Witnesses and their churches. Known members of the American Legion participated in 176 of these outrages.[50]

Finally in 1943 the Supreme Court acknowledged that patriotism could not be coerced and excused those children who, because of sincere religious conviction, would not participate in flag-salute exercises. In a stirring decision, Mr. Justice Jackson pointed out that the flag-salute exercise compelled students to declare a belief. "The flag salute is a form of utterance," he said, and "symbolism is a primitive but effective way of communicating ideas. . . ." He added, "If there is any fixed star in our constitutional constellation, it is that no official, high or petty, can prescribe what shall be orthodox in politics, nationalism, religion, or other matters of opinion or force citizens to confess by word or act their faith therein."[51]

Despite the Court's decision, violence and expulsions continued.

---

49 *Cf.* MANWARING, RENDER UNTO CAESAR—THE FLAG-SALUTE CONTROVERSY (1962). The Jehovah's Witnesses brought at least twenty-five important cases to the Supreme Court between 1938 and 1948.

50 *Id.* at 175.

51 Board of Educ. v. Barnette, 319 U.S. 624, 632, 642 (1943).

The Justice Department was compelled finally to circularize all United States attorneys, alerting them to their obligations to "uphold religious freedom as Constitutionally guaranteed."[52]

A significant aspect of this case is that it marked a turning point in the Supreme Court's exercise of self-restraint where basic human liberties were involved. In the first flag-salute case, which had denied the right of school children to refuse the salute on religious grounds, the Court had asserted that "in a field where courts possess no marked and certainly no controlling competence . . . to the legislature no less than to courts is committed the guardianship of deeply-cherished liberties and . . . [it is constitutionally appropriate] to fight out the wise use of legislative authority in the forum of public opinion and before legislative assemblies rather than to transfer such a contest to the judicial arena."[53]

Now realizing, perhaps, that minorities cannot always overcome the hysteria of the moment and induce reasoned consideration of their views, the Court asserted:

> The very purpose of a Bill of Rights was to withdraw certain subjects from the vicissitudes of political controversy, to place them beyond the reach of majorities and officials and to establish them as legal principles to be applied by the courts. One's right to life, liberty, and property, free speech, a free press, freedom of worship and assembly, and other fundamental rights may not be submitted to vote; they depend on the outcome of no elections.[54]

It is of interest to note at this point that Catholics sharply rebuked the Court for its earlier decision. Mr. Justice Frankfurter's reluctance to have the judiciary usurp the responsibility of the legislature and his insistence that the people and the representatives themselves ought not to rely on the Court "for the impossible task of assuring a vigorous, mature, self-respecting and tolerant democracy . . ."[55] provoked unanimous criticism from Catholic law journals. Representative of their viewpoint was the editorial of Reverend Paul L. Blakely in the Jesuit magazine *America*. Citing the valuable role of the Court in defending the right of Catholics to attend private schools, as in the Oregon case, Blakely

---

52 MANWARING, *op. cit. supra* note 49, at 243.

53 Minersville School Dist. v. Gobitis, 310 U.S. 586, 597–98, 600 (1940).

54 319 U.S. at 638.

55 From a letter of Felix Frankfurter to Harlan F. Stone, Apr. 27. 1940, quoted in MANWARING *op. cit. supra* note 49, at 137.

questioned Frankfurter's conclusion that "the courtroom is not the arena for debating issues of educational policy." "If that be true," queried Blakely, "where is our protection when the next campaign to close our schools through the Oregon method begins?"[56]

In another case brought to the Court by the Jehovah's Witnesses, the Court upheld the right of a religious group to distribute literature and to seek converts in spite of the "probability of excess and abuses." In this case the Court, for the first time, clearly extended the protection of the Fourteenth Amendment to the religious liberties protected by the First Amendment. It thereby gave itself jurisdiction over those actions of state authorities that, in its judgment, abridged religious freedom.[57]

By these decisions concerning the Jehovah's Witnesses, the Court catapulted itself into the center of the democratic process by which accommodations and adjustments are made among religious groups in our pluralistic society and by which the state regulates its relations to the church. The Court not only assumed a share with the legislature in developing patterns of church-state relationship; it set itself up as the ultimate arbiter of conflicts among religious groups in this pluralistic society.

Jewish Community Benefited by Supreme Court

The Jewish community in the United States has benefited very much in recent years by the Court's active involvement in church-state issues. Jewish parents and Jewish agencies have been party to almost every First Amendment case that has made its way to the Supreme Court. The particular concerns of Jews have been the place of religion in public education and the right of Sabbatarians to exemption from restrictive Sunday closing laws.

There was a time, however, when the Jews were too frightened to litigate. Anxiety over anti-Semitism kept them from risking the national public exposure consequent to the use of the courts. Besides, Jews were not certain that American jurists would appreciate their particular concerns. In former decisions, both the Supreme Court and to an ever greater degree the state courts had included in their judgments assertions that this was "a Christian

---

[56] Quoted in MANWARING, op. cit. supra note 49, at 156.
[57] Cantwell v. Connecticut, 310 U.S. 296 (1940).

nation" or "a religious country."[58] Jewish opposition to religious exercises in public schools and to Christian symbols on public property could easily be misrepresented as an attack on religion and Christianity.

As early as 1904, Rabbi Joseph Krauskopf, president of the Central Conference of American Rabbis (CCAR), in his presidential address asserted:

> As American citizens and in the name of American citizens of Jewish and non-Jewish persuasion, we must protest against this sectarianizing of our public schools. As profoundly as we respect the Christian creed, and as sacredly as we venerate the Bible, and as heartily as we approve of the study of the Bible as literature in connection with the study of classical literature, so strenuously must we oppose their introduction for religious purposes into institutions which are maintained by the commonwealth. Respectfully but emphatically we must say to all who trespass upon our citizenship rights in public institutions: Have all the Christianity you wish, cherish it as much as you can, enthrone it in your church, but keep it from the public schools. Let us be Protestants or Catholics, agnostics or Jews in our churches or homes; in our public institutions, however, let us be Americans.[59]

The next year, 1905, a newly organized CCAR church-state committee cautioned the Jews against instituting legal test cases with regard to sectarian practices in the public schools. Pointing out that all state constitutions are not explicit on this issue, the committee warned: "Defeat in such matters is so baneful that the risk of it had rather not be incurred. It is best that we concentrate our efforts on the education of public opinion on this very important subject."[60] The CCAR then engaged in a vigorous campaign of public education, but without very significant effect.

Despair concerning the effect of education, negotiation, and dialogue as means of achieving social change was also evident in later decisions made by the CCAR. In 1917, for example, the Re-

---

58 In 1824 the Pennsylvania Supreme Court held: "Christianity is a part of the common law of this state. It is not proclaimed by the commanding voice of any human superior, but expressed in the calm and mild accent of customary law." Updegraph v. Commonwealth, 11 Serg. & R. 394, 406–07; see also Vidal v. Girard Executors, 2 How. (43 U.S.) 127 (1844); Church of the Holy Trinity v. United States, 143 U.S. 457 (1892).

59 CENTRAL CONFERENCE OF AMERICAN RABBIS, YEARBOOK (1904).

60 Id. (1905).

form rabbis endorsed released time. According to this plan, public school children were to be excused for one or two hours a week for religious instruction at their churches or synagogues. This was by far a superior arrangement, in the judgment of the rabbis, than the providing of religious teaching within the public school curriculum. But by 1940 the rabbis realized that the program of released time had been much abused throughout most of the United States. Schools were involved in the recruiting of students for the released-time classes. Children were separated according to religion. Those who refused to take released-time classes were often humiliated and found themselves with nothing but "busy work" to do, and, most importantly, in many communities the released-time classes were conducted right on school property with no provision made for the dissenter. Rabbi Emil Leipziger, speaking the mind of the CCAR church-state committee, said, "Even the most seemingly innocuous project of released time cannot be practically applied without danger of becoming an opening wedge for the violation of the American principle of church-state separation."[61]

Thus, when the Supreme Court, demonstrating a new sensitivity to minority rights, extended its authority over infringements on religious liberty in the states, Jews who had despaired of educating Christian leadership in their local communities or of achieving change through local and state legislation were ready to make use of litigation. The use of litigation by Jews even at this point in American history still entails some physical risk. The record indicates that Jewish parents who have protested Christian religious practices in the public schools have had to endure cross-burnings on their lawns, harassing telephone calls, the threat of economic boycott, and the mass distribution of anti-Semitic hate literature. But it must also be admitted that these acts of violence have been mild compared to past incidents in American history. Evidently Americans now reserve for interracial relations the physical passion that once accompanied interreligious conflicts.

THE LAW SERVES AN EDUCATIONAL FUNCTION

The debate over the Court's decisions on prayer and Bible reading in the public schools and the testimony rendered at the congressional hearings on a constitutional amendment to permit

---

61 *Id.* (1940).

such practices has provided an education for all American citizens on the meaning of religious freedom that the Jews never could have achieved by the publication of pamphlets or the organization of conversations among clergy of different faiths.

This is not to deny that there is a widespread disobedience of the Court's decisions at the grass-roots level. Studies undertaken in co-operation with the National Conference of Christians and Jews (NCCJ) reveal that the majority of school systems, particularly in the rural parts of the United States, will continue the regimen of religious practice, prayers, and Bible reading at the opening of their school day.[62] But, at the same time, educational and religious leaders have pointed to the crisis in morality occasioned by the fact that a public school will seek to instruct children in respect for the law and then break the law itself with an act of prayer.

Without doubt we are entering a new period in the history of church-state relations in this country. As I have admitted, the founding fathers probably never intended by the First Amendment to exercise federal control over state actions or to remove from education its responsibility to communicate a religiously sanctioned morality. While the instrumentalities of state and church were not to be intermingled, there was never any thought of creating barriers for the spiritual interpenetration of society. I have no doubt, however, that the Court acted properly when it considered liturgy in the public school, composed, sponsored, or sanctioned by the state, whether voluntary or not, to be an establishment of religion. For the pluralism of our nation in this post-Protestant, even post-Christian, era required such a decision.

As Mr. Justice Brennan observed in the *Schempp* and *Murray* cases:

> . . . our religious composition makes us a vastly more diverse people than were our forefathers. They knew differences chiefly among Protestant sects. Today the Nation is far more heterogeneous religiously, including as it does substantial minorities not only of Catholics and Jews, but as well of those who worship according to no version of the Bible and those who . . . worship no god at all. . . . Practices which may have been objectionable to no one in the time of Jefferson and Madison may today be highly offensive

---

62 A summary of these surveys is to be found in the "Year in Review" section of this volume, *infra* pp. 243–48.

to many persons, the deeply devout and the non-believers alike.[63]

But it is also important to note that in its prayer decision the Court recognized that it cannot separate religion from the state absolutely without itself becoming party to the establishment of a functional secularism as the philosophy that undergirds governmental action. The Court invoked the creative concept of "wholesome neutrality"[64] instead of the concept of absolute separation of church and state, recognizing that the Court can be so rigidly separatist as to be detrimental to religion. Some freedom must remain for co-operation between religion and state so that the secular purposes of the state may themselves be served and the religious needs of the American people respected and accommodated. In the *Schempp* and *Murray* cases Mr. Justice Goldberg stated the issue well. He observed:

> . . . untutored devotion to the concept of neutrality can lead to invocation or approval of results which partake not simply of the noninterference and noninvolvement with the religious which the Constitution commands, but of a brooding and pervasive devotion to the secular and a passive, or even active, hostility to the religious. Such results are not only not compelled by the Constitution, but, it seems to me, are prohibited by it. . . . Government must inevitably take cognizance of the existence of religion and, indeed, under certain circumstances the First Amendment may require that it do so.[65]

Apparently there is a vast political consensus that approves of such co-operation. Witness, for example, the lack of restriction against the use of public funds for secular instruction in church-related schools in the recent congressionally approved grants for higher education, the National Defense Education Act, and the Poverty Bill.

The fine line between wholesome and unwholesome neutrality, public service grants and aids to the church, teaching *about* reli-

---

[63] School Dist. of Abington Township v. Schempp, 374 U.S. 203, 240–41 (1963) (Brennan, J., concurring).

[64] Writing for the Court, Mr. Justice Clark said: "In the relationship between man and religion, the State is firmly committed to a position of *neutrality*. Though the application of that rule requires interpretation of a delicate sort. . . ." 374 U.S. at 226 (emphasis added).

[65] *Id.* at 306 (Goldberg, J., concurring).

gion as an aspect of secular education and the teaching *of* religion, remains hard to define. It is conceivable now that the Court will be confronted with a rash of lawsuits seeking adjudication of every fine point and that Americans will become litigious on the church-state issue.

In his review of the Supreme Court Term of 1963, in the *Harvard Law Review* (November, 1964), Philip B. Kurland suggests that a consequence of the Court's work during this decade has been "the enhancement of judicial dominion at the expense of the power of other branches of government, national as well as state." Although pointing out that the Court's thrust for equality is deserving of approbation, Professor Kurland nevertheless suggests that "the most recent expansion of judicial authority has had a longer life than usual and shows no immediate likelihood of recession. At least there are no indications of self-restraint." I would hope, however, that the Court will exercise self-discipline, realizing that there has been a benefit for democracy in our country that derives from the local control of public school policy. Having set down broad principles, the Court ought not to seek to act as a national school board but should now allow the American people to work out some degree of consensus, if at all possible, through the process of dialogue.

THE EMERGENCE OF INTERRELIGIOUS DIALOGUE

For the first time in American history, religious and community leaders are now talking to each other. We have reached such a point of maturity that each religious group has felt free to voice its opinion and seek justice for itself without fear of violent consequence and with some degree of assurance that views will be heard, understood, and reacted to civilly, whether in agreement or disagreement.

Under the auspices of the NCCJ, dialogue groups of clergy meet monthly in fifty-five cities of the United States to discuss the issues of religious freedom; and with the co-operation of educational associations, national denominational bodies, and academic institutions, new approaches to the problems of religion in education and the financing of education are being explored.

Recourse to litigation alone as the ultimate arbiter of interreligious conflict substitutes "constitutionality" for "righteousness" as the central political value. It diminishes the obligation of all to consider with each other that which is in the public good, and it delegates to the judiciary a responsibility that should be shared by all citizens.

In recent years, Catholics particularly have been eager to seek political solutions to their requests for public funds for children in church-related schools, in contrast to adjudication. In the tension between the conflicting "good" of church-state separation and the excellence of the education of all American school children, Catholics have wished to pin their hopes on the understanding and sympathy of the American people rather than on the courts. For the courts, because of the nature of adjudication, may have to choose among these goods, sacrificing one to preserve another, whereas the American people, through the process of dialogue, may discover programs that will somewhat satisfactorily remain faithful to both concepts.

In a major address before an NCCJ-sponsored institute on religion and law at the University of Chicago Law School, Senator Abraham Ribicoff supported such a viewpoint:

> It is safe to predict that if the difficult cases in this field are one day decided by the court it will either set aside much of the public support now going to private education, or more likely it will indicate a much wider area of permissiveness than is now in effect. This raises the question of do we really want a series of definitive answers from the court on these most perplexing questions. Or more pointedly, do we want such answers now? Would it not be better to pursue the political process further to explore new approaches to the problem and try to develop a consensus within this country as to what should be done?[66]

This review of history reveals that much of the conflict among America's religious communities resulted from prejudice and mistrust existing between them. The emergence of a secular policy in education and a governmental policy of religious neutrality enables us to achieve public purpose without becoming entangled in religious wrangling. Is it not possible, therefore, to conceive that in an age of new trust more will be allowable and less will have to be restricted? Co-operation between the church and state need not be seen as threatening if we trust the churches to be *servants of all mankind* rather than the *executors of institutional*

---

[66] The National Conference of Christians and Jews, Background Report, April, 1964, p. 10.

investment. Dialogue might help us to achieve that degree of trust and promote an interreligious competition in sacrificial service instead of membership recruitment and church-building.

Interreligious dialogue, however, is still in its beginning and it may be too soon to spin such dreams for it as a method of social change. Our democratic system properly still provides us recourse to legislative enactment and to judicial review. All these methods —legislation, litigation, and dialogue—have their strengths and weaknesses. Of this we may be sure: we are living in a markedly new period of history in the relation between America's religious communities. It behooves us to consider carefully how best we may bear witness to the vitality of the democratic process and demonstrate that love and service are still the true characteristics of religion.

PHILIP WOGAMAN

THE NCC NATIONAL STUDY CONFERENCE ON CHURCH AND STATE

The first National Study Conference on Church and State, convened by the National Council of Churches in Columbus, Ohio, on February 4–7, 1964, may be remembered by many of its participants as a model of ambiguity. If so, time may prove the conference to have been an accurate barometer of thought on church-state matters among American Christians. Most of the conflicting currents of thought were well represented there, both in their points of firm conviction and in their uncertainties. It is to the credit of the NCC's Department of Religious Liberty, which staged the conference, and of its able executive director, the Reverend Dean M. Kelley, that no effort was made to stack the conference or to blunt the sharp conflict of virtually irreconcilable positions. Moreover, the uncertainties which have crept into Christian discussion were not glossed over for the sake of public "image." Contributing to the ambiguity of the conference was the fact that its brevity produced a mood of haste in which adequate reflection on complex issues was most difficult. This was compounded during the final plenary session, at which the statement entitled *General Findings* (the sole statement discussed and adopted by the conference as a body) was adopted, by the absence of more than half the official delegates and by steady attrition as the hour of adjournment neared.

Philip Wogaman is Associate Professor of Bible and Social Ethics, University of the Pacific.

This article is an effort to interpret the conference and is written in the belief that the conference was important despite the elements of ambiguity. It was important as a first effort of its kind. It was important because of the careful preparatory process which preceded it, involving numerous denominational groups and some of the best minds in the country. It was important because it provided some clue to the actual situation of Christian thought on church and state relations and some stimulus to the further clarification of that situation. But it was also important because the quest for creative new direction was at least partly successful.

THE STRUCTURE OF THE CONFERENCE

Some background information on the study conference may help in understanding and interpreting it. While this was the first NCC study conference to be devoted to questions of church and state, it was preceded by other study conferences dealing with other areas of social concern—notably war and peace and economic affairs. While every effort is made by the National Council of Churches to make these conferences representative and to involve all the churches in serious discussion of their findings and recommendations, the conferences have no official standing and do not, therefore, speak for the NCC or for its member denominations.[1] The value of the conferences, accordingly, must rest upon the intrinsic quality of their discussions, publications, and recommendations. While this may weaken their direct importance, it doubtless minimizes the intrusion of short-range ecclesiastical considerations and contributes to their creativity.

Preparation for the Columbus conference began two years before the actual meeting and consisted of three stages: (1) Six preparatory commissions were appointed to help guide the thinking of the writers of six preparatory papers each dealing with a different topic. These commissions were widely representative of the diversity and competence of the churches in the area of church-state relations, and the six writers were among the best available. (2) After the first meetings of the commissions and the preparation of preliminary drafts, the papers were printed and submitted to nine regional conferences meeting at retreat centers across the

---

[1] This fact was widely overlooked by critics who attacked the NCC World Order Study Conference, which recommended consideration of the admission of mainland China to the United Nations.

country. The regional conferences produced fifty pages of comments. (3) The commissions then met again to review the comments, and the writers prepared their final drafts. In final form, the papers remained the sole responsibility of their writers, although the influence of the commissions and regional conferences is clearly discernible in most of them. As distributed to delegates a few weeks before the conference, the preparatory papers each appended a distillation of the regional conference comments to stimulate further reflection and to dispel the notion that the ideas were beyond debate.

The conference was attended by delegates in three categories and by consultants and observers who were permitted to participate but not vote.[2] It was organized into twelve "sections." The sections had three principal tasks: First, they were to indicate categorically whether they considered the preparatory papers worthy of publication without further amendment as contributions to Christian discussion of church-state relations. (All the papers were thus approved, although few of the delegates would have accepted all the ideas contained in all the papers.) Secondly, the sections were to advise the General Findings Committee on the content of the *General Findings* of the conference. To facilitate this, four proposals for general findings were outlined by as many speakers on the first evening. Discussion in the sections then centered on these four proposals and others suggested on the spot.[3] Thirdly, each section was assigned a unique topic on which it was to submit a report. The section reports became a part of the official record of the conference. They could not be rejected or

---

[2] Two hundred and forty-five delegates represented member denominations of the National Council of Churches; 36 delegates represented such non-member communions as the American Lutheran Church, the Lutheran Church—Missouri Synod, and the Southern Baptist Convention; 22 delegates (including the present writer) were designated by city and state councils of churches; there were 14 observers from the National Catholic Welfare Conference and 9 observers from the Synagogue Council of America, the National Association of Evangelicals, and the Church of Christ, Scientist. Finally, there were 17 invited consultants and 21 advisers representing the staffs of NCC departments. There were, thus, 303 delegates and 61 non-voting participants.

[3] The four proposals were designed to represent four logically distinct possibilities ranging from an absolute separationist position of "no government aid, no government recognition to religion" to the position "some government aid, some government recognition to religion," with the intervening options "no government aid, some government recognition" and "some government aid, no government recognition." The design never quite got off the ground, partly because the individuals chosen to present these options saw their task in larger terms and partly because the typology itself seemed to obscure deeper philosophical differences. The *General Findings* will be given more attention below.

amended by the plenary session, although the plenary session could, and in two or three cases did, record dissents.

Besides reviewing the work of the sections, the plenary session debated, amended, and approved the *General Findings,* the one document which fairly could be said to represent the thinking of the entire conference.[4] This statement, initially proposed by the representative General Findings Committee, was subjected to wide-ranging comments at the first plenary session. It was then quickly revised and mimeographed for presentation to the final plenary session for amendment and adoption.

On the basis of this background, one can appreciate that interpretation of the conference must include understanding of the preparatory process and the mechanics of the conference itself. The materials to be interpreted include the preparatory papers, presentations to the conference, section reports, and the *General Findings.* As the culmination of the process, the latter is most important.

A BASIS FOR A PROTESTANT-ORTHODOX[5] POSITION ON CHURCH-STATE RELATIONS

While popular interest in the conference focused on the specific controversial issues, discussion of the *basis* upon which the churches should approach religious liberty and church-state relations was more fundamental and, in some respects, more revealing. The conference was clearly and thoroughly committed to religious liberty "as man's right and indispensable condition of a free society."[6] To a lesser degree, it continued also to affirm the traditional position of theoretical opposition to religious establishment in every form. One could discern, however, an obvious weakening of three time-honored supports for these positions.

In the first place, anti-Catholicism had clearly lost its power to

---

[4] Such a statement must, of course, be qualified by the atmosphere of haste in which it was discussed and the fact that only 121 were present to vote on it when it was finally adopted. See Fey, *Separate but Interacting,* THE CHRISTIAN CENTURY February 19, 1964, pp. 231–32.

[5] Through membership on the National Council of Churches, Eastern Orthodoxy was, of course, represented at the conference by voting delegates. It was a surprise to some observers to discover that the participation by these delegates was indistinguishable from that of other delegates on most matters. Hence, it is proper to refer to the conference as having been in search of a "Protestant-Orthodox" position.

[6] *General Findings.* This six-page (single-spaced) report is available in mimeographed form from the National Council of Churches, or it may be found in 6 JOURNAL OF CHURCH AND STATE 147–53 (1964). The quoted words are at 148.

determine Protestant-Orthodox thinking. The fourteen participating observers from the National Catholic Welfare Conference
were well received and listened to attentively. And, although the
conference as a whole rejected some viewpoints on particular
issues which have generally been espoused by Roman Catholic
leadership (e.g., relating to parochial schools and birth control),
there was little evidence of competitive concerns. This mood
doubtless owed much to the recent reign of Pope John XXIII, the
Vatican Council, and the administration of the first Roman Catholic President, John F. Kennedy. It also reflected the influence
which a generation of Protestant writers, including John C. Bennett, Franklin H. Littell, Robert McAfee Brown, Martin E.
Marty, and others have exerted in interpreting the good intentions of Roman Catholics as fellow Christians. With this new
mood there was appreciably more self-criticism and less willingness to adopt the kind of double standard which considers governmental aid to religious institutions a violation of "separation of
church and state" only if it benefits Roman Catholicism.

The rejection of anti-Catholicism found most articulate expression in the preparatory paper, "Christian Witness and Culture-
Religion" by Franklin H. Littell. Pointing out that Protestants
have in fact received considerably more advantage than Roman
Catholics in the federal government's surplus disposal program,
he commented that "obviously there is widespread confusion in
the matter of church-state relations, and the criticism directed
toward other religious groups for seeking or accepting governmental subsidy does not substantially affect the willingness of a
church to accept favors for itself."[7] Analyzing contemporary anti-
Catholicism in particular, Littell argued that it serves within
Protestantism as a substitute for the difficulties of church discipline.

> Although anti-Catholicism is waning as a political force, pro-
> fessional anti-Catholicism has a support in some Protestant
> church circles which it has not enjoyed for many years. We
> have reached the point in our history where the chief need
> in our statistically successful churches is for the recovery of
> discipline—in worship, creeds, morals and ethics, elementary
> church order. But such a recovery of integrity, granted the
> extraordinary popularity of "cheap grace" (Bonhoeffer's

[7] Littell, *Christian Witness and Culture-Religion*, PREPARATORY PAPERS FOR THE
NATIONAL STUDY CONFERENCE ON CHURCH AND STATE 3 (privately published by the
National Council of Churches, 1964).

phrase) among millions of "new Christians," calls for a vigorous rededication and agonizing effort in the training of the whole people of God (*laos tou theou*). An easy alternative is found by some in the negativism of an unreasoning anti-Catholicism. By this route, an "easy identity" can be found which does not cost the effort of recovery of a worthy witness and disciplined discipleship.[8]

In its writings and most of its discussions, the conference clearly avoided the temptations of this kind of "easy identity" in its search for the basis of its position.

Secondly, the conference marked a diminishing Protestant-Orthodox reliance upon the United States Constitution as the basic authority for its position. While discussion of constitutional issues was not lacking (indeed, several eminent constitutional authorities were present as delegates or consultants), an effort was made to base the position on deeper ground. Thus, the possibility of changing the Constitution to accord with new insight was not categorically excluded, as it has been from much previous Protestant discussion of church-state relations. This was, incidentally, illustrated implicitly and negatively when the conference recorded its "opposition to any proposal such as the so-called Christian Amendment which seeks to commit our government to official identification with a particular religious tradition."[9]

The First Amendment was, however, used here and there to support positions taken—as, in the discussion of government's duty toward religion in the *General Findings*, where it is said that "the clause of the First Amendment prohibiting an establishment of religion must be balanced against the clause prohibiting interference with the free exercise of religion. . . . Any concept of 'neutrality' must take into account the proper balancing of the establishment and free exercise limitations."[10] But, despite a few such appeals to the Constitution as authority, it was not generally employed to settle important questions.

Thirdly, one may record a diminishing commitment to what has been described as the mythical concept of separation of church and state.[11] The word "myth" is here used not to suggest that separation of church and state is meaningless or that the commonly accepted stories about the origin of the concept among our

---

8 *Id.* at 9.

9 *General Findings*, 6 JOURNAL OF CHURCH AND STATE 148 (1964).

10 *Id.* at 151.

11 Wogaman, *The Changing Role of Government and the Myth of Separation*, 5 JOURNAL OF CHURCH AND STATE 61 (1963).

founding fathers are merely fairy tales. Rather, it has a more technical reference to "a popular belief which is not *literally* true but which may symbolize realities or systems of value in nonpropositional terms."[12] The problem with a myth, however, is that, while it may symbolize important truths or values, it can be highly misleading if it is taken literally at face value. This danger clearly attaches to a literal reading of Jefferson's phrase "a wall of separation between church and state" (which is, after all, a metaphor), or to an oversimplified understanding of the actual situation in the early days of the Republic when, after all, there was a considerable amount of governmental support, and recognition of religion and religious liberty was not as dependable a right as most of us think it should have been.

Illustrating the much more sophisticated examination of the slogan "separation of church and state" than Protestantism has generally given, the *General Findings* points out that

> in the American experience, relations between church and state have generally been affirmative, friendly and marked by mutual respect. In view of the nature of these relationships any attempt to express church-state relations in terms of an absolute and complete separation or of a wall of separation between church and state serves only to obscure the fullness of their relationship rather than offering a fruitful basis for an understanding of the present situation. The history of church-state relations in the United States refutes such a rigid conception.[13]

Yet, a statement of this sort is significant precisely because the conception *has* been rigidly held. One might even say that until fairly recently it has indeed *dominated* most Protestant discussions of church-state relations. Commitment to the absolutist position was expressed articulately by a number of delegates, but it was clear that the majority were no longer willing to make this position the basis for all Protestant-Orthodox discussion on church-state relations.

In part, the diminishing commitment to the myth of the "wall of separation" reflected growing recognition that it is indeed a metaphor. Logically, church and state must interact in numerous ways if members of the church make up the state and if the jurisdiction of the state includes the institutions of the church. The conference, moreover, reflected a growing awareness of the

---

12 *Ibid.*
13 *General Findings*, 6 JOURNAL OF CHURCH AND STATE 149 (1964).

difficulty of *uncritically* applying ideas born in the early days of the Republic to the vastly more complex America of the twentieth century. The first draft of the *General Findings* asserted that "in 1964 both the church and state are infinitely more complex than they were 162 years ago when Thomas Jefferson introduced the metaphor of 'a wall of separation between church and state.'" While this specific statement was removed prior to submission of the final draft, its point was a generally accepted one.

In part, also, the diminishing commitment to the metaphor of "separation" as an authority reflected growing awareness that Protestantism in America has not historically been as separate from government as many have thought. As suggested above, there was considerably more self-criticism than Protestant discussions of church-state relations have generally evoked in the past. Many delegates who had rather uncritically accepted the principle of separation of church and state, and in the name of that principle condemned Roman Catholicism as its chief violator, were challenged with a broader perspective. In Littell's words, this perspective is that

> religious liberty is not so much something that we once "had" which has suddenly been put in jeopardy, as it is something to be gone out after. Neither Protestants nor Catholics nor Jews have as yet realized the full implications of the standard, nor in practice accepted them fully. Since we are trying to find our way in a difficult situation, one quite new in the history of mankind, the sloganizing use of the phrase "a wall of separation" obfuscates the real issues and decisions as much as other phrase-making references to some imaginary American past.[14]

This perspective also led to a statement in the *General Findings* that

> the nation which adopted the First Amendment, at the same time considered itself both Christian and Protestant and saw no contradiction in passing laws which required Sunday observance, prayer and Bible reading in the public schools. Its actions attested to historical interaction as well as to separation of church and state.[15]

A number of the section reports also reflected this note of Protestant self-criticism as they called attention to areas wherein the

---

14 Littell, *supra* note 7, at 5.
15 *General Findings,* 6 JOURNAL OF CHURCH AND STATE 147–48 (1964).

churches may be receiving too much governmental assistance, thereby endangering their own independence and diluting the integrity of any witness for "separation." Indeed, one section report—that dealing with the military and institutional chaplaincy—produced spirited debate in the conference plenary session because it seemed to manifest too *little* self-criticism of an area of current ecclesiastical practice.[16] Twenty-five delegates requested and received permission to record their dissent to the entire report of that section.

Along with the weakening of anti-Catholicism, normative reliance upon the United States Constitution, and commitment to the myth of separation, the conference was generally characterized by more relativism in its approach to questions of church-state relationship. In part, this may be attributed to the weakening of the more traditional bases of authority, as has been suggested. In part, however, it also reflected greater awareness of the "pluralism" of American religious life and a new sensitivity to the differences between the American experience and conditions elsewhere in the world. For example, in a paragraph affirming the importance of separation of church and state, the *General Findings* contains the statement that "*in the American society* we hold the most desirable relationship between church and state is one in which each is distinct and free to fulfill its separate role and so to enrich the common culture." (Emphasis supplied.) For decades Protestant writing on the subject would generally have abhorred such a use of the first four qualifying words because separation was seen as a universal, not a local principle. "Pluralism," denoting the presence of more than one dominant religious group, similarly received much new recognition—although Protestant writing for the past few years has increasingly taken cognizance of a new pluralism in American religious life. The *General Findings* states as a generally agreed-upon conclusion the "recognition that ours is a pluralistic and not simply a Protestant society." Likewise, the *General Findings* calls attention to "the transition of this nation

---

[16] Report of the National Study Conference on Church and State 26–28 (New York: Dept. of Religious Liberty of the National Council of Churches, mimeographed, 1964). This section report concluded that "the structures of the chaplaincy as currently organized and administered in our country are in general a viable response to the common need of both religious bodies and the government to provide for the free exercise of religion without an establishment of religion. Both religious bodies and the agencies of government, however, in working with the chaplaincies, are operating in a changing, dynamic situation which demands vigilant concern on the part of both."

from a predominantly Protestant to a religiously pluralistic society" and asserts that "both the new pluralism and the expansion of governmental functions require re-examination of the role of the state respecting religion and the churches." Similar quotations from preparatory documents and section reports could be multiplied. Their net effect would seem to be generally a relativizing one.

It would be a mistake, however, to conclude from all this that religious liberty and separation of church and state no longer seemed important to the delegates. Rather, there was an increased feeling that these traditional concerns are only weakened and distorted if they are not more deeply grounded in the central meaning of the Christian faith and in a defensible social philosophy. This feeling helped to define the whole preparatory process and the conference itself. It was in the search for a relevant theological basis and for a more adequate expression of natural law that the most basic discussion occurred.

In the judgment of the present writer, the conference was more successful in its grappling for a philosophy of church-state relations than it was in its quest for a more adequate theological basis. Theological observations are notably sparse and inadequately related to immediate issues, particularly if one regards the *General Findings* as the basic document. Thus, it is recorded that the delegates "view both state and church as standing under the sovereignty and love of God," that "the mission of the church is to make known the purpose of God to bring salvation to all men through Jesus Christ, and to manifest God's kingdom of love and justice among all men," and that "the church offers intercessory prayers for those in authority, supports the state in its proper functions, holds the state accountable to the sovereign law of God and encourages responsible citizenship."[17] But such observations could be made to support conclusions far different from those any delegate would have approved. For instance, if both state and church stand "under the sovereignty and love of God," and if it is the function of the church "to make known the purpose of God to bring salvation to all men through Jesus Christ, and to manifest God's kingdom of love and justice among all men," why could one, as a Christian, object to the church's using the state for its high purposes, even to the point of silencing those who make the church's witness more difficult? Why religious liberty? Surely even the narrowest Christian opponents of religious liberty have

---

17 *General Findings*, 6 JOURNAL OF CHURCH AND STATE 147, 149 (1964).

construed their actions as serving both the sovereignty and the love of God. The fact that the *General Findings* actually rings with concern for religious liberty only underscores the failure of the conference to root this concern theologically.

During the preparatory process and in the sections, theological discussion may have come closest to providing a foundation for religious liberty when, in the name of the sovereign love as well as the transcendent otherness of God, it was most critical of man's tendencies toward idolatrous pretension.[18] Does not the sovereign transcendence of God suggest that *no man knows all about God* and hence that all men must be free to witness to their partial understandings? Does it not also suggest that God, the sovereign Creator of all, is at work in all in ways which it would be blasphemous for any man or any government to prejudge? If God is sovereign and loving, to whom, may we say, he cannot speak? If God is sovereign and transcendent, to whom, may we say, he has said everything? If God has possibly spoken to one with whom we are in disagreement, do we not risk idolatry by making absolute claims about our version of the points at issue? And, on what basis then could one possibly designate in advance the *necessary* means through which God wills to effect the salvation of his children?

Such theological reflection, though present in some of the reports only by implication, would seem to strike closer to the heart of a distinctively Protestant-Orthodox contribution to the dialogue on church-state relations. It would provide a theologically principled basis for religious liberty and help to relieve the nagging suspicion that when churchmen speak of religious liberty they do so for prudential reasons only. Moreover, it would raise serious questions about the casual manner in which the term "pluralism" is used in some of the conference reports and in much contemporary Protestant writing. From the perspective of God's transcendence and God's immediate access to every man, is there not a sense in which *every* society and every historical epoch must be seen as religiously pluralistic? The encounter of every man with God, by this reckoning, is unique and unrepeatable. Religious liberty and the independence of state authority from ecclesiastical authority then can become bound to the relativities of the human situation as such rather than simply to the relativities of a passing social era.

If theological discussion of the basis for a Protestant-Orthodox position on church-state matters left something to be desired, bet-

---

[18] See especially the report of Section I and the first three of the preparatory papers.

ter results were obtained in the quest for a more adequate expression of relevant natural law—a philosophy of church-state relations which would communicate to Christians and non-Christians alike. Many of the delegates, influenced by the more Barthian atmosphere of contemporary Protestant thought, would want to avoid the term "natural law," although much of the discussion plainly was concerned with the "nature" of the state and of other realities of common experience in the natural world and with the search for the best possible ordering of the affairs of this world. Indeed, one of the preparatory papers made sweeping statements regarding the most desirable social arrangements at the same time that it characterized the "public philosophy" as an "invented god."[19]

In its more philosophically oriented discussion, the conference produced considerably more satisfying bases for religious liberty and the independence of church and state. In part, separation is grounded in a functional analysis of church and state and in part it is seen to be instrumental to the superior value of religious liberty. One paragraph in the *General Findings* illustrates this:

> Recognition of the separate functions of church and state finds expression in the principle of separation of church and state. As a constitutional principle it serves the great and central objective of preserving, protecting and promoting religious freedom for all, churches and individuals. At the same time, it assures the freedom of the state in exercising its secular authority to promote democratic values and to sustain essential political institutions.[20]

Such a statement, of course, has obviously been influenced by the school of constitutional interpretation which sees the no-establishment portion of the First Amendment as instrumental to the free exercise portion.

One of the most distinctive contributions which the conference made to a philosophy of church-state relations was stimulated by a paper by W. Astor Kirk, one of those designated to outline proposals for the *General Findings* on the first night of the conference. As background to his proposal, Dr. Kirk called attention to the modern trend toward "increasing promotion through public policy of social ends which heretofore were achieved primarily through

---

19 Forell, *Christian Freedom and Religious Liberty*, Preparatory Papers for the National Study Conference on Church and State 20 (privately published by the National Council of Churches, 1964). *Cf.* critiques of this paper at 23.

20 *General Findings*, 6 Journal of Church and State 149 (1964).

the programs of the church or of other nonpublic institutions and agencies."[21] Occasionally, this leads government to consider making use of church-related agencies to further its ends. The Kirk paper was not opposed to this possibility, but it went on to take the position that if government is true to its nature as the servant of all of the people, "the sole purpose of any governmental policy in this respect must be the promotion of a clearly identifiable *public* interest, as against a *private* interest of an individual or group."[22] Particular programs would be disallowed to the extent that they serve as channels for "(1) inculcating religious doctrines, (2) conserving religious practices or (3) dissuading religious belief or behavior," and to that extent, accordingly, they should not be supported by government. Specific criteria then were proposed to establish whether or not "publicly aided programs are in fact conducted in the public interest."

Key portions of Kirk's proposal were incorporated virtually intact into the body of the *General Findings,* which stated that

> under some well-defined circumstances, government may legitimately support specific programs of church-affiliated health and welfare agencies. The sole purpose of any governmental policy in this respect must be the promotion of a clearly identifiable public interest as against a private interest of an individual or religious group. The important considerations here are (a) that the governmental program must not be aimed primarily at the support of religious institutions or objectives, (b) that any support of church-affiliated agencies must be an incidental part of a large program directed to appropriate public interests, (c) that the agency does not discriminate on the basis of race, color, creed, or national origin, and (d) that revisionary clauses, limited to a fixed and reasonable period, be written into all contractual arrangements to insure that funds, buildings and equipment are not diverted from the purposes from which they were originally acquired.[23]

The logic of this general position would seem to require, as indicated in this statement, that one of the standards for governmental use of a religious agency for public purposes would be that religious as well as other forms of discrimination would not be practiced. The word "creed," however, was not included under (c) in the draft of *General Findings* which was presented for adop-

[21] Kirk, Proposal for General Findings 2 (mimeographed copy for the press) (1964).
[22] *Ibid.*
[23] *General Findings,* 6 JOURNAL OF CHURCH AND STATE 151 (1964).

tion to the final plenary session of the conference. This omission led to one of the more fundamental debates of the conference when Dr. Kirk himself moved insertion of the word in the clause. Objection was immediately raised that this would affect personnel policy as well as policy regarding clientele of a given religious agency. The insertion carried, however, by a vote of 107 to 34, and it was also sustained by a wide margin on a later motion to reconsider. There is, thus, no question but that the conference acted in full recognition of the implications of its position. The full logic of the position was completed by the next to last paragraph of the *General Findings,* which reads as follows:

> Government must never coerce church-affiliated health, educational or welfare agencies into acceptance of public support of any of their programs. Such coercion would constitute an unwarranted infringement of the freedom of church-affiliated agencies. However, so long as church-affiliated agencies have the freedom to accept or reject government support of any of their programs, it is not an unwarranted restriction of their discretion to require them to conform to governmentally prescribed policy and program standards as a condition for voluntarily receiving the public support. Government must never abdicate its responsibility to protect the public interest in the expenditure of public funds. If church-affiliated agencies accept public support of any of their programs, they must be prepared to conform to program standards designed to protect the public interest.[24]

It requires little imagination to see how this orientation could affect most of the issues having to do with acceptance of public financial aid by religious institutions. In all cases, they would be able to do so only to the extent of their willingness to abdicate their peculiarly religious functions and to assume public status and control.

For present purposes, however, it is the presupposition lying behind this orientation which is most interesting: that is the notion that government ought to be responsible to all the people. Although no effort was made to do so at the conference, this assumption seems easily relatable to the idea of the "responsible society" which has been the hallmark of the ecumenical movement among Protestant and Orthodox churches' social thought since the formation of the World Council of Churches at Amsterdam in 1948. The Amsterdam Assembly defined the "responsible society" as one

---

24 *Id.* at 152.

"where freedom is the freedom of men who acknowledge responsibility to justice and public order, and where those who hold political authority or economic power are responsible for its exercise to God and the people whose welfare is affected by it."[25] Here, too, there is reflected the importance of freedom. But at the same time, there is an understanding of the wider dimensions of responsibility which accompany public authority and a caution against any use of that authority for distinctively private ends—however concealed those ends might be. In this connection, religion is implicitly identified as a "private" end, although the conference properly rejected the notion that this means that religion is therefore only a subjective personal matter.

Here, then, there is a philosophy of church-state interaction which explains why, in the name of responsibility to its people, the state must now begin to assume many of the welfare responsibilities which heretofore have seemed the special province of the churches, why the state in fulfilling those responsibilities must hold the public interest foremost, why the state may make some use of religious agencies, provided it carefully safeguards the public interest, and why the state ought not to prohibit religious groups from engaging in like services on their own terms when there is no public financial involvement.[26] The clarity of this position was, again, somewhat obscured by a lack of coherence running through the *General Findings* and the various section reports, although this point of view is often implicitly and sometimes explicitly reflected in statements on particular issues.

A Protestant-Orthodox Response to Specific Issues

While the search for a basic theoretical orientation, both in its successes and failures, was undoubtedly the most important aspect of the conference and preparatory discussions, popular in-

---

[25] This definition is from the report of Section III, "The Church and the Disorder of Society," at the Amsterdam Assembly.

[26] It should be recorded that there were at least some delegates who, while in complete theoretical agreement with this orientation, expressed the fear that religious institutions, practically speaking, would have too much power for government to be able to police the standards designed to guard the public interest. For instance, some felt that reversionary clauses in contractual arrangements between public and religious agencies would prove quite unenforceable in practice. Could the government actually be expected to reclaim title to a science building or a dormitory located in the middle of a church-related college campus when the college defaulted on its loan? Would it not be more likely that violations of public standards would be overlooked or that special legislation would be introduced on behalf of such institutions unable to fulfill the financial obligations of their contractual arrangements?

terest centered on what position the conference would take on specific controversial questions. Much of the preparatory work, most of the discussions in the twelve sections, and some of the general findings of the conference were devoted to analysis of such questions. The amount of material thus produced is too great for systematic treatment in a paper of this kind, but some of the specific issues must be discussed here if one is to form an accurate judgment of the impact of the conference.

RELIGION IN THE PUBLIC SCHOOLS

In the wake of important Supreme Court decisions prohibiting devotional exercises in public schools, and of the popular storm which these decisions evoked, the question of religion in public school education was especially significant. Indeed, the report of Section V, "Public Schools and the Moral and Religious Training of Children," was much longer than that of any other section. Whereas a vocal minority at the conference was highly critical of the trend of court decisions, the *General Findings* clearly represented the dominant mood of the conference in its "acceptance and support of Supreme Court decisions insofar as they prohibit officially prescribed prayers and required devotional reading of the Bible in public schools" and its "recognition that the Court's decision underscores the primary responsibility of the family and the church for religious education."[27] This position was considerably enlarged upon in the report of Section V, which affirmed its support of the Supreme Court decisions as follows:

> We believe . . . that Christians should welcome the decisions. Christians do not believe that the question of authentic religion can ever be decided by formal rites and words alone. Neither is the presence of God in his world nor valid Christian service to Jesus Christ dependent upon a formally Christian observance. In addition, the decisions are consistent with our concern for the religious liberty of all men and our unwillingness to coerce in any way a person's response in faith to the gift of God's grace in Jesus Christ. Far from being antireligious, these decisions offer us a real opportunity to ex-

---

27 *General Findings*, 6 JOURNAL OF CHURCH AND STATE 148 (1964). An earlier draft of the first of these statements, however, read "prohibiting" instead of the more qualified "insofar as they prohibit" as finally accepted. Endorsement of the decisions, thus, was not entirely unqualified, although the conference obviously approved their substance.

plore in a new way the relationship of religious values to the *total* program of the public school.[28]

The report continues, then, to point out that the Supreme Court has carefully reaffirmed the constitutionality of teaching *about* religion. "Objective teaching about the influence of religion in history and in contemporary society is not restricted."[29] Indeed, "education which lacks or omits effective, objective dealing with these subjects is truncated and incomplete" because "no person is truly educated for life in the modern world who is not aware of the vital part played by religion in the shaping of our history and culture, and of its contemporary expressions."[30] A number of suggestions are then advanced concerning the best means of meeting this need for objective teaching about religion. Section V, thus, agreed wholeheartedly with the Supreme Court on the inappropriateness of devotional exercises in the public schools, but likewise affirmed the importance of recognition of religion and its decisive place in all human culture.

The section pursued the logic of its position by discussing such religious observances as Christmas nativity pageants and baccalaureate services, which have not been singled out by the Supreme Court. These observances, it held, are likewise properly functions of the church and home, not of the public schools. Such functions, it suggested, might actually weaken rather than strengthen the distinctive witness of the church. Where, however, such observances are held in the public schools, the report cautioned that churches and school officials should "protect the rights of minorities whether or not such minorities protest."[31]

In the name of religious liberty and the integrity of the church's own witness, then, the conference was committed to a point of view which has recently encountered heavy criticism throughout the United States. It would seem to the present writer that, in doing so, it continued to serve not secularism but an understanding of the transcendent sovereignty of God and of the state which is equally responsible to all its people. The key question separating those who attack religion in the schools in the name of secularism and those who do so in the name of a religious faith is whether religion ought to be taken seriously. According to the first, all re-

---

28 Report of the National Study Conference on Church and State 17 (1964).
29 *Ibid.*
30 *Id.* at 18.
31 *Id.* at 21.

ligion ought to be avoided because it is not to be taken seriously;
but to the second, religious worship (implying a participation in
faith) is to be avoided precisely because the religion (or ultimate
faith commitment) of *all* is taken seriously. To the latter, objective consideration of religion (which implies nothing about the
faith participation of students) is important because, indeed, there
could be no more important thing to study. To the secularist,
however, even objective study about religion is viewed with indifference or even apprehension. One could argue that the secularist
actually has less respect for the personalities of students because
he takes less seriously what they take most seriously. Under sensitive classroom leadership, it would seem that one could avoid all
the problems attached to prayer and devotional reading, but at
the same time so thoroughly explore the diversity of religious commitments that each student would understand himself better and
have a deeper appreciation of the commitments of his fellow students.

One should make the additional distinction between those who,
because they take religion seriously, wish to avoid devotional
exercises in public schools (while placing new emphasis upon objective teaching about religion) and those who, because they fear
secularism in education, believe that prayer, devotional Bible reading, baccalaureate services, etc., have a real place in the public
schools. Although the latter group was very much represented at
the conference, its numerical strength there was not large. Nationally this group is most anxious to adopt some sort of "Christian
amendment" to the Constitution which would free the state to be
frankly Christian. By rejecting this position in favor of the former,
the conference, one might argue, acted on the assumptions discussed above in relation to the responsible society. If a democratic political philosophy includes the postulate that the state is
equally responsible to all its members, then there is no foundation
for the direct or indirect coercion of any of its members to pre-
tend to participate in worship exercises which are alien to their
personal faith. Moreover, the government which engages in such
coercion does by that token substitute private ends for public
ones. These considerations are philosophical. Theologically, it
could, of course, also be argued that there are profound risks of
idolatry wherever ceremonial forms of any kind are taken to be
efficacious in themselves without reference to the state of mind of
participants.

STATE AID TO CHURCH-RELATED INSTITUTIONS

The discussions of state aid to church-related institutions were particularly timely and controversial where they touched the parochial school question. Section VIII, which considered this issue, was one of the real storm centers of the conference, and the debates on general findings which dealt with this issue were among the hardest fought. The conference was sharply divided between two groups. One included those who felt that any public aid given to the furtherance of religious teaching is wrong in principle and who, on the basis of this, were opposed to all public aid to parochial schools beyond the bare minimum of health and welfare services for their students. The other was made up of those who were concerned about the plight of the parochial schools and wished to do something, through the state, to strengthen their contribution to American life. In between, as evidenced by somewhat illogical fluctuations in voting patterns in plenary session, were doubtless many who were still uncertain. The conference plenary session attempted to arrive at a consensus through the following paragraph:

> Since parochial elementary and secondary schools are maintained by churches so that "religion permeates the entire atmosphere" of the school, government funds should not be authorized or appropriated for overall support of such schools as distinguished from aid in support of specific health and welfare programs conducted by such institutions to meet particular public needs. While we acknowledge the right of parental choice of schools, we do not admit that a choice by parents of parochial or private schools imposes on the state any obligation to support such choice through the granting of public funds in overall support of such schools. In recognition of the seriousness of the financial problems of the parochial schools, we propose shared time as the most creative measure for solving this problem and are willing to explore other legal means for solving it.[32]

In the original draft, the first sentence read simply "specific programs" rather than "specific *health and welfare* programs." (Emphasis supplied.) An effort was made to delete the word "overall" and all the words following "such schools," the effect of which would be categorical disapproval of *all* aid. When this mo-

---

[32] *General Findings,* 6 JOURNAL OF CHURCH AND STATE 152 (1964).

tion failed by a close margin, a second motion was adopted which inserted the words "health and welfare." At stake here was the question whether aid to religious schools might be given in the form of subsidies of non-religious teaching and buildings not to be devoted to religious instruction—such as science buildings or gymnasiums, or whether aid should be limited to "health and welfare" services for the children.

The report of Section VIII is less analytical than the *General Findings* on the question of public aid to parochial schools, but the section did report the results of a detailed poll conducted among its own members on various kinds of aid. According to this poll, fewer than one-fourth of the section members supported state aid for teachers' salaries, buildings (even if used for secular subjects), or tuition. A large majority favored such indirect programs as lunches and medical care, and the group was more nearly divided, though negative, on the questions of transportation and books.[33]

Perhaps the most significant thing about this report or the relevant part of the *General Findings* is that both reveal considerable division within Protestantism on issues which Protestants have traditionally approached with more unanimity. On the supposition that a united Catholicism should be able to make considerable headway toward further public support for parochial schools in the absence of united Protestant opposition, one is tempted to speculate that the political tide on the issue may shift somewhat. This is a difficult situation to interpret, partly because of the uncertainty of the Protestant-Orthodox position (which has also been compromised considerably by the acceptance of aid through public loans and "purchase of services" for Protestant colleges), but partly also by uncertainty in the Roman Catholic position. Catholic leadership, by bending its efforts toward achieving a breakthrough for *some* aid, has yet to agree upon a principled position as to *how much*. As one of the Catholic observers at the conference put it in his report:

> . . . the Catholic observers are of a mind that Catholics must formulate a much clearer policy to answer the question of just what they want. Do Catholics seek full aid? Or is there a modification of terms by reason of the teaching of religion? Do Catholics seek a political solution, a compromise, a minimum recognition of rights in education, a legal solution? Are

---

[33] Report of the National Study Conference on Church and State 32–33 (1964).

they convinced, as are so many Protestant thinkers, that tax
aid is a matter of public policy and not a constitutional barrier and consequently the matter is quite open to negotiation
and compromise? Catholics must address themselves to both
the Protestant and Orthodox objections and their own as-
pirations, convinced that men of good will can solve these
problems.[34]

The principle of responsibility, discussed earlier in this paper,
could provide theoretical guidance to Protestant-Orthodox leadership as it continues to move in this difficult field. If the state is responsible to all the people, and if it is to be restricted to public
rather than private ends, then blanket grants to religious institutions unaccompanied by duly administered standards to guard the
public interest would seem improper. Insofar as religious institutions, even serving educational functions, are willing to accept the
full implications of public agency (a problematical question), it is
conceivable that a solution might be achieved. In the case of
schools, would this not require non-discriminatory policies (even
with respect to creed) and an educational approach which would
take seriously and sensitively the differing religious commitments
of the students? Ironically, in proportion to its willingness to accept such terms, the justification of parochial school education
would seem to recede.

The section of *General Findings* dealing with aid to religious
schools alludes to a further dimension of this problem, however,
by saying that "support of such institutions at the primary and
secondary levels of education may well have the result of further
fragmentation of the educational system and weaken the role and
position of the public schools." If this were to occur, the cultural
consequences in American society would surely be enormous.
Would other religious denominations be encouraged to develop
their own schools, subsidized by public grants? If they did, would
not all American education be weakened through fragmentation?
What would happen to the traditional "melting pot" function of
the public schools—the practical education in democratic living
which public schools provide by bringing youngsters of widely
differing heritages into direct contact with one another? Such
questions, which do not proceed from a doctrinaire orientation,
point to the enormous social significance of the way in which this
delicate issue is finally resolved. The conference itself was able to

---

[34] Hurley, *Sees Protestant Re-evaluation,* The Monitor, February 14, 1964, p. 2.

go little further than proposing "shared time" as "the most creative measure for solving this problem."[35]

CHURCH-STATE PROBLEMS IN AMERICAN FOREIGN RELATIONS

Consideration of the international dimension of church-state relations represented a relatively new aspect of Protestant-Orthodox thinking. In the past, many people who have held relatively doctrinaire convictions regarding separation of church and state have largely been oblivious to the intricacies of involvement between their churches and their own and other governments abroad. This is understandable, of course. Both the web of international governmental activity and the widespread growth of the Christian missionary movement represent developments which could hardly have been anticipated when the First Amendment and the doctrine of separation were born. The problem in this area, as Section XII recognized,[36] is to make a new, creative application of the deeper values and assumptions which gave validity to the doctrine of separation at the time of its origin.

In staking out a position, the section report warns mission efforts against "every appearance of dependence upon U.S. governmental support." Although no objection to governmental protection of missionaries is voiced, special privileges to missionaries are opposed because "the proclamation of the Gospel should not be, and in the end is not, advanced effectively by the power or prestige of the state."[37] In recognition of the fact that the Church is now indigenous to most countries, the report cautions against the effort to supply American solutions to non-American situations. In particular, the question of support by governments abroad should "be determined by nationals of the country concerned." This principle is also applied to other forms of aid, including the United States Peace Corps. Accepting the possibility that church schools might be supported by the countries in which they are located, the report suggests that any such school "should accept its responsibility to contribute to the development of public education."[38] While calling attention to dangers in church use of public relief commodities, the report concludes that the "positive re-

---

35 *General Findings*, 6 JOURNAL OF CHURCH AND STATE 152 (1964).

36 Since the *General Findings* largely ignores the international dimension of church-state relations, the report of Section XII represents the principal conference expression on the subject.

37 Report of the National Study Conference on Church and State 43 (1964).

38 *Ibid.*

sults of these activities far outweigh the dangers." Quoting from
Article 18 of the Universal Declaration of Human Rights on freedom of conscience, the report finally urges the United States government to act to defend freedom of religion for United States
citizens abroad.

It is interesting to note a degree of inconsistency between some
of the particular recommendations of this report and parts of the
General Findings—particularly in the section dealing with religious
schools. The inconsistency is heightened by the fact that the rejection of public aid to parochial schools in the *General Findings*
is generally approached on principle and not simply as good advice
for the American situation. No principle, however, is any better
than the range of its applicability, and the significance of the report of Section XII may lie largely in its implicit challenge to the
universality of the separation principle. On the other hand, it can
be argued that the countries in which American missions are most
generally at work are areas of rapid social and political transition.
Only potentially are they fully responsible societies, however much
the leadership of emerging nations may be committed to democracy. Therefore, principles which are relevant to a fully democratic society may not be as practicable in the immediate flux of
a changing era as they would and will be in more stable times. As
the new nations of Africa develop universal public school education, for instance, it is conceivable that mission schools could and
ought to rely less and less upon governmental support. In any
event, the world-wide dimension of the problem of church-state
relations, as opened up by this report, poses new practical and
theoretical problems which now must be integrated into any further discussion.

DEFINITION OF RELIGION

Section II was devoted to the question of proper legal definitions of such key terms as "religion," "church," and "minister,"
upon which the framing of laws and important legal decisions must
necessarily turn. Another largely neglected area in the past, its importance is attested by the wide variety of definitions used for
these terms. The definitions developed by Section II are based
upon the key idea that religion refers to beliefs "which are held to
be of ultimate importance by the believer." According to this
understanding, everyone has a religion of some sort or other. To
understand a person's religion, one must ask which of his beliefs
are of most ultimate importance to him.

This approach has the merit of cutting through every definition of religion which is slanted toward the faith commitments of any given religion. In terms of religious liberty, it has therefore the value of making a basic right applicable to all the people. Religious liberty could not, under such a definition, be restricted to the activities of "religious" people as against the activities of other kinds of people. All people are religious in the sense that all have ultimate beliefs and values, and such beliefs and values are to be respected equally by the law. Moreover, in terms of the establishment clause of the First Amendment, such a definition places in new light the old question whether that clause was intended to refer to state support for religion per se or whether it was merely intended to exclude partiality among the religions. It does so by being inclusive of all groups which regard certain shared beliefs to be of ultimate importance. Thus, under the establishment clause, there would be no ground for government to support, say, all Christian churches while excluding a society for the propagation of atheism. At the same time, however, a constitutional case could now be made for forms of public support for groups of persons holding ultimate beliefs in common which were absolutely not conditioned upon any governmental partiality toward what ultimate beliefs are truest or of greatest value.[39]

RELIGION IN CIVIC LIFE AND PUBLIC POLICY

While the conference, and its principal product, the *General Findings,* were so largely concerned about matters of relationship between church and state—and therefore with the largely negative task of defining limits, it was strikingly evident to participants and observers that most of the people present were aware of other fundamental problems of Christian witness to a world torn and suffering. Other concerns, particularly in race relations but also relating to war and peace and economic life, weighed heavily upon the deliberations. Occasionally, these concerns leaped into the discussions of church and state. The *General Findings,* for instance, sought to make clear that agencies receiving funds from public coffers ought not to discriminate on the basis of race,

---

[39] As a matter of public *policy,* the variant forms of ultimate belief held by groups in the United States bring certain difficulties to mind. To illustrate the point, however, there seems to be little practical or constitutional reason to deny any religious group the use of public meeting rooms just because the group is formed by its adherence to ultimate beliefs.

color, or national origin—as well as the "creed" that was, as noted above, later inserted. Section III, which considered the problem of conflicts between religious conscience and civil authority, set this problem squarely and controversially in the context of race relations and participation in war: "The present crisis in race relations—a struggle for human dignity—has lifted up with new urgency the question of disobedience to civil authority, a question which has also arisen in the past over such diverse issues as conscientious refusal to bear arms, to pay taxes for purposes of war, or to salute the flag."[40] Discussion of the question of public aid to religious schools was conducted with the awareness that there had been recent moves in some of the southern states to use private schools to avoid compliance with the 1954 Supreme Court school desegregation decision, and a deep concern was expressed that the church, at least, ought never to allow itself to be used in such a way.

The question of religious influence on the great questions of public policy came to a focus in Section IV. In response to the question "whether churches *should* seek to influence public policy," the section argued that "churches *do* influence public policy, regardless of their intentions. As office-holders and citizens, church members influence public affairs. No person ceases to be religious merely because he operates in the political or civil sphere."[41] In light of the numerous involvements of the church, as an institution, in the life of community, "the question becomes not whether churches and churchmen will act in civil affairs but *how*."[42] The basis of a Christian involvement in civil affairs is laid in the nature and mission of the church.

> Christians believe that God is at work in society as well as in the church. Christians are called to love the world as God has loved it, in giving His Son to reconcile it to himself. They believe it to be God's intent that men and nations be governed by his righteous will. They believe themselves called to radical obedience to this will and resolute service of "God's poor."[43]

Churchmen, however, "need greater understanding of the political process," particularly recognizing that "social change results from the exercise of power." To be effective, the report counsels, re-

---

40 Report of the National Study Conference on Church and State 12 (1964).
41 *Id.* at 14.
42 *Ibid.*
43 *Id.* at 14–15.

ligious groups need to study, to consult with competent persons, and to involve themselves more directly in actual situations.

In saying these things, Section IV largely reflected and confirmed a point of view which has been characteristic of the ecumenical movement for fifty years. It is, all the same, a point of view which has frequently been under fire within the churches—particularly when churches have attempted to provide leadership in controversial areas. Churches and churchmen have sometimes been enjoined from providing such leadership on the ground of "separation of church and state." The report of Section IV was a helpful reminder that, although churches are not public policy-making institutions, Christians and their churches have public responsibilities in a democratic society.

The Net Effect of the Conference

It remains to ask what over-all effect the National Study Conference may have had upon the future course of church-state relations and the religious dialogue. As I remarked at the beginning of this paper, the conference reflected, perhaps overreflected, the ambiguous situation of Protestant-Orthodox thought at the present time. Yet, as we have noted, the conference clearly did make some contributions and illustrate trends.

It would be interesting to interpret the conference on the basis of Leo Pfeffer's thesis regarding the role of the three great faiths on church-state issues in this country. According to Pfeffer,[44] the strict separationist position—or the "broad" interpretation of the no-establishment clause of the First Amendment, has been anchored historically by secular humanists in alliance with Protestantism and, more recently, Judaism. This position has generally prevailed. In recent decades, however, it has been challenged by a "narrow" interpretation of the First Amendment which has been espoused by a growing Roman Catholicism. The "narrow" interpretation holds that, while government should be impartial among the churches, it may properly support religious institutions in their work. This interpretation has also gained substantial Protestant support. In the future resolution of church-state issues, Protestantism will represent the decisive factor because it is numerically predominant and also because it represents the balance

---

44 Pfeffer, Creeds in Competition: A Creative Force in American Culture *passim*, particularly chs. 1 and 9 (1958).

of power between contending extremes. The direction of future Protestant movement, thus, becomes the key question in projecting the coming shape of church-state relations in America.

Following this thesis, did the conference shed any light on the role that Protestantism will, indeed, play? Pfeffer, who was there as a consultant, might well have been discouraged by some aspects of the conference—not because it repudiated the separationist position, which it certainly did not do in any clear sense, but because it did illustrate a growing tendency within Protestantism to relativize "separation" as a principle. It was not, for example, the fact that some of the votes in plenary sessions were carried by advocates of public aid to religious schools, etc.—for in most cases actual voting was carried by advocates of more traditionally Protestant postures on such questions—but it was the fact that such issues were debated seriously with numbers of influential persons lined up on both sides that was significant. For Protestantism to help preserve separation, Pfeffer would doubtless argue, it must be more *united* on such questions. At the conference, Protestantism-Orthodoxy obviously was not united enough. Could this now mean that the pendulum will swing away from separation?

Still speaking in Pffeffer's terms, however, forces inimical to the doctrine of separation could scarcely take much comfort from the conference either; for, on a level deeper than specific policy issues, it had rejected the notion that government should ever be used to support any religious ideas in competition with other religious ideas—and it had defined religious ideas in such a way that the ultimate concerns of every man should be included. It had, moreover, grappled with the meaning of responsible government in such terms that no religious group, having accepted public aid for any purpose, would ever be able to use that aid with the conference's sanction for any but clearly public purposes. In effect, the conference had accepted the principle that religious institutions accepting public support must become, to that extent, public institutions which are no longer responsible simply to religious leadership but to all the people. And, while only a hint of this was clearly evident, there was the underlying theological conviction that God, as sovereign Lord of nature and history, must be permitted to speak to every man on His terms—a conviction which relativizes every claim of the church in relationship to the concentrations of public power.

In the judgment of the present writer, the conference is not so much to be understood as having taken a clear or an ambiguous position in terms of the old polarity of separation versus interaction or mutual support as it is to be understood in a new perspective altogether. It clearly signalized disenchantment with "separation" as an absolute, not because it rejected all that separation has meant historically, but because it was in search of deeper absolutes. In part this search reflected awareness of the vast historical changes which have occurred in the less than two centuries since the doctrine of separation was born. To this extent, the conference sought to be honest with new complexities. In part, however, the search was also motivated by deeper theological grappling throughout Protestantism and Orthodoxy in relation to all questions before modern man. Thus, the conference refused to restrict itself to principles or commitments which do not arise from the heart of Protestant-Orthodox understandings of the Christian faith.

This would lead, then, to the final observation that the conference probably made a splendid contribution to the on-going religious dialogue. Superficially, this was clearly evident from the active, friendly participation there by observers from non-member religious groups. More fundamentally, the conference made some contribution to the clarification for Protestant and Orthodox communions of the witness they must bear and the questions they must ask as they move into closer dialogue with their brethren of Roman Catholic, Jewish, and other faiths. In this, as in all other respects, the conference must be interpreted as only a beginning.

PETER R. SALADIN

RELATIVE RANKING OF THE PREFERRED
FREEDOMS: RELIGION AND SPEECH

Freedom of religion and freedom of speech are both guaranteed in the United States by the First Amendment of the Constitution. Similar wording is used in granting both rights, and it would appear upon preliminary examination that both are entitled to the same degree of protection. First Amendment freedoms, taken as a whole, are generally regarded as holding a "preferred" position in the American hierarchy of constitutionally protected personal rights. However, freedom of religion is the one singled out from the rest with the greatest frequency and referred to as enjoying a particularly "preferred" position. It will be the purpose of this article to investigate whether or not freedom of religion has been granted such a pre-eminently preferred position when compared with other First Amendment rights.

Since one is hard put to imagine situations in which freedom of speech and freedom of religion might come into direct conflict, our inquiry is not of immediate practical concern. The American courts will probably never be faced with choosing between these two values. Nonetheless, it is of theoretical interest to determine, if we can, which of the two freedoms is valued more highly. The United States Supreme Court has been criticized in many quarters for detracting from the nation's spiritual heritage and advancing

Peter R. Saladin is a lawyer with the Swiss Federal Department of Justice. The author wishes to acknowledge his indebtedness to the editor for his suggestions about the implications of some of the more recent state cases.

the cause of a secular humanism by its recent decisions. If this is true, one would expect the Court to be guided by a secular ethos which accords freedom of speech a position higher than that given freedom of religion. If, on the other hand, freedom of religion has been accorded higher rank in the case law, this would blunt such criticism and indicate that the Court pays due respect to the spiritual sensibilities of American society, currently one of the most religious in the world by modern standards.

In the following pages we shall undertake to analyze the relationship between freedom of speech and freedom of religion according to the jurisprudence of the American courts, and particularly the Supreme Court. Our investigation will proceed on four fronts: (1) a comparison of the respective standards of protection granted freedom of speech and freedom of religion to determine the extent to which American society is more prepared to sacrifice other values in order to protect one or the other; (2) a comparison of the respective standards in free speech cases involving the dissemination of religious ideas and free speech cases involving other ideas to see if greater protection is granted in the former; (3) a comparison of the respective protection granted freedom of religion and free speech in the context of the military draft; (4) a consideration of the degree to which the courts permit the other branches of the government positively to promote the free exchange of ideas as compared with the free exercise of religion.

SOCIETY'S TOLERATION FACTOR

In attempting to determine whether freedom of speech or freedom of religion is granted a higher place in American jurisprudence, one is inclined to begin by comparing the standards used by the courts in free speech cases with those in freedom of religion cases. The thought would be simply that if a stricter standard of protection is used more frequently with regard to one freedom than to the other, the former is given a higher place in American society's official hierarchy of values.

If this is to be our measure, freedom of speech would appear to be the more important value. It has been in this area that the "clear and present danger" test has been used most frequently.[1]

---

[1] The "clear and present danger" test was first enunciated by Mr. Justice Holmes in 1919 in the *Schenck* case. Schenck v. United States, 249 U.S. 47 (1919). In subsequent cases involving politically subversive speech it was rejected by a majority of

This test rather forcefully suggests that there must be an immediate and pressing danger of harm before free speech can be inhibited. It would seem, at first, a more protective standard than the "balancing of interests" test generally followed by the courts in religious freedom cases.[2] The idea of "balancing" religious liberty against competing interests does not suggest that the scale is heavily weighted in favor of the individual's freedom, as the "clear and present danger" test readily suggests.

In support of a claim of at least equal status for freedom of religion, one could point to the trend of relying on a balance of interests test in recent cases involving claims of free speech, and particularly free association.[3] Apart from this development, however, the prevalence of different standards is not actually indicative of the relative weight given to each freedom. The deviation in standards can readily be explained in light of the different claims that these two freedoms make upon society because of the dissimilar modes by which they are realized. The kind of risks that society must tolerate with regard to unqualified free speech are limited to those that flow from more or less unrestrained utterance of one's thoughts. Although a wide variety of dangers can be fore-

---

the Court in favor of a test of "sufficient danger of substantive evil," with Justices Holmes and Brandeis urging its adoption in a series of dissents. *E.g.,* Gitlow v. New York, 268 U.S. 652 (1925). The test was then adopted by a majority of the Court in a number of cases, including ones involving public comment on pending litigation (*e.g.,* Bridges v. California, 314 U.S. 252 [1941]; Pennekamp v. Florida, 328 U.S. 331 [1946]; Craig v. Harney, 331 U.S. 367 [1947]) and in cases involving speech tending to incite a breach of the peace (*e.g.,* Thornhill v. Alabama, 310 U.S. 88 [1940]; Terminiello v. Chicago, 337 U.S. 1 [1949]; Feiner v. New York, 340 U.S. 315 [1951]). Although the "clear and present danger" test was formally adopted in the field of national security in the *Douds* case in 1950, the Court in effect applied a balancing test. American Communications Ass'n. v. Douds, 339 U.S. 382 (1950). The Court confessed as much when it stated: "In essence, the problem is one of weighing the probable effects of the statute [requiring officers of labor unions to file non-Communist affidavits with the National Labor Relations Board as a condition for recognition of their unions under the Labor Management Relations Act] upon the free exercise of the right of speech and assembly against the Congressional determination that political strikes are evils. . . ." 339 U.S. at 400. In the *Dennis* case the "clear and present danger" test was refined in the area of national security to a test requiring the Court to measure the "gravity of the evil discounted by its improbability." Dennis v. United States, 341 U.S. 494 (1951) (upholding the convictions of leaders of the Communist party for teaching and advocating the violent overthrow of the government and for organizing a group to propagate such teachings and advocacy).

[2] *E.g.,* Jamison v. Texas, 318 U.S. 413 (1943); Schneider v. Town of Irvington, 308 U.S. 147 (1939).

[3] *E.g.,* Barenblatt v. United States, 360 U.S. 109 (1959); Uphaus v. Wyman, 360 U.S. 72 (1959); Konigsberg v. State Bar, 353 U.S. 252 (1957).

seen, ranging from libel and obscenity to incitement to riot and political subversion, they are quite restricted when compared to the risks that unqualified free exercise of religion would entail. Those risks would be as various as the kinds of socially questionable behavior that some religions in the course of history have required of their adherents, ranging from polygamy and the use of narcotics to ritualistic suicide and even murder.

The clear and present danger test is to a large extent premised on the idea that in most cases words by themselves cannot do great damage.[4] It is only when there is serious danger that the words will lead to some socially harmful action that the government can prohibit them. But in religious liberty cases the courts have held, as a matter of constitutional compulsion, that the state must in some cases exempt persons from duties imposed on society generally if those obligations conflict with their religious scruples. In other words, whereas society must tolerate only substantial risks that undesirable conduct may come about in free speech cases, in some freedom of religion cases it has tolerated the actual incidence of such conduct for the sake of religious liberty.

The recent Supreme Court decision in *Sherbert v. Verner*,[5] and particularly the way it is being applied in the state courts, illustrates the degree of tolerance society extends to religious interests generally. In the *Sherbert* case a Sabbatarian was constitutionally entitled to receive unemployment compensation benefits despite her refusal to take employment requiring Saturday work because it interfered with her observance of the Sabbath. The Court required South Carolina to extend the benefits to her despite a state requirement that claimants must stand ready to take positions involving Saturday work.

The manner in which state courts are applying the *Sherbert* case demonstrates quite dramatically the much wider protection given freedom of religion than freedom of speech in particular situations. The Minnesota Supreme Court has interpreted *Sherbert* as requiring excusal from jury duty of those who have religious objections to it.[6] The California Supreme Court has held that persons who use peyote, a non-toxic hallucinogen, for a vital part of their religious ceremonies must be excused from observing a state

---

4 See CHAFEE, FREE SPEECH IN THE UNITED STATES 35 (1941).

5 Sherbert v. Verner, 374 U.S. 398 (1963).

6 *In re* Jenison, 125 N.W.2d 588 (1963).

criminal statute prohibiting its use generally.[7] There are no cases according comparable exemption from the criminal laws to permit the exercise of free speech.

With regard to the use of peyote one can easily imagine a situation where the claims of free speech probably would have to give way because free discussion of a certain kind was leading people to use the drug. Although there is little doubt that California would be constitutionally obliged under the First Amendment to tolerate the activities of an institute that favored peyote, publicized the benefits and pleasures of its use, attempted to gain public acceptance of this practice, and endeavored to bring about a change in the state law, it would be a closer question if the institute were engaged in giving courses instructing its members in the techniques of using the various hallucinogens. Recent free speech cases have been reformulating the clear and present danger test in a way that tends to limit its scope. Under the recent cases it would be enough if the gravity of the evil in using peyote, discounted by the improbability of its use by members of the institute, justified invasion of free speech. This is essentially the test used in the *Dennis* case,[8] in which the defendants were sent to prison for organizing the American Communist party and advocating violent overthrow of the government. Nonetheless a state might not be able to prohibit the teaching about hallucinogens by one institute under this test because of the isolated character of the threat, unlike the threat posed by the Communist conspiracy in the *Dennis* case.

But if the program of instruction were aimed at preparing and encouraging members of the institute for immediate use, then the institute would have gone beyond advocating "abstract doctrine" and would be more vulnerable to governmental restraint.[9] If, in addition to advocacy of use, there were facts on the record showing that members of the institute were regularly using hallucinogens because of the encouragement and teaching of the institute, the clear and present danger test in its most vital form would not permit the speech. As originally formulated by Mr. Justice Holmes, it provided that speech could be restrained when it created "a clear and present danger that . . . [it would] bring

---

[7] People v. Woody, 394 P.2d 813 (Cal. 1964).
[8] Dennis v. United States, 341 U.S. 494 (1951).
[9] *Cf.* Yates v. United States, 354 U.S. 298 (1957).

about the substantive evils that Congress has a right to prevent."[10] It can safely be assumed that the California legislature has the "right" to ban the use of peyote generally; the due process clause does not protect the liberty of drug users as a class. This being so, once there is proof that the institute's activities are causing or substantially aiding people to turn to drugs, its teaching and other promotional activities could be restrained.

If the above analysis is sound, the consequence would be that California need not tolerate the use of drugs by a somewhat restricted group in order to protect the free communication of ideas by some or all within it, whereas it would have to tolerate such use by a similarly restricted group in order to protect the religious liberty of the members within it.

The fact that society tolerates more undesirable kinds of conduct in the interest of freedom of religion than it does in the interest of free speech does not of itself necessarily mean that the former has been officially recognized as having greater value than the latter. It may only indicate that the right of free speech essentially requires only the opportunity to give effective utterance to one's views and that this right can be ringed about with a number of reasonable restrictions to protect other interests of society without depriving it of its necessary vitality. Thus the time, place, manner, and other circumstances attendant upon the exercise of free speech can be subjected to reasonable regulation without destroying an individual's opportunity to communicate with others and influence their views.

Free access to the market place of ideas in order to persuade society to adopt certain views sums up the essence of free speech. Granted that the one who speaks wants others to act, insofar as he wants action contrary to law he must rely on the force of his ideas to carry the day in the political arena and bring about lawful change. In the words of Mr. Justice Holmes, one is permitted the right to advocate criminal action only because "we should be eternally vigilant against attempts to check the expression of opinions . . . unless they so imminently threaten immediate interference with the lawful and pressing purposes of the law that an immediate check is required to save the country."[11]

In contrast with the limited range of protection required by

---

10 Schenck v. United States, 249 U.S. 47, 52 (1919).
11 Abrams v. United States, 250 U.S. 616, 630 (1919) (dissenting opinion).

freedom of speech, if particular conduct is theologically central to an individual's religious observances or obligations, society must tolerate the conduct or destroy completely the individual's opportunity to exercise his religion.

The conclusion that the clear and present danger test is used more frequently in free speech cases because of the limited claims made on other social interests is borne out when one examines the nature of the claims made in the relatively few religious liberty cases adopting this broadly protective standard. In these cases the claims that the religious interest was making on society either were closely related to free speech or involved conduct not significantly more dangerous than words. For instance, in *Cantwell v. Connecticut*[12] the activity involved was proselytizing, an obvious form of free speech, and the Court spoke interchangeably of freedom of speech and freedom of religion. In *Board of Educ. v. Barnette* the Court required a showing of "grave and immediate danger to interests which the state may lawfully protect"[13] before the state could order school children to salute the flag despite strong religious objections to doing so. Here again the majority of the Court spoke interchangeably of freedom of religion and freedom of speech, finding that the compulsory flag salute "transcends constitutional limitations on . . . [the state's] power and invades the sphere of intellect and spirit which it is the purpose of the First Amendment to our Constitution to reserve from all official control."[14] Justices Black and Douglas in a concurring opinion rested the decision squarely on the freedom of religion clause.

It would appear then, that freedom of religion is given at least the same protection as freedom of speech, and in some cases it is given even greater protection when society tolerates the actuality of undesirable conduct for the sake of religious liberty.

THE COMPARATIVE PROTECTION GRANTED RELIGIOUS SPEECH

Free exercise of religion depends at times upon unrestrained speech. This is true, for instance, in cases where those holding certain religious beliefs wish to influence public decision-making and have it conform to the ethical tenets of their religion. It is particularly true in cases where members of a religion are en-

---

12 310 U.S. 296 (1940).
13 319 U.S. 624, 639 (1943).
14 *Id.* at 642.

gaged in proselytizing. One possible way of measuring the relative value of freedom of religion and free speech is to examine the case law and see whether speech which is religious in content is given greater protection than non-religious speech.

Where important social interests, such as public order or the basic individual rights of others, are opposed to free speech, the content of the communication should make no difference. Such basic social interests should prevail in all cases because of their importance and because normally one has rather wide opportunity to communicate his ideas effectively under circumstances that do not threaten either breaches of the peace or serious deprivations to others. The cases are in accordance with this reasoning and generally apply the same standards in such situations regardless of whether the speech has religious content.[15]

But there are situations in which lesser social interests are opposed to free speech, such as the promotion of the cleanliness and quiet of public streets and parks, the licensing and other restriction of door-to-door solicitation, or public distribution of literature. If freedom of religion ranks higher than freedom of speech, one would expect the American courts to treat the former freedom as more resistant to the demands of such interests than the latter.

There is no case which clearly demonstrates such a ranking. As a rule, the courts have treated all cases of this kind as involving freedom of speech primarily and have not granted special protection in the case of religious ideas.[16] There are, however, several decisions that suggest to a considerable extent that freedom of religion has greater stature in this area. In *Martin v. City of Struthers*,[17] for instance, an ordinance forbidding anyone distributing handbills and circulars to summon home dwellers to the door was held unconstitutional when applied to a Jehovah's Witness circulating leaflets advertising a religious meeting, whereas in *Breard v. City of Alexandria*[18] an ordinance prohibiting peddlers from soliciting orders from home dwellers without first obtaining their

---

15 Taylor v. Mississippi, 319 U.S. 583 (1943); Chaplinsky v. New Hampshire, 315 U.S. 568 (1941).

16 *Cf.* Jamison v. Texas, 318 U.S. 413 (1943); Cox v. New Hampshire, 312 U.S. 569 (1941). In these cases the activities of Jehovah's Witnesses were involved, yet the result in each, and the reasoning for the most part, was largely unaffected by the fact that religion was involved. For a discussion of these cases that compares a free speech approach with a religious liberty approach, see KURLAND, RELIGION AND THE LAW 54–57 (1962).

17 319 U.S. 141 (1943).

18 341 U.S. 622 (1951).

permission was upheld when applied to solicitors for subscriptions to literary periodicals.

The somewhat contrary results in the two cases can be explained on grounds other than the religious factor. Mr. Justice Black, who wrote the majority opinion in the *Struthers* case and placed that decision squarely on the free speech clause, simply regarded the *Breard* case as overruling the earlier decision. Mr. Justice Reed, who wrote the majority opinion in *Breard,* recognized that the *Struthers* case presented difficulties, but he did not expressly overrule it. He suggested it could be distinguished: "As no element of the commercial entered into . . . [the] free solicitation [involved in the *Struthers* case] and the opinion was narrowly limited to the precise fact of the *free* distribution of an invitation to *religious services,* we feel that it is not necessarily inconsistent with the conclusion reached in this case" (emphasis supplied).[19]

The language is somewhat ambiguous with regard to assessing the importance which the Court ascribed to religious liberty in distinguishing the two cases. I doubt that much can be made of it to support the proposition that religious liberty stands higher than free speech. Mr. Justice Reed does not refer specifically to freedom of religion, only to "religious services." Moreover he rather strongly suggests that if distribution of notices announcing a meeting involving philosophical, political, literary, or similar discussion open to the public without charge had been similarly restricted, this too would be unconstitutional.

The reasoning, and possibly the results, in two other cases involving Jehovah's Witnesses could be interpreted to mean that religious freedom does receive greater protection than freedom of speech. One, *Murdock v. Pennsylvania,*[20] involved a license tax on the sale of periodicals and the other, *Follett v. Town of McCormick,*[21] involved a tax on book agents. In both cases the Supreme Court held that Jehovah's Witnesses who were distributing religious literature had to be exempted from the taxes. The language of Mr. Justice Douglas, who wrote the majority opinion in the *Murdock* case, indicates that freedom of religion was in the forefront of his mind and may have been critical:

> The hand distribution of religious tracts is an age-old form of missionary evangelism. . . . It is more than preaching: it

---

19 *Id.* at 643.
20 319 U.S. 105 (1943).
21 321 U.S. 573 (1944).

is more than distribution of religious literature. It is a combination of both. Its purpose is as evangelical as the revival
meeting. This form of religious activity occupies the same
high estate under the First Amendment as do worship in the
churches and preaching from the pulpits. It has the same
claim to protection as the more orthodox and conventional
exercises of religion. It also has the same claim as the others
to the guarantees of freedom of speech and freedom of the
press.[22]

Although mention is made of freedom of speech and of the
press in the opinion, Mr. Justice Douglas goes to great lengths
to establish that the distribution of devotional literature is an important religious activity for Jehovah's Witnesses. That this element may have been of controlling significance, rather than the
free dissemination of ideas, is suggested by the language immediately following that quoted above:

The integrity of this conduct or behavior as a religious
practice has not been challenged. Nor do we have presented
any question as to the sincerity of petitioners in their religious
beliefs and practices, however misguided they may be thought
to be. Moreover, we do not intimate or suggest in respecting
their sincerity that any conduct can be made a religious rite
and by the zeal of the practitioners swept into the First
Amendment.[23]

The reason why the Court considered distribution of literature
by Jehovah's Witnesses as presenting a case for special treatment
is that the Court equated this activity with worship, as do Jehovah's
Witnesses. The case therefore cannot be read for the broad proposition that dissemination of religious ideas holds a higher place
than dissemination of other ideas. Nonetheless, the favored treatment accorded freedom of religion in this instance is of greater
significance in establishing its higher rank over freedom of speech
than is the preferred position it has been granted in the peyote
cases. For although a non-discriminatory tax would place some
burden on a rather important religious activity of Jehovah's Witnesses, it would not destroy it, or even seriously restrict it. The
Court, however, did not engage in an analysis requiring the balancing of interests. It simply viewed the case as involving a tax ex-
acted for the privilege of engaging in a religious activity and found
it *ipso facto* unconstitutional.

---

22 319 U.S. at 108–09.
23 *Id.* at 109.

It is somewhat problematical, however, whether the *Murdock* and *Follett* cases do in fact rank religious freedom over free speech. In the course of his majority opinion in the former case, Mr. Justice Douglas said: "Freedom of press, freedom of speech, freedom of religion are in a preferred position."[24] He contrasted these activities with the "wares and merchandise of hucksters and peddlers," thus possibly implying that it would be unconstitutional to place a tax on the activities of selling or distributing literature by non-profit organizations primarily interested in the free exchange of ideas, such as subsidized university presses.

A Supreme Court decision tending to undercut rather seriously the hypothesis that religion is granted a position of special preference is *Prince v. Massachusetts*.[25] In that case it was held that the state could prohibit the sale of literature by young children on the public street, even when they were accompanied by an adult and the purpose of the activity was to perform a religious service. Again Jehovah's Witnesses were involved. The freedom asserted was that of the child to preach the gospel by public distribution of religious publications in accordance with the biblical scripture: "A little child shall lead them."

The appellant conceded that freedom of speech could not protect the child's activities if Massachusetts determined as a matter of general policy that to keep children from selling on the public streets would promote their welfare. But it was argued that an exception had to be granted when the "sale" was a mode of religious exercise.

Mr. Justice Rutledge rejected this argument in the following words:

> If by this position appellant seeks for freedom of conscience a broader protection than for freedom of the mind, it may be doubted that any of the great liberties insured by the First Article can be given higher place than the others. All have preferred position in our basic scheme. . . . All are interwoven there together. Differences there are, in them and in the modes appropriate for their exercise. But they have unity in the charter's prime place because they have unity in their human sources and functionings.[26]

This language, particularly in the context of the decision made, would appear to establish conclusively the proposition that free-

---

24 *Id.* at 115.
25 321 U.S. 158 (1944).
26 *Id.* at 164–65.

dom of religion is entitled to no greater protection than freedom of speech. However, it should hardly be taken as the final word on the subject. In *Sherbert v. Verner*[27] the Supreme Court has given freedom of religion a new dimension. The state is now proscribed not only from taking action making free exercise of religion impossible but also from taking action making it unnecessarily difficult. To determine whether the difficulty is unnecessary, one must assess the state's interest in acting to see if it justifies the interference with religious liberty.

If the very recent state cases applying *Sherbert* have read the intentions of the Supreme Court correctly, then the state must adduce evidence showing that the interference with religious freedom is in fact necessary to protect important public interests. Because the state failed to establish in *People v. Woody*[28] that the religious use of peyote by members of the American Native Church would actually harm public health or safety, or make enforcement of the narcotics laws administratively difficult, the California Supreme Court held that the religious use could not be proscribed. Similarly, in the *Jenison*[29] case, the Minnesota Supreme Court decided that a woman who declined jury duty because it would violate her religious scruples had to be excused until such time as the state could demonstrate that its judicial processes were actually being impaired because of the number of people excused from jury duty for religious reasons. In effect, these decisions require more than the usual "rational basis" to justify the state's exercise of the police power if substantial religious interests are being seriously impaired.

It is conceivable, therefore, that extension of the *Sherbert* rationale would lead to the overruling of the *Prince* case. It may be true that child preaching is not vital to the full exercise of religion by a Jehovah's Witness, particularly if the restriction applies to the public streets only. A court may be very reluctant to make this type of finding, however, insofar as it must look into questions of theology. On the other hand, it would be very easy for a court to find that under proper safeguards distribution of religious literature by children on the public streets does not pose grave dangers to the welfare of the young.

If the *Prince* case were to be overruled, dissemination of religi-

---

27 374 U.S. 398 (1963).

28 394 P.2d 813 (Cal. 1964).

29 *In re* Jenison 125 N.W.2d 588 (1964).

ous ideas would be free from restraint under circumstances where dissemination of other ideas would be limited, even though there might be substantial and respectively equivalent substitute avenues for the communication of both kinds of ideas. This would be the consequence flowing from utilization of the rational basis test to assess the "evils" to be "prevented" and justify use of the police power in free speech cases, as was done in the *Prince* case, and from requiring the state to show actual and imperative need in freedom of religion cases, as was done in the *Woody* and *Jenison* cases.

It should be emphasized, however, that this clearly privileged position for religious speech would apply only to those limited kinds of communication which take on something of the character of religious services or which are considered the fulfillment of a rather clearly defined religious obligation.

THE RESPECTIVE FREEDOMS AND THE MILITARY DRAFT

There is one sphere of governmental action in which the supreme position that American political society grants religious liberty has been outstanding: it is the military draft. Exemption from military service has been traditionally given to those who genuinely claim that it would conflict with the dictates of their religion.[30] Thus far the exemption has been treated as a statutory privilege extended by act of Congress, and not a constitutional right flowing from the free exercise clause.[31] Be that as it may, in both world wars of this century the United States has deemed the

---

[30] The First Continental Congress in 1775 resolved it would protect the rights of those who could not bear arms because of their "religious scruples." 2 Journals of the Continental Congress 189 (1905). During the Civil War a federal draft act was passed without exempting conscientious objectors. Act of Mar. 3, 1863, ch. 75 §2, 12 Stat. 731. The next year a conscientious objector provision was enacted providing for non-combatant duty. Act of Feb. 24, 1864, ch. 13 §17, 13 Stat. 9. During World War I Congress passed the Draft Act of 1917 exempting conscientious objectors who were affiliated with historic peace churches. Act of May 18, 1917, ch. 15, 40 Stat. 78. Similar exemptions were provided by Congress in both the Selective Service Act of 1940 and the Selective Service Act of 1948. 50 U.S.C. App. §453 (Supp. 1963).

[31] The majority opinion in *United States v. Macintosh* contains dictum to the effect that a conscientious objector on religious grounds does not have a constitutional right to be exempted from military service. 283 U.S. 605, 623–24 (1931). This dictum has never been rejected by the Court but has on the contrary been significantly reinforced by the Supreme Court in *Hamilton v. Regents of the Univ. of Cal.*, which held that a state university could require all male students to take a course in military tactics and science as a condition for enrollment, regardless of the religious objections of a student to military service. 293 U.S. 245 (1934).

demands which a religiously formed conscience make on the individual should be protected, even at the risk of weakening the war effort to some degree. No comparable exemption has been given, as a matter of either constitutional right[32] or legislative grace,[33] to those who claim that military service conflicts with other individual liberties. Consequently the military draft takes precedence over the individual's exercise of freedom of speech.

We are not confronted here with a situation in which the modes of religious free exercise necessarily require that the demands of military conscription be overridden, whereas the modes of free speech do not. Regardless of whether we define free speech narrowly as freedom of communication or broadly as the freedom "of the intellect and spirit," military service all but destroys the individual's opportunity to exercise that right. This is particularly true if we grant freedom of speech the broadest definition. Some cases, particularly the second flag-salute case,[34] have suggested that in some instances freedom of speech transcends the freedom to communicate ideas; it also prohibits the government from unnecessarily imposing social duties inconsistent with the individual's philosophical and political beliefs.

American political society has up to now taken the position that the demands of military conscription must necessarily override the individual's political and philosophical principles even though religious principles are granted precedence over national security. Mr. Justice Hughes summed up the reasons for this in his dissent in the *Macintosh* case:

> When one's belief collides with the power of the state, the latter is supreme within its sphere and submission or punishment follows. But, in the forum of conscience, duty to a moral power higher than the state has always been maintained. The reservation of that supreme obligation, as a matter of principle, would unquestionably be made by many of our conscientious and law-abiding citizens. The essence of religion is belief in a relation to God involving duties superior to those rising from any human relation. As was stated by Mr. Justice Field, in Davis v. Beason, 133 U.S. 333, 342: "The

---

32 Selective Draft Law Cases, 245 U.S. 366 (1918).

33 Attempts in Congress to extend exemption to conscientious objectors who relied on other than religious grounds failed in both 1917 and 1940. See Conklin, *Conscientious Objector Provisions: A View in the Light of Torcaso v. Watkins*, 51 GEO. L. J. 252, 260–61, 269–70 (1963).

34 State Board of Educ. v. Barnette, 319 U.S. 624 (1943).

term 'religion' has reference to one's views of his relations to his Creator, and to the obligations they impose of reverence for his being and character, and of obedience to his will." One cannot speak of religious liberty, with proper appreciation of its essential and historic significance, without assuming the existence of a belief in supreme allegiance to the will of God. . . . There is abundant room for enforcing the requisite authority of law as it is enacted and requires obedience, and for maintaining the government, without demanding that either citizens or applicants for citizenship shall assume by oath an obligation to regard allegiance to God as subordinate to allegiance to civil power.[35]

Congress apparently concurred in the view that the individual should be excused from military service only when a law higher than the civil one commanded him not to participate in war or its preparations. In 1940 Congress exempted from the military draft anyone who "by reason of religious training and belief, is conscientiously opposed to participating in war in any form."[36] Then in 1948, to make the basis of exemption clearer, Congress defined by statute what it meant by "religious training and belief":

Religious training and belief in this connection mean an individual's belief in relation to a Supreme Being involving duties superior to those arising from any human relation, but does not include essentially political, sociological or philosophical views or a merely personal moral code.[37]

Recent judicial development have cast some doubt on the special place granted to religious scruples. This is due in large part to the free-wheeling definition given to religion by Mr. Justice Black in *Torcaso v. Watkins*[38] when he designated secular humanism and ethical culture as religious beliefs and required that they be given status equal to theistic beliefs under the free exercise clause. The seed then planted has taken root quickly. The Court of Appeals for the Second Circuit has held in the recent *Seeger*[39] case, that it would be unconstitutional to deny exemption to a person having conscientious scruples not based on belief in a Supreme Being. The

---

[35] United States v. Macintosh, 283 U.S. 605, 633–34 (1931).

[36] Selective Training and Service Act of 1940, ch. 720 § 5 (g), 54 Stat. 889.

[37] 50 U.S.C. App. § 456 (j) (Supp. 1963).

[38] 367 U.S. 488 (1961).

[39] United States v Seeger, 326 F.2d 846 (2d Cir. 1964), *cert. granted,* 377 U.S. 922 (1964).

inductee in the *Seeger* case opposed war because it would be destructive of all "moral life" and would "betray the cause of freedom and humanity."

What is most significant about these decisions from our point of view is that the distinction between "religion" and "ideology" is breaking down in the American case law. If this should proceed apace, freedom of religion and freedom of speech in the sense of "freedom of intellect and spirit" would merge. This could conceivably lead to the anomalous result of a Communist's being granted the status of a conscientious objector because to engage in a war to further imperialistic capitalism would violate his most highly prized ethical and philosophical views.

Even the cases making the most radical departure in this regard implicitly or explicitly recognize that some distinction must be made between religion and ideology. In the *Seeger* case the government in argument conceded that the inductee's views fell within a fairly broad definition of "religion" enunciated in an earlier decision by the Second Circuit, *United States v. Kauten.*[40] In the *Kauten* case, decided prior to the 1948 statutory clarification requiring belief in a Supreme Being, the court said:

> There is a distinction between a course of reasoning resulting in a conviction that a particular war is inexpedient or disastrous and a conscientious objection to participation in any war under any circumstances. The latter, and not the former, may be the basis of exemption under the Act. The former is usually a *political objection,* while the latter, we think, may justly be regarded as a response of the individual to an inward mentor, call it *conscience or God,* that is for many persons at the present time the equivalent of what has always been thought a religious impulse [emphasis supplied].[41]

Although it is not clear how the court would distinguish between religious beliefs and political or other ideological beliefs, the quoted language expresses recognition of the need for the distinction.

The trend to broaden the definition of religion in the recent cases should be sharply limited, if not reversed. Beliefs classified as religious should be restricted to those involving a transcendental element.

---

40 133 F.2d 703 (2d Cir. 1943).
41 *Id.* at 708.

This is particularly true where preference over vital interests of the state itself are at stake, such as national security during a war. The individual who supports secular philosophies, theories, and ideologies keeps himself on the same plane of human non-transcendental truths as does the religiously neutral state. In a democracy there is no reason why his own fallible judgment on what is good for society should take precedence over what the majority deem is appropriate for the commonweal.

But with freedom of religion, the relationship between God and man is involved. The individual's judgment is now based on a higher spiritual plane than that of the state. This does not mean that the democratic state must accord such views any greater respect than it does secular views in deciding what is good for society. Social values grounded on a religious base will prevail in this respect only to the extent that they commend themselves to the majority. The transcendental element in a truly, religious belief, however, places the individual in an intolerable position when the state demands of him what his God sternly forbids.

The court in the *Seeger* case recognized that commands of the Deity impose a special burden from the individual's point of view. But it also maintained that for many the interior voice of conscience can be as compelling in its demands. If the *Seeger* case signifies a development whereby the scope of freedom of religion is to be expanded generally, Americans adhering to traditional religious beliefs have little cause to complain. But if such broad protection should prove impossible to administer and lead Congress to repeal the exemption for conscientious objectors in its entirety, the courts will have unwittingly done a disservice to religious liberty. It will be an unecessary and unjustifiable disservice. No matter how much one admires and respects conscientious objections based on ethical considerations of the value and sanctity of human life, they are the products of human judgments based on what is good and necessary for human life in society. Even though it is desirable to defer to these objections as far as possible, when their assertion endangers the collective security, they must in a democracy defer to the collective wisdom. The dissenter must suffer because of his unique sensitivities which place him in opposition to the majority.

Conscientious objections based on religious grounds must also give way at some point. But if the individual genuinely asserts he is under an inflexible divine command, his sensitivity derives from an external source over which he himself has no control. The views of other men can move him only at the cost of violating a higher obligation.

Because of this added dimension of obligation there appears good reason to distinguish between the ethically formed conscience and the theistically formed one and to make special effort to protect the latter. Granted that it would be desirable to protect both, there should not be simply the alternative of having both yield in cases of necessity. If society cannot stand the strain of tolerating both, no injustice is suffered should only the theistically formed conscience be protected. There can be little doubt that this kind of preferential treatment is in accord with the values of American society, which has traditionally been a Christian one.

THE RELATIVE SOCIAL VALUE OF THE TWO FREEDOMS

From our discussion thus far we could tentatively conclude that American society officially ranks freedom of religion at least as high as, and probably higher than, freedom of speech. This is because we have emphasized the degree to which the courts require state action to be limited so that it will not interfere with the individual's exercise of these rights. A somewhat different conclusion may be reached if we consider the extent to which the state may positively advance the realization of these rights.

There can be no doubt that the state may use its resources to the fullest extent to promote the free exchange of ideas. The substantial financial support given to both public and private universities is witness to this. In supporting such institutions the state has as its primary purpose the education of a responsible citizenry. But in view of the tradition of academic freedom behind the university and its demand that inquiry for the truth be unrestrained, the state in effect is greatly expanding the opportunities for and the occasions of free exchange of ideas. Indeed, one can safely say that the state may decide, and in fact has done so, that an educated citizenry in a democracy is one that has been exposed to the free clash of ideas and that universities should be actively supported because they increase the occasions for such exchange.

There is also precedent holding that governmental authorities may not withhold use of publicly owned facilities for the dissemination of particular views when those facilities are adapted for and have been used by the public for the exchange of other ideas.[42]

When one examines the extent to which the state may positively promote the occasions for the free exercise of religion, one finds it is significantly limited by the establishment clause. The manner in which this limitation has been interpreted and applied has led many public officials, and a few scholarly commentators, to conclude that the Supreme Court is hostile to religion. A close examination of the Court's decisions and its reasoning does not bear out this conclusion, but it does raise the question whether the Court ranks freedom of religion significantly lower than freedom of speech as a social value.

Critics of the Court's action have claimed that the decisions in the *McCollum*,[43] *Engel*,[44] and *Schempp*[45] cases prohibiting religious instruction, prayers, and devotional Bible reading in the public schools have unnecessarily sacrificed the religious liberty of the majority.[46] This is a highly dubious conclusion. If students or their parents are desirous of organizing daily communal prayer, there is wide opportunity for them to do so outside the public school at times and places where they do not impose in any way on the minority. It is the Court's concern for preserving the individual religious liberty of all equally that accounts for its doctrine of "neutrality" toward religion. This was forcefully brought out by the concurring opinions of both Mr. Justice Brennan[47] and Mr. Justice Goldberg[48] in the *Schempp* decision.

The restriction that these opinions place on the role which religion may play in the public education of the child, however, would seem to belittle its stature as a social good. Has not the Court thrown in its lot with the rationalists of the eighteenth-century French Enlightenment? Relying on man's reason as the ultimate guide to determine what is good and proper for him and society, the Court appears to be more concerned about advancing freedom of speech than freedom of religion, in order to insure

---

[42] American Civil Liberties Union v. Board of Educ., 359 P.2d 45 (Cal. 1961); Danskin v. San Diego Unified School Dist., 171 P.2d 885 (Cal. 1946).
[43] McCollum v. Board of Educ., 333 U.S. 203 (1948).
[44] Engel v. Vitale, 370 U.S. 421 (1962).
[45] School Dist. of Abington Township v. Schempp, 374 U.S. 203 (1963).
[46] RICE, THE SUPREME COURT AND PUBLIC PRAYER (1964).
[47] 374 U.S. at 230 ff.
[48] *Id.* at 305 ff.

that society will be predisposed to attain and preserve other basic values.

This may be the private opinion of some of the justices, but it does not accord with their public utterances.[49] Theoretically, there are at least two lines of justification for the Court's position in these cases even if one postulates, as some theologians do, that vital commitment to religion is necessary to attain the good society. Both lines of justification stem from the general principle of separation of church and state, one emphasizing its theological aspects, the other its political ones. As a matter of private opinion, some or all of the justices on the Court may believe, as do some churchmen,[50] that religion is more vital and more effective in forming the moral and spiritual character of individuals in a society when it is wholly voluntary and wholly independent of state support. Even if the justices would not subscribe to such an opinion, they could justify their actions on the ground that governmental neutrality is the only way in which religious liberty can truly be secured in an open, pluralistic society like the American one.[51] Following this approach the Court would not see three choices before it: a state that actively promotes free exercise, one that inhibits it, or one that protects it from inhibition by remaining neutral; only the last two would be viable alternatives.

Just as the protection of religious freedom tends to make wider claims on society than does protection of free speech, the promotion of religious exercises tends to interfere to a greater extent with individual rights than does promotion of freedom of speech. Religious liberty implies not only freedom to exercise one's own re-

---

49 In the majority opinion of the *Schempp* case Mr. Justice Clark referred to the "exalted" position of religion. *Id.* at 226. Mr. Justice Brennan, concurring, ended a long opinion quoting with approval Chief Justice Black of Pennsylvania, who had maintained that the citizenry would be more religious if separation of church and state were maintained. *Id.* at 304. Mr. Justice Goldberg, who was joined in his opinion by Mr. Justice Harlan, stated that "many of our legal, political and personal values derive historically from religious teachings." *Id.* at 306.

50 *E.g.,* Kelley, *Beyond Separation of Church and State,* 5 JOURNAL OF CHURCH AND STATE 181 (1963).

51 In the *Schempp* case Mr. Justice Clark, speaking for the majority, stated: "The place of religion in our society is an exalted one, achieved through a long tradition of reliance on the home, the church and the inviolable citadel of the individual heart and mind. We have come to recognize through bitter experience that it is not within the power of government to invade that citadel, whether its purpose or effect be to aid or oppose, to advance or retard. In the relationship between man and religion, the State is firmly committed to a position of neutrality." 374 U.S. at 226.

ligion but also freedom from imposition of unwanted religious exercises. There is little question that compulsory attendance at chapel in a state university would violate the constitutional guarantee of religious liberty. Contrariwise, freedom of speech does not at all imply freedom from exposure to highly offensive ideas. The convinced royalist or Marxist cannot complain if he is required to take courses in a public university which present the virtues of democracy or capitalism. Indeed the entire social value of free speech depends upon the exposure of the individual to various points of view.

Underlying the *Schempp*[52] decision prohibiting Bible reading and prayers in the public schools was the fact that young, impressionable children were involved, so that the element of coercion lurked in the background, even though the children could ask to be excused from the exercises. Mr. Justice Brennan in his concurring opinion thought this element was so important—since it was too much to ask children to act with the social confidence and independence necessary for them to seek excusal from an officially sanctioned rite of the majority—that he concluded the prescribed exercises violated the free exercise clause of the First Amendment as well as the establishment clause.

But even if one discounts the element of coercion entirely in the *Schempp* case, the fact that the state would be putting the weight of its authority and prestige behind the voluntary exercises creates a special problem, particularly where children are concerned. The religious rights of the minority would be infringed to the extent that the government would be favoring majority religious beliefs and practices. It is, of course, true that the state can actively favor certain political and ideological beliefs, such as democracy and capitalism. The majority can use the agencies of government to promote their political beliefs and ideas, such as prescribing patriotic exercises in the public schools. The proper conclusion to be drawn is that whereas the government prizes the individual's right to religious liberty so highly that it will not promote the exercise of religious rights by the majority, the same does not hold true in the case of freedom of speech. This is undoubtedly due to the nature of the social value of free speech. Presumably, majority acceptance of ideas in a democracy is a test of their worth. The government is obliged to throw its weight behind these ideas. Freedom of speech requires primarily that voices of dissent be

52 School Dist. of Abington Township v. Schempp, 374 U.S. 203 (1963).

heard so that they may influence the majority; it certainly does not require that equality of resources be put at the disposal of the minority.

That freedom of speech depends so much on its social value to democracy may paradoxically lead to the conclusion, therefore, that it does not provide as much protection to the individual as freedom of religion. This conclusion finds much support in those free speech cases, notably in the area of obscenity, which hold that the communication of ideas that do not have any social value is not within the area protected by the First Amendment. Thus in the *Roth* case[53] the majority opinion did not examine whether the literature involved created a clear and present danger of some antisocial consequences. It held such an inquiry irrelevant if the material were found to be obscene, because if it were so classified it would not be protected under the First Amendment.

In the early freedom of religion cases a similar approach was taken. Religion was defined so as to exclude antisocial conduct from the protection of the First Amendment. Thus the Mormon claim on religious grounds to a dispensation from the requirement of monogamy was rejected on the theory that a creed worthy of the title "religion," at least for First Amendment purposes, would not put forward such a claim.[54] Even this approach differs significantly from the one taken in free speech cases involving obscenity, since the former excludes only that which is socially harmful whereas the latter excludes that which is not socially useful.

Of greater consequence is the shape of things to come as revealed by the peyote decisions.[55] For in these cases behavior which is generally considered socially harmful is given protection under the claim of religious liberty. In view of this difference it is not at all inconceivable that the courts might require the state to leave undisturbed a group of adults who collectively viewed subjects of hard-core pornography as part of a religious ceremony but would permit the restraint of adults who collectively viewed the same subjects simply for vicarious sexual gratification.

In conclusion, if one considers freedom of speech in the narrow sense of the free exchange of ideas, it is an important social value in the American democracy. But it is more important as a means

---

53 Roth v. United States, 354 U.S. 476 (1957).

54 *E.g.*, Davis v. Beason, 133 U.S. 333 (1890).

55 *E.g.*, People v. Woody, 394 P.2d 813 (Cal. 1964).

to other ends (perhaps such higher values as full religious liberty) than as an end in itself. But freedom of religion is an important end in itself, and because of this its integrity must be respected even when society looks to it to achieve other social ends. The social value of religion, therefore, must be realized in the United States through the activities of the individual and the private voluntary groups he belongs to, not through the activities of the state.

CONCLUSIONS

There can be little doubt that freedom of religion is accorded the supreme place in the hierarchy of American civil rights. No other right is as successful in overriding other social interests; no other freedom is considered as important to the individual person.

Freedom of speech is also granted a very high estate, indeed a preferred one over most other civil rights. But this is in large part due to its importance to society generally. When the Supreme Court is convinced that a particular communication has little social value, it will not include the dissemination of such ideas within the ambit of free speech, no matter how great the satisfaction some individuals might derive from them. On the other hand the Court has not examined—in recent years at least—the social utility of an individual's beliefs to determine whether or not they qualify for treatment as a religion within the scope of the free exercise clause. It is enough if the individual genuinely finds religious fulfillment in adherence to these beliefs for them to warrant protection.

Because of the importance of religion to the individual, it is necessary for the courts to define it with clarity and precision. Lines should not be so loosely drawn that beliefs which do not merit or require the highest protection are included thereunder. Claims based on secular truths and seeking secular goals should defer to the secular interests of temporal society; only claims with a transcendental basis should be accorded the very high protection accorded religious interests. Otherwise, indiscriminate reliance on freedom of religion may place too great a strain on other social interests and lead in the long run to a net loss to this civil right.

The high estate of religious freedom is not diminished by the

Supreme Court's insistence that the state may not promote the free exercise of religion. The Court's intransigence on this point stems not from indifference to the social value of religion but from a deep concern that the religious liberty of all individuals be protected fully and that this is best accomplished by the principle of separation of church and state.

RECENT DEVELOPMENTS

PATRICIA BARRETT, R.S.C.J.

BOOKS ON RELIGION, LAW, AND SOCIETY
SEPTEMBER, 1963, TO SEPTEMBER, 1964

The relation of church and state is a "limit-problem" in the sense that Danielou applies the term to the problem of God. It cannot be correctly viewed solely from one side or the other or, for that matter, from a single dimensional approach. Theological, philosophical, legal, sociological, and historical aspects must be carefully meshed into a comprehensive theory which can serve as a guide in resolving real conflicts. Books in the church-state field published during the past year cover this entire spectrum. A persistent theme is the summons to religion as prophet, as "disturber of the undisturbed," as challenger of existing institutions and complacent attitudes. Modern man's awareness of history has aroused anxiety about the increasingly ominous pressure of contemporary events. Thus, the search is for a philosophical framework, a clue to the transhistorical meaning of contingent happenings which is also respectful of the role of human freedom in the molding of these events. As contemporary man assumes greater personal responsibility in deciding for or against God, he realizes ever more clearly that his decision is not just private but fraught with immense social consequence. The irreversible secularization of public life poses for institutional religion the problem of nurturing its members and, for the members, the challenge of expressing their faith within neutral social structures.

Mother Patricia Barrett, R.S.C.J., is Professor of Political Science, Maryville College of the Sacred Heart, St. Louis, Missouri. Acknowledgment is hereby made to AMERICA, National Catholic Weekly Review, 920 Broadway, New York, New York 10010, for permission to use parts of the following reviews: OAKS (ed.), THE WALL BETWEEN CHURCH AND STATE, January 18, 1964; MILLER, PIETY ALONG THE POTOMAC, July 4, 1964; and CALLAHAN (ed.), FEDERAL AID AND CATHOLIC SCHOOLS, August 8, 1964.

On the American scene, the "wall mythology" continues strong in some minds, though there have been important yieldings on crucial issues, mainly for pragmatic reasons. Prolonged controversy over the proposed prayer amendment indicates the current danger of an American culture-religion as an alternative to an aggressive secularism.

The burgeoning ecumenical spirit is undoubtedly influencing interreligious relations, though the extent of its impact is still tentative and unclear. Thoughtful writers agree that religion must come to terms with secular society and give up the practice of equating the secular with evil and the sacred with good. Voluntary withdrawal of church from society is no more desirable than forced exclusion or total union. Creative encounter seems to be emerging as the most sought-after goal.

THEOLOGICAL, PHILOSOPHICAL, SOCIOLOGICAL, AND POLITICAL STUDIES

Professor Thomas G. Sanders' *Protestant Concepts of Church and State*[1] is a valuable historical survey of five main Protestant approaches to church-state theory. Intimate knowledge of Protestantism and long familiarity with Catholic teaching have equipped the author for the perceptive comparisons he makes on salient points. Protestants, for instance, seem to be moving toward more systematic conceptualization while Catholics are striving for less rigid formulas and more flexibility in response to the signs of the time. Three fundamental principles which Protestantism shares with Roman Catholicism and Eastern Orthodoxy are the dualism of church and state, the sovereignty of God over both church and state, and a concept of the state as both good and evil. On this last subject, Catholics generally hold that the state is a natural and necessary society which would have existed even if Adam had not sinned. The consequence of the Fall is that political authority must now be coercive as well as directive.

The five types of Protestant approach singled out by Dr. Sanders are (1) the Lutheran; (2) the Anabaptist-Mennonite; (3) the Quaker; (4) the separationist; and (5) the transformationist.

Luther realistically recognized the tension between the authority of God and man's perversions of that authority. Because he was an activist in dealing with social and political controversies, his directions to the people were informed by a conservatism predicated

---

[1] New York: Holt, Rinehart & Winston, 1964. Pp. 339. $7.50.

on an assumed continuation of existing structures. By the late seventeenth and eighteenth centuries, Lutheranism, according to Professor Sanders, had almost entirely abdicated responsibility for political and social problems and adjusted to the regime in power. Luther's own teaching, however, contained a corrective to abject submission to the leader, though it was gradually forgotten over the years.

In the United States Lutheranism adjusted to church-state separation and, currently influenced by new trends of thought, is well on the way to overcoming a traditional passivity toward the political order. Focus on the theological dimension is, perhaps, its most significant contribution to Protestant church-state perspectives. Life as a response to the Will of God offers a satisfying alternative to secularistic rationalism. Happily emerging is an effort to recapture the sense of social responsibility, defined in theological terms consistent with Reformation insights.

Dr. Sanders turns next to the sixteenth-century Anabaptists from whom the present-day American Mennonites are descended. The radically religious commitment of this group precluded a concept of formal disestablishment, though they fought against Zwingli for the freedom of the church within the political order. Resistance to the existing form of national religion constituted their contribution to the growth of religious liberty. Until the twentieth century American Mennonites lived on the outskirts of society, content with their sixteenth-century teachings and distinctly sectarian attitude toward the state. Current historical research and theological reconstruction is directed toward a more varied Mennonite approach to society. Dr. Sanders hopes that there will be no weakening of the essentially Protestant stance of witnessing to the primacy of the kingdom of God over this world. A legalistic, strictly integrated outlook has motivated Mennonites to demand separation of church and state as a matter of church doctrine in order to secure religious liberty.

Departing from an earlier quietism and withdrawal, modern Quakers have shown active concern for such social goals as world peace and civil liberties. Premising their actions on a theological notion of the presence of the Inner Light in every man, they have supported specifically humanistic causes which proclaim the dignity and worth of every person. Although this strong ethical imperative precludes acceptance of extreme church-state separation, they have yet to analyze the implications of their convictions for the American pluralistic system. A major Quaker contribution to

Protestant church-state theory consists in this stress on the potentiality of government, in contrast with the Lutheran and Mennonite emphasis on the shortcomings of the political order.

The American Friends Service Committee and the Friends Committee on National Legislation have been very effective in promoting national and international social justice. Eschewing pressure methods of legislative lobbying in fidelity to the principle of nonviolence, the Friends prefer to arrange persuasive and courteous exchange of views. Richard K. Ullman, influenced by the Lutheran Dietrich Bonhoeffer, rejects the unqualified emphasis on pure principles and urges his fellow Quakers to be more aware of the ambiguity of their pacifism in a world torn by tension between good and evil. He suggests a nuanced approach, sensitive both to the effects of sin in man and the action of God in history through man.

Since the late 1940's American Protestants have tended to follow either a separationist or transformationist policy in church-state matters. The first, represented by the Protestants and Other Americans United for Separation of Church and State (POAU), interprets separation in strict terms. The second, developed in response to this, adopts a moderate church-state separation and a restrained attitude toward Roman Catholicism. Beginning with the English Puritan sects of the sixteenth and seventeenth centuries, Professor Sanders traces the complicated web of history, noting the successive impact of religious fragmentation, the rise of secularism, revivalism, rationalism, the social gospel, individualism, the attitude toward Catholicism, and contemporary revisionism. Within the seventeenth-century establishment-of-religion context, dissenting sects made a valid protest against the church's use of political power to maintain its privileges. The more flexible American system does not warrant an unmodified adherence to separation as an ideological principle. Thus, Professor Sanders thinks that those who crusade for such a concept are not really consistent with the American tradition or authentic representatives of Protestant concerns. Theirs is a time-conditioned emphasis, elevated now into a secular dogma which is out of touch with the original religious motivation. Articulate opposition to unfair manipulation of the "wall" doctrine is coming from such new-breed separationists as Winthrop Hudson, Franklin H. Littell, and Dean M. Kelley. They underline the sharp distinction between the function of the church and that of the state and feel that the integrity of the former is compromised by too close association with the political.

Transformationism, the fifth Protestant church-state approach, is carefully traced from its Calvinist beginnings to its contemporary embodiment in the position represented by the respected periodical *Christianity and Crisis*. A strong sense of Christian social responsibility and a moderate attitude toward Roman Catholicism characterize the members of this group. Transformationism allows for the influence of religion on public policy, prefers a theistic to a secularistic view of American culture, supports religion in public education, and co-operates with Catholics and Jews on common projects. Transformationist writers have recently shown considerable diligence in probing the theological dimension of church-state relations. Prominent in this regard are Merrimon Cuninggim, executive director of the Danforth Foundation; John C. Bennett, president of Union Theological Seminary; and the members of the Department of Religious Liberty of the National Council of Churches of Christ. All are searching for theologically founded principles in dealing with church-state issues. Their chief contribution, in Sanders' judgment, is a reassertion of the church's prophetic role, a desire to rekindle the ancient dynamic spirit.

On the whole, transformationism is the most promising contemporary Protestant approach to church-state problems. It is open to dialogue on the sensitive subject of government benefits to church-related, public-purpose projects. It is aware of the continued challenge in interpreting pluralism and maintaining church-state independence. Its willingness to co-operate in dealing creatively with issues which plague the nation should serve as a model for all Americans.

Church and State under God,[2] edited by Albert G. Huegli is a historical-theological study by a group of Lutheran scholars of the New Testament roots, changing patterns, and emergent trends in church-state relations. The book is premised on the Lutheran view that co-operation between the God-ordained instruments of church and state is desirable and that absolute separation is untenable. Scriptural concepts are meant not to provide an operative technique for handling contemporary issues but to cultivate an attitude of mind and inculcate a set of principles governing man's relationship to God. The insights of Reformation thinkers, as well as subsequent theological expressions in Europe and the United States, provide the necessary historical background for the American experience. According to Professor Lewis W. Spitz, Jr., the Reformation's great contribution was an element of stability, derived from

---

[2] St. Louis: Concordia Publishing House, 1964. Pp. 516. $8.00.

its purely theological message and expressed in the courageous and determined faith of its adherents. Professors Richard H. Klann and William H. Lehmann, Jr., are understandably skeptical about any real change in the position of the Roman church regarding the church-state question. The comprehensive theoretical structure supporting preferential status for Catholicism has, they claim, been definitively formulated and never repudiated by Rome. Subsequent adaptations to meet changing social conditions are operational only, they say, and designed for tactical ends. This is another instance of the urgent need for authoritative recognition that there is no single, doctrinally prescribed Catholic ideal in church-state relationships.

Much considered attention is given to the main tension areas on the American scene: religion in public schools; government aid to parochial schools; military chaplaincies; tax exemption; zoning; and Sunday closing laws. There is a willingness to make public welfare benefits available to all children, but not to use tax monies for teachers' salaries or school construction in the case of parochial schools. Such financial support is judged to be an illegitimate aid to religion.

Of the several ways of resolving church-state conflicts, Martin Marty lists three alternatives: radical separation, overlapping of spheres, and the favored interpenetration and tension between the church and state. This seems to him the most practical for the American system of realized pluralism, where the old formulas— "wall of separation," "union of church and state"—are fading away and may even die some day.

A concluding chapter by Huegli calls attention to the emerging new dimensions in American church-state relations which are increasingly brought into public view. Burgeoning interfaith dialogue groups, for example, give evidence of a shared respect for governmental authority, concern for the moral and spiritual foundations of society, interest in the dignity and worth of the individual, support of the principle of voluntarism. Unanswered, however, is the question of what contacts with government the churches will find acceptable.

Regarding the state's attitude toward the church, there is agreement that genuine pluralism requires government impartiality. To some, as Professor Huegli notes, this means strict separation and an effective secularization of society. To others it means, simply, treating all religions alike but not ignoring them. Changing social and political conditions call for re-examination of the traditional benevolent attitude of government toward religion in order to ascertain how best to realize the American principles of religious liberty, pluralism, and co-operation. Churches are a long way from speaking with one voice in these matters, but they are at least speaking with one another about them.

The Christian Witness to the State,[3] by John Howard Yoder, is an example of the current Mennonite research and theological reconstruction mentioned by Dr. Sanders. The material in this study was originally prepared for a conference on "The Lordship of Christ over Church and State," held in July, 1955, in Puidoux, Switzerland. It was later reworked by Mr. Yoder in collaboration with an advisory group. The New Testament concept of the state, he claims, provides theological justification for Mennonite criticism of the way in which a particular state carries out its responsibilities. Mr. Yoder is convinced that a Christian pacifist position, rooted not in pragmatic but in Christological considerations, is profoundly relevant to the social order. He wants to show the "possibility of speaking to the state from the posture of New Testament nonresistance, rather than arguing the case for nonresistance in its own right" (p. 26). Nevertheless, he concedes the necessity, when addressing the statesman, of using such secular terms as liberty, human rights, democracy, since the statesman is separated by the barrier of unbelief from the single true standard of justice rooted in the love of Christ. Thus, the Christian can bring his distinctly religious insights to bear on the social order by expressing them in middle axioms familiar to the statesman but without ascribing to them any metaphysical value apart from Christ.

Religion's failure to promote the political, industrial, and intellectual revolutions that have transformed the modern world accounts, in part, for its eclipse as an acknowledged force. Thus, Herbert J. Muller, in *Religion and Freedom in the Modern World,*[4] indicts the historical record of the churches but admits their present support of a free society. The legacy of political corruption and injustice, for example, so characteristic of religiously orientated states in Latin America and Southeast Asia, aggravates the contemporary problem of combating communism. The inquiring, restless, probing spirit has been so smothered, according to Dr. Muller, by layers of ritualism and legalism that one can hardly blame the moral and political decay of our time

---

3 Newton, Kans.: Faith & Life Press, 1964. Pp. 90. $1.50.
4 Chicago: University of Chicago Press, 1963. Pp. 129. $3.95.

on a decline of religious faith. Churchmen, by and large, have failed to meet the challenge of relativism. A growing historical-mindedness and the awareness that institutions are products of culture, have left many people with troublesome questions. Is a given religious faith merely a local custom? Are the ideals of freedom, social justice, and human rights cultural prejudices or permanent principles flowing from man's nature? As he reads Western history, Mr. Muller is impressed with the dangers of Christian absolutism which is more readily disposed to authoritarianism than to defense of civil liberties and the free society. Although this can be documented as fact, it can also be challenged as misleading in that it brings contemporary insights to bear as exclusive criteria for judging former historical eras.

Mr. Muller suggests, as a possible middle ground, that both philosophical relativists and absolutists pay greater attention to standards of excellence. Free Americans, in his opinion, are presently neither good relativists nor good absolutists. They seek to be "well adjusted" with little independent thought about the kind of life, of people, or of God that they are adjusting to. It is not clear to him that religion is particularly helpful in this respect. The growth of secular independence, on the other hand, has made possible a breadth and variety of interest, a tolerant pluralism more conducive to freedom than the restraints of an established Christian culture. He wisely notes that churchmen would do well to cease labeling the secular irreligious and begin to realize that it may be in the light of secular ideals of a free society that Christianity can have the greatest appeal today. Those who cannot agree with the Christian faith may unite in asserting the primacy of love. A common commitment to this principle could serve to reconcile the absolutists and the relativists, since, in the words of Paul Tillich, love "can transform itself according to the concrete demands of every individual and social situation without losing its eternity and dignity and unconditional validity" (p. 117).

The thoughts in this provocative little book are sometimes fragmentary and inconclusive, aimed more at prodding religious people out of a slackness or smugness into which they may have slipped than at providing closely reasoned and comprehensive solutions.

In *The Fourth American Faith*,[5] Duncan Howlett, Pastor of All

5 New York: Harper & Row, 1964. Pp. 239. $4.50.

Souls Church, Washington, D.C., describes the unstructured, existentialist-inspired faith of a growing number of Americans. Discontented with the gulf between religious orthodoxy's official dogmas and the "beliefs of the heart," these people are seeking to liberate religion from the chains of tradition which alienate it from contemporary man's needs. They reject the very idea of orthodoxy and strive constantly to reformulate what they believe in accordance with changing times. Theirs is a faith of adventure in contrast to the faiths of stability. Whether it can be institutionalized without losing its distinctive genius is an unanswered question. It places no reliance on the doctrine of revelation but claims that truth emerges from an open encounter of mind with mind. It denies any distinction between sacred and secular and affirms that all experience is *human* experience—which alone can indicate what is worthy of worship. Adherents of the fourth faith are honest, inquiring, and insistent that a man can believe only what seems to him to be true. The reason why religion should concern itself about God, they say, is that God is ultimate meaning which constantly unfolds before us.

As Dr. Howlett describes the fourth faith, it seems to be essentially a mood of rebellion against confinement, a surge of man's religious spirit toward that complete freedom which he can never find in this world. The fact that it exists, as something distinct from secularism, further attests the emergence of a realized religious pluralism in America. Its challenge should not be underestimated.

That the vital testing areas of a democracy are the points of conflict and tension is the message of *Religion and Social Conflict,*[6] edited by Robert Lee and Martin E. Marty. The book contains the 1962 lectures of the Institute of Ethics and Society at San Francisco Theological Seminary. Each of the contributors explores one facet of the theme in order to show the positive functions of conflict. They do not contend that religion's sole function is to produce disquiet but that human conflict is part of the life of faith-bearing and may be "the matrix in which God's grace is expressed" (p. 7).

Charles Y. Glock's chapter, "The Role of Deprivation in the Origin and Evolution of Religious Groups," contains a refinement and development of the "sect-church" theory. The organizational response to felt-deprivation, he claims, may be either reli-

---

[6] New York: Oxford University Press, 1964. Pp. 193. $3.50.

gious or secular. If religious, it tends to develop as a church or a sect depending upon the kind of deprivation. Such movements, if they are to survive, must be relevant to long-term trends in society. The growing secularization of American life, for example, is seen as a major cause of the growth of Unitarianism. The author does not mean to reduce religion to a sociological variable or confine it to a relief function but means simply to show that this is *one* thing it does.

Charles S. McCoy, in "The Churches and Protest Movements for Racial Justice," supplies an analysis of the impact of organized religion on the movement toward racial justice. To him, religion means "that center of ultimate commitment and loyalty from which men derive their understanding of reality, of themselves and their companions, and of what is truly of value" (p. 38). It is basically an individual affair, only secondarily social. Thus, it is likely to play an ambiguous role in social conflict situations. Only secondarily and in rare circumstances can we look for decisive and courageous leadership from the churches. Their record in the protest movements for racial justice, unhappily, bears out this contention. They did not initiate the Montgomery bus boycott of 1955, the "sit-in" movement, or the freedom rides, though they have provided guidance, encouragement, and interpretations of the profound upheaval that these developments give witness to. Dr. McCoy suggests that this is likely to be the prevailing pattern as the struggle for racial justice moves ahead at a quickening pace. The need to put theory into practice finds the churches lagging behind, he asserts, perhaps because actual integration demands mass support and not just the notional assent of a minority. Devotion to this cause has not yet extended sufficiently beyond an enlightened leadership.

In a long and well-documented chapter, Seymour Lipset tackles the complex problem of the "religious factor" in American politics. Rejecting the assumption of some moderns that a relationship between religion and politics violates separation of church and state, he traces the development of the religious-political pattern in the United States from the formative years of the Republic to the present day. Statistical tables provide support for the conclusion that religion affects political choices insofar as it is a source of beliefs and a determinant of class status. The first is a theological factor and the second a social one.

In spite of steady improvement in interfaith understanding, Mr. Lipset notes two types of anti-Catholicism which appeared in

1960: the traditional, rural, lower-class variety which has been evident throughout American history; and an anti-Catholic sentiment among higher-status Protestants in response to their growing minority-consciousness. In some respects this feeling may have been more acute after the 1960 election than before. Material circulated during the campaign showed that the chief hesitation of higher-status Protestants about voting for a Catholic candidate was the sincere fear of the power and purposes of the Catholic Church. An influential group of liberal-minded Protestants, aware of the diversity within Roman Catholicism, made a successful effort to allay this fear and to promote respect for individual freedom and personal belief. Their achievement contributed significantly to the Kennedy victory and, perhaps, to the Protestant minority-consciousness.

Concluding his discussion of the influence of religion on politics, Mr. Lipset suggests that more important than its effect on party loyalty may be its contribution to the American tendency to enforce morality by law. He, too, is of the opinion that tolerance and secularism are closely related. Although ample practical evidence supports this view, it need not and should not follow that a religiously committed person is less likely than anyone else to respect the rights of those he believes to be in error. Rights belong to human beings and authentic religious commitment requires recognition of others' right to freedom of conscience and the exercise of religious liberty. Mr. Lipset is surely on safe ground in predicting that future analysts of American political life will continue to find evidence of religion's impact, no matter what its mode of manifestation.

The chapter "Church and State in America: A Theological Inquiry" by Professor Benjamin A. Reist of San Francisco Theological Seminary focuses on two aspects of the problem of relating Christian faith to the American church-state situation: Calvin's view of the positive nature of the state, in contrast with Luther's position that the political order is a result of man's sin; and the contextual character of the New Testament ethic which summons Christians to *witness* and "not to attempt to apply universally applicable principles to the given complexities of human existence (p. 129).

Agreeing with Dr. John Bennett and Professor Thomas Sanders that there is no single Protestant doctrine of church-state relations, Professor Reist takes up the challenge to develop one which will be intelligible to the modern world. The prototypes, he says, are all pre-modern and of little use to the task at hand. Any attempt to impose yesterday's insights on today's problems is doomed to failure. This, he says, is what happens when church-state relations are considered within the framework of natural-law philosophy. He mistakenly identifies Catholic church-state teaching with natural-law doctrine; medieval society with some sort of abstract ideal; and natural law with a rigid standard to be inflexibly applied. All, he asserts, are to be rejected, and with this we agree but not with the inadequate understanding or oversimplified dismissal of Catholic thought on church-state matters. He is evidently familiar only with the older, static view, to the neglect of the newer, dynamic stance which could very well meet his prescriptions for a theory both respectful of the transcendent aspect of religion and responsive to the exigencies of particular historical situations.

The contemporary coexistence of Christianity and the secular state poses the problem of how, precisely, to live as a Christian in such an independent order and bear witness to the lordship of Christ. Reist endorses J. H. Oldham's proposal that we develop "middle axioms" as guides in relating general ethical principles to concrete situations. He cites as an example of such a decision-making aid the committee report called "Relations between Church and State" submitted to the 174th General Assembly of the United Presbyterian Church, U.S.A. On the issue of religious observances in public schools, for instance, it is recommended that these schools should not be hostile to religious beliefs or favor one religion over another. Thus, specific observances should be eliminated, but ministers, rabbis, and priests should be allowed to speak in public schools for purposes other than religious indoctrination. Implementation of this and other recommendations, according to Reist, would serve the cause of "disestablishment for the sake of authentic encounter," the extrication of the church from its prevailing comfortable innocuousness in favor of a prophetic and dialectical mission to the nation.

In a new chapter, "Religious Group Conflict," Will Herberg elaborates and updates his celebrated study, *Protestant, Catholic, Jew*.[7] Group tensions are more manifest between Protestants and Catholics, he finds, than between Jews and Gentiles. The former grow out of the ongoing social change which is rapidly transforming America from a Protestant to a three-religion country, with Catholics emerging as a pivotal middle-class community. Height-

---

7 A revised edition of this book has recently been published; Gloucester, Mass.: Peter Smith, 1964.

ened tensions thus appear in the short run, but will probably yield, in the long run, to a reduction of aggravation.

Jewish-Gentile conflicts arise from the widespread conviction among Jews that they can best preserve their freedom and equality in a thoroughly secular society. Herberg thinks this "Jewish schizophrenia" of orthodoxy in private life and radical secularism in public life is going to be more and more difficult to maintain. He hopes that this will also apply to "Protestant paranoia" and "Catholic claustrophobia." The strength of our system, Herberg concludes, resides in its "pluriunity," the ability to maintain diversity in unity.

A provocative epilogue by Martin Marty notes the criticism of organized religion so frequently heard in the United States today, lists the elements of the religious settlement which minimize conflict, and weighs the assets and liabilities of conflict. In the eyes of many, he observes, the creative vitality of religion has been so dissipated that church groups are reactors to, rather than initiators of, needed social change. Believers too often settle for the false sense of security and distraction from life's sorrows which such pseudo-religion offers.

The ways in which religion minimizes conflict include: (1) a "buffer" function in the face of social change, (2) a bulwark to protect existing values, (3) a harmonizing and even quiescent role, and (4) an institutionalism which may lead to irrelevance in relation to crucial human issues.

Dr. Marty's own incisive judgments are worth pondering. Theologically, he says, religious pluralism may not be in accord with God's will, but existentially it is sure to be with us for a long time. Conflicts which arise therefrom could be minimized or eliminated by capitulation of one of the contestants, conditional surrender, compromise, coexistence, consensus through the promotion of knowledge and understanding, or by fulfillment—which can be completely achieved only beyond history. Within history, however, we might all draw more heavily on the theological resources which minimize conflict and maximize Christian fidelity and integrity. Our witness to Christ should be one of service and self-giving rather than superiority and self-seeking, in imitation of Christ's own mode of action.

The emergence of a religiously tripartite America and the growth of the urban majority have caused the gradual implementation of the ethical concept of the "equality of man." According to

Alan P. Grimes, in *Equality in America*,[8] the establishment of this principle as the basis for majority rule has been due as much to pragmatic liberalism in politics as to the imperatives of our natural-law heritage. The securing of equal religious liberty in the modern environment is largely a problem of education. Still, as the author observes, it is precisely over public policy in education that the most intense religious disputes occur. He is opposed to public funds for church schools and is not clear about the distinction between *school* and *church*. He is surely correct, however, in observing that the best safeguard for the equal exercise of religious liberty lies in the diffusion of religious power and not merely in an appeal to religious principles.

The sociological context of American church-state relations is considerably clarified by Milton M. Gordon's *Assimilation in American Life*.[9] According to his findings, the American situation is fundamentally one of *structural pluralism,* and a declining cultural pluralism. The three major religious groups and the racial and quasi-racial groups maintain separate subsocieties for various purposes. The intellectual community is the only one in American life in which people of different ethnic and religious backgrounds interact in primary group relations with considerable frequency and ease. The undesirable civic effects of structural pluralism are minimized by the fact that individuals are generally left free to select their friends and organizational affiliations on whatever basis they choose. Mr. Gordon sees this as a factor in the progressive lowering of racial and religious ghetto walls. A major challenge to American democracy is the problem of maintaining healthy subcommunities which will be, at the same time, vital contributors to an open, pluralistic society. Leaders of the major religious groups set an example in this matter by the formation of the National Conference on Religion and Race. Multiplication of local interfaith projects in areas of need further attests the effort to meet the challenge realistically.

René De Visme Williamson, professor of government at Louisiana State University, says in the preface to *Independence and Involvement*,[10] that this book is a presentation of the basic concepts of political science in the light of the Christian faith. He deals with the alleged impotence of natural and social sciences to meet the problems of survival and world peace and with the Christian con-

---

8 New York: Oxford University Press, 1964. Pp. 136. $4.00.

9 New York: Oxford University Press, 1964. Pp. 276. $5.25.

10 Baton Rouge: Louisiana State University Press, 1964. Pp. 269. $7.50.

cept of the state, of law, of civil rights and citizenship. The chapter "Separation and Stability" reveals Professor Williamson's uncompromising rejection of the radical church-state separation espoused by the Supreme Court in *McCollum*[11] and subsequent decisions. His position is based on a commitment to the Christian faith which he believes provides the best standard for analyzing church-state relations. Thus, he criticizes the 1962 *Report of the United Presbyterian Church in the U.S.A.* for its endorsement of the extreme separationism of Madison and Jefferson. It fails, too, he judges, because it uses the American Constitution, rather than the Christian faith, as a norm for determining what is a "true state." This substitution of standards, Williamson holds, is an embrace of liberal secularism which prevents a church from bearing witness to Christ through political, economic, social, and cultural life.

He marshals a strong two-pronged argument against the elimination of religion from public schools. First of all, he declares, secular education is incomplete without some reference to Christianity and its place in Western culture. Secondly, if diverse groups in a pluralistic society are to live together, they must know something about one another and something about how to handle controversial issues. The sad results of radical separationism he finds evident in the numbers of public school graduates who are religiously illiterate, morally confused, prone to low and elastic standards of conduct, and surfeited by the feeling of frustration and alienation. Although this is a reflection on the church, it is also a concern of the state which could be met, in part, by reinstating religion in public schools on an optional basis.

Williamson's case for government aid to parochial schools is based solidly on the public function argument. He can find no valid reason against public support for the teaching of subjects like English, science, history, mathematics, and foreign languages, unless one holds that everything related to religion in any way must be radically divorced from government. He is convinced that, from a Christian point of view, the main purpose of the constitutional provisions about religion is to guarantee the *freedom* of the church. In a world of competing faiths, every man must choose one and take the consequences. Williamson has made his choice and is forthright in facing the consequences.

Religious Conflict in America,[12] provides a compact and convenient collection of previously published studies on church-state

---

11 McCollum v. Board of Educ., 333 U.S. 203 (1948).
12 New York: Doubleday & Co., 1964. Pp. 231. $1.25.

matters. In an introductory chapter, "The Nature of the Conflict," the editor, Earl Raab, claims that interreligious differences tend more and more to crystallize around church-state issues. Tensions seem to be sharpened as the state extends its presence into ever widening areas of private life. What appears to be developing may more accurately be described as the "religious-secular" conflict in America instead of the church-state conflict. Selections in the volume are taken from the writings of Gerhard Lenski, Clark E. Vincent, Seymour Lipset, James S. Coleman, Will Herberg, Jaroslav Pelikan, Gustave Weigel, Emil L. Fackenheim, Sidney Hook, Leo Pfeffer, Wilber Katz, and John Courtney Murray.

Conflict is also a central concern of Alan Geyer's *Piety and Politics*,[13] a study of American Protestantism in the world arena. He argues that church-state doctrine has too often ignored the dimension of conflict *among* states in its preoccupation with domestic issues. But the church has a transnational life, and realistic discussion in this universal theater where contemporary history is being made would be better labeled "church-and-states." Like Sanders and Williamson, the author attempts to build some conceptual bridges between religion and politics. A relevant Christianity, he claims, must be the source of a continuing creative conflict between itself and the political community. Puritan-inspired "privatization" is no longer adequate in the swift current of "politicization," with almost every aspect of personal and social living a direct concern of government. Professor Geyer urges the immediate involvement of religious people in the work of opinion-forming. This will mean a restructuring of inner church resources in order to bring the cherished values of our free society to bear on the decision-making process. Groups of trained churchmen are urgently needed to carry the prophetic message of Christianity into the secular areas where the real battles of religion are being fought today. The world, says Geyer, is waiting for such men who will take upon themselves all human conflicts and, on this inner battleground with the help of Divine Power, win the greatest of victories.

Among the significant signs of our time noted by Pope John XXIII in *Pacem in Terris* are the growth of human self-consciousness and the consequent demand for limited or constitutional government to protect inalienable rights. Professor Carl J. Friedrich, in *Transcendent Justice*,[14] shows the rise of Western constitutional-

---

13 Richmond, Va.: John Knox Press, 1963. Pp. 173. $2.25.
14 Durham: Duke University Press, 1964. Pp. 116. $3.50.

ism in response to the medieval concern for human dignity, under-lines its indigenous religious and philosophical roots, and raises the question of its survival in a climate of religious decline. Co-gently argued chapters deal with medieval constitutionalism, which was based on the recognition of a higher law; Protestant constitu-tionalism, mainly in its Calvinist expression; Deist and Theist constitutionalism with the emphasis shifting from revelation to reason; and rights, liberties, and freedoms in a discussion which traces the development of human rights—from natural rights through civil liberties to social freedoms. As Friedrich points out, the emerging international community is forcing governments to give at least lip service to human rights. However formulated, this amounts to an assertion of intrinsic human dignity and the consequent right of every man to an opportunity for self-fulfill-ment. The question is whether this assertion can be maintained if the belief in man continues to be divorced from belief in God and in an order of transcendent justice.

That the future needs the past, especially the recent past, is amply demonstrated by William Lee Miller in a collection of essays on politics and morals in the 1950's, *Piety along the Potomac*.[15] Written during the decade of "attempted repose," they provide keen comment on the moral crusade of the Eisenhower years, the merchandising of government, the debating career of Richard M. Nixon, the religious revival in America, and dilemmas of foreign policy in a nuclear age. The fifties, according to the author, showed us at something like a counterfeit of our best. During the heralded religious revival, for instance, writers and preachers concentrated on formulas and techniques for achieving desired ends, such as peace of mind, security, and success. Few bothered to challenge the goals, personal or social. The interna-tional struggle was conceived simply as a war against atheistic communism, with God on our side and religion the uncritical ally of American purposes. The revivalist heritage with its illusion of American omnipotence stimulated enthusiasm and passion but little wisdom and less patience. This was but a pale foreshadowing of the fanatic frenzy of contemporary patriots of the radical right.

Mr. Miller reminds his readers that politics is the "art of the possible," that it is a serious, worthy, and important activity, an honorable and necessary part of a community's quest for justice and the common good.

15 Boston: Houghton Mifflin Co., 1964. Pp. 236. $4.00.

Political Morality,[16] a volume by Jeremiah Newman, professor of sociology in Maynooth, Ireland, deals with the origin of political authority, modern war and pacifism, ethics of conquest, revolt and self-determination, church and state, religious toleration, democracy, and a Christian constitution. On church-state doctrine, the author espouses the view that, ideally speaking, the state should accord special recognition to the Catholic Church, the true church. This need not, he says, take the form of constitutional establishment but ought to include whatever the people's spiritual interests require. The presentation is a striking illustration of the abstract, categorical, deductive, non-historical approach. No attention is given to the development of doctrine, which was unmistakably set forth in the teaching of John XXIII. Says Newman: "The demands of the Church of Christ on the State are fundamentally doctrinal; they stem from the uncompromising source of theological truth" (p. 240).

Detailed criticism is leveled against the thought of Jacques Maritain and Father John Courtney Murray, S.J. The former is accused of excluding from consideration, in church-state matters, the "absolute ideal," of denying its "practical relevancy" and its consistency and "validity as a concept" (p. 267). Father Murray is indicted for using a historically oriented approach. A few of the specific points at issue are worth noting. Newman defends the competence of the public power to extend special care to the *true* religion. Murray prefers to limit its competence to the safeguarding of religious liberty, both individual and institutional. Newman insists on the primacy of theological considerations in church-state relations. Murray believes that the constitutional question is as primary as the theological-moral question. Newman seeks to clarify the concepts of "thesis" and "hypothesis," which, he claims, have been much misunderstood. Murray abandons these categories, since they are based on the abstract notion of the exclusive rights of truth. He prefers to focus on the human person with his legitimate demands for individual and corporate freedom under a limited government. Newman insists that Leo XIII's teaching calls for more than mere freedom from state interference for the church. Included should be submission to the moral judgment of the church. Murray refuses to accord to Leo the final word on church-state doctrine. He points, in addition, to Pius XII's juridical concept of the state as an advance over Leo's ethical notion, and to John XXIII's affirmation of the institution of religious freedom.

---

16 Dublin: Scepter Publishers Ltd., 1963. Pp. 459. $6.25.

The implications of these contributions are indeed a genuine and praiseworthy development of Catholic doctrine.

Fundamentally, the difference between Newman and the position he criticizes is between the abstract, categorical mind-set and a more flexible historical consciousness. The dichotomy is profound and evidently irreconcilable.

Highlights of the 16th National Conference on Church and State conducted by POAU, can be found in *We Hold These Truths*.[17] Introducing the pamphlet, Executive Director Glenn Archer pinpoints the current threats to the absolute separation of church and state his organization was founded to safeguard. He finds the biggest potential danger in the growing ecumenical spirit which tends to soft-pedal interfaith differences and nourish the ambition of religious leaders in social and political causes. At the same time, he favors an ecumenism which might eradicate the Catholic teachings he finds unpalatable, such as the rules of the Index, promises in mixed marriages, and restrictions on common worship. He summons Protestant leaders to intelligent and courageous action whenever religious freedom is threatened.

Associate Director C. Stanley Lowell reports on the Vatican Council and religious freedom from his vantage as an accredited correspondent. The great failure of the second session, as he sees it, was the refusal to budge on church-state matters. In his judgment, too much is at stake for the church in its complex of concordat arrangements, financial subsidies, and preferred status to do anything more than reiterate the right of freedom of conscience.

The real significance of the Council, Lowell says, is the complete change of strategy adopted by the Roman Catholic Church in its attitude to non-Catholics. Instead of trying to widen the chasm, it is seeking to minimize it. This raises the disastrous possibility that all churches might come under one big ecclesiastical tent.

POAU's endemic anti-Catholic bias is evident in these and the other contributions by F. Gerald Ensley, Luther A. Smith, Penrose St. Amant, H. B. Sissel, James E. Wood, Jr., and Franklin C. Salisbury.

CONSTITUTIONAL LAW STUDIES

Religion and American Constitutions[18] is a superb example of the "open-mind" as it comes to grips with recurring problems

---

[17] Washington, D.C.: P.O.A.U., 1963. Pp. 59. $1.00.
[18] Evanston: Northwestern University Press, 1964. Pp. 114. $3.50.

of church and state. Professor Wilber Katz of the University of Wisconsin has consistently acknowledged the development of his own thought in accordance with the changing realities to which the First Amendment clauses are addressed. The essays in this book comprise the 1963 Rosenthal Lectures, Northwestern University School of Law, and cover "Religion and the Conflict of Freedoms"; "Public Education—the Establishment of American Religion?" "Religious Schools—the Price of Freedom?" "Epilogue: Neutrality as of June 1963."

Professor Katz considers the neutrality principle the core doctrine, best suited to prevent both government sponsorship and government restraint of religion. It is interesting to compare his explanation with that of Professor Philip B. Kurland in *Religion and the Law*.[19] The latter, in applying the principle which prohibits government "classification in terms of religion either to confer a benefit or to impose a burden," tends to ignore the fact that many people *are* organized on the basis of religion. The functions which such groups perform may or may not be "religious." To exclude them automatically from either benefit or burden might inhibit the free exercise of religion to which they are entitled.

As Katz sees it, the neutrality principle does not require the state to ignore religion, as witnessed by Supreme Court decisions dealing with religious exemptions from Sunday closing laws, military service, and other obligations. Classification on the basis of religion in these cases serves to protect religious freedom in those areas where the government has power to legislate. An ever expanding state activity makes it more and more difficult to safeguard this freedom under a policy of strict separation. Hence the necessity of positive government protection which may appear to some people as unjustifiable "aid."

Attacks on the neutrality principle by advocates of non-preferential-aid-to-religion stem from an interpretation of the First Amendment which sees it as outlawing only an "established church." Careful consideration of the congressional history of the establishment clause leads Katz to the cautious conclusion that all we really know of the original meaning is that Congress was forbidden to disestablish as well as to establish religion. He notes, significantly, that under the neutrality principle, the state is a

---

19 KURLAND, RELIGION AND THE LAW: OF CHURCH AND STATE AND THE SUPREME COURT (1962).

secular entity, incompetent in religious matters but not, therefore, unaware of or hostile to the religious allegiance or lack of religious allegiance of its members.

The alternative attack by the strict separationists is judged unacceptable because of its cost in terms of religious liberty. Applying the separationist view to the problem of religion in public schools, he says that it is not the function of state schools to teach religious doctrine or promote religious worship, *or* rigorously to exclude all references to religion from public school programs. Difficult as it may be to work out, some information should be presented about the main religious and non-religious beliefs.

On a related topic and in agreement with Arthur E. Sutherland and Mark DeWolfe Howe, Dr. Katz concludes that religious schools need not be counted out of a general federal aid program, even though this may entail indirect help to religious teaching and practice. Encouraged by the inclusion of religious liberty on the agenda of the Vatican Council and by doctrinal writings of Catholic scholars, he says: "Ten years ago I thought that the ambiguity of the Catholic stand on religious freedom might be sufficient reason for the withholding of equality in programs of aid to education. Today, I am certain that it is not" (p. 85).

This calm, comprehensive, and comprehending discussion of religion and the public order contrasts markedly with Charles E. Rice's bitterly critical *The Supreme Court and Public Prayer*.[20] The author, professor at Fordham University Law School, reaches a number of unwarranted conclusions from inadequate premises. For example, he states categorically that the 1962 and 1963 prayer decisions of the Supreme Court were wrong. The result, he insists, is the denial of what was conceded until that time, namely, that the United States Constitution is based on "a profession that, in fact, there is a God and there is a divine law to which men and nations are subject" (p. ix).

Professor Rice deplores what he terms the Court's erection of agnosticism into the official American public religion. He thinks, moreover, that it severely handicaps the United States in its current momentous struggle on behalf of freedom against the atheistic Communist tyranny. Enactment of a constitutional amendment along the lines of the Becker proposal he sees as the best way to restore the American birthright and rearm the country in the face of a powerful enemy.

20 New York: Fordham University Press, 1964. Pp. 202. $5.00.

For Rice, a disturbing aspect of the school prayer decision is the notion of government neutrality between theistic and non-theistic beliefs. He prefers to think of the First Amendment as allowing government to acknowledge God's existence, while maintaining impartiality among theistic creeds. He claims that the "Court has ordained as a constitutional imperative that the agnostic approach is true, and, therefore, that the theistic is wrong" (p. 85). The book abounds in such single-line polemics. Satisfactory treatment of the complex question of American church-state relations requires greater sensitivity to the constitutional, legal, and human aspects of the problem that Daniel Callahan called a "briar patch" through which we must cautiously and skillfully make our way, bit by bit.

In Rice's mind, the Supreme Court has clearly misinterpreted the First Amendment and the only feasible way to restore its real meaning is to amend the Constitution. Since public apathy is the main obstacle to this desirable goal, all true Americans, he says, should join the drive for an appropriate amendment. Unfortunately, the author's antagonistic presentation is likely to harm rather than help his rightful concern about the erosion of America's religious heritage.

In *The First Amendment*,[21] William H. Marnell makes a strong case against the Supreme Court's doctrine of absolute separation. He contends that the prevailing doctrinaire interpretation of the establishment clause seriously endangers the free exercise of religion by large numbers of Americans. Truth, justice, and freedom require that one clause be accommodated to the other. That such is not the case at present is the logical conclusion of a clear, forthright, and thought-provoking argument. To acknowledge this, one need not, however, agree with all of Dr. Marnell's points. In spite of well-documented evidence to the contrary, he is quite definite that an "establishment of religion in the historic sense is the creation of an established church" (p. xi). Consequently, he is not pleased with the dilution which the expression has undergone in the course of its expansion. The American principle of church-state separation, he insists, was a practical arrangement in the interest of religious peace, not a product of secularism. Thus, he is persuaded that the Supreme Court has misread history in attributing to the "wall of separation" an original position in the American experience.

---

21 New York: Doubleday & Co., 1964. Pp. 247. $4.50.

Two phases in the developing pattern of American church-state relations are the gradual disestablishment in the states and the application of the First Amendment to the states by way of the Fourteenth. Dr. Marnell is not opposed to the latter as long as minority religious rights are protected. This principle, he claims, was vindicated in *Meyer v. Nebraska*[22] and *Pierce v. Society of Sisters.*[23] Until 1947, in fact, the Court regularly drew a distinction among the people, the state, and the church. It saw no violation of the Fourteenth Amendment in the type of state aid that benefits the people and the state, and, only incidentally, the church. *Everson*[24] marked the beginning of a new doctrine which is shifting the emphasis from prohibition against an *establishment* of religion to prohibition against an establishment of *religion*. This dangerous debarment of government service to religion, finds its most recent expression in the prayer and Bible-reading decisions. *The First Amendment* was written in response to this disturbing trend in order to promulgate the author's conviction that there is and ought to be a deep and often disregarded relationship between the Christian church and the American state.

The role of religion in public education and tax aid for parochial schools are the concerns of Father Joseph Costanzo, S.J., in *This Nation under God.*[25] He believes that public schools should transmit the American religious heritage as that heritage is embodied in our basic national documents. He holds, also, that private and church-related schools have a valid place in the American educational system and should be so recognized in any congressional aid policy. His premise is that American democracy is more than a process, that its roots are primarily religious, and that its authentic endurance depends upon the reassertion of these theological and moral foundations. He asserts unequivocally that the no-establishment clause of the First Amendment is instrumental to the free exercise counterpart. Thus, he condemns as not really neutral all attempts to exorcise religion from public schools or to exclude church-related schools from federal aid programs. National educational policy should be freely determined, he says, by the elected representatives of the people and not precluded from debate by a prior assumption about constitutional prohibitions.

Father Costanzo is exigent in urging believers to overcome their

---

22 262 U.S. 390 (1923).

23 268 U.S. 510 (1925).

24 Everson v. Board of Educ., 330 U.S. 1 (1947).

25 New York: Herder & Herder, 1964. Pp. 448. $7.50.

lethargy and take vigorous action in behalf of their spiritual heritage. Otherwise, he questions the survival of American political freedom with its panoply of religious and civil liberties. Positions are sometimes overstated and the thinking not as carefully nuanced as that of Professor Katz. There is not much point at this stage in our history, for instance, of assigning to non-theists a secondary place in American society or of easily identifying the secular with the godless or antireligious. There is, however, the intractable problem of achieving in practice a just balance between the no-establishment and free exercise clauses of the First Amendment. Father Costanzo's contribution provides ample material for thought and action.

The Wall between Church and State,[26] edited by Dallin H. Oaks, is a collection of essays whose prime purpose is to promote dialogue rather than diatribe on the currently crucial church-state issues: aid to parochial schools, tax exemption for religious activities, the religious factor in the adoption of children, religion in public schools. The arguments are not new, but it is helpful to have opposite points of view ably presented within one book.

Participants in the original discussion, sponsored by the University of Chicago Law School, include Robert F. Drinan, S.J., Harold E. Fey, Murray A. Gordon, William Gorman, Robert M. Hutchins, Paul G. Kauper, Philip B. Kurland, and Monrad G. Paulsen. In a fine introduction, Dallin Oaks indicates that the various positions represented in the assembled papers stem from disagreement about the proper relationship between the free exercise and the establishment clauses of the First Amendment. Should "no establishment" give place to freedom in case of conflict? Or is the paramount aim to avoid an establishment, with freedom one of the consequences thereof? Again, should the two phrases be read together as prohibiting government from making any classification in terms of religion?

Mr. Fey believes that freedom of religion can be secured only by the most scrupulous care in keeping the institutions of church and state separate. Mr. Hutchins sees very little future for the "wall of separation," since he holds that the object of the First Amendment is to guarantee and promote religious freedom, including freedom from religion. Professor Kurland supports the neutral principle which prevents government from using religion

---

26 Chicago: University of Chicago Press, 1963. Pp. 179. $6.75.

as a standard for action or for inaction. Mr. Gorman argues against
the use of the no-establishment clause to protect irreligion. Father
Drinan argues that private (including parochial) schools are
charged with a public responsibility and thus could qualify for
a share in public funds. Mr. Gordon is convinced of the uncon-
stitutionality of aid to parochial schools, because the services they
render are performed or controlled by a religious institution and
facilitate the propagation of religious doctrine. Thoughtful reading of this book will probably lead to agreement with Mr. Oaks
that we are not yet ready as a people to decide answers to constitutional questions across the board in church-state matters.

RELIGION AND EDUCATION

Paul Blanshard's *Religion and the Schools*[27] provides useful and detailed information about the 1962 and 1963 prayer and
Bible-reading decisions of the Supreme Court. These are viewed
as incidental to the larger American controversy over the place of
religion in the educational process and the even larger issue of the
alleged "world policy of the rulers of the Roman Catholic Church"
to get public subsidies for their schools. Although considerably
more accurate than earlier works, this book suffers from the same
rigid, legalistic mind-set which prevents the author from grasping
any but the juridical aspect of the Catholic Church. The vibrant,
dynamic element which makes it a living thing escapes him. He
readily acknowledges the Supreme Court's right to move beyond
the founding fathers in interpreting the Constitution, but denies
any such prerogative to interpreters of canon law.

A staunch separationist, Mr. Blanshard, predictably, opposes the
granting of tax funds to church-related schools. Posing the issue in
terms of a "Catholic versus American battle," he pictures world
Catholicism as monolithically committed to periodic or permanent treasury raids. If they should succeed in the present federal
aid drive, he foresees two serious social consequences: an increase
of religious narrow-mindedness and the weakening of public
schools with the possible sectarian fragmentation of the whole
educational pattern. In contrast to Professor Rice, Mr. Blanshard
thinks a constitutional amendment the *least* acceptable solution to
the controversy, since it might alter the basic policy of church-

---

[27] Boston: Beacon Press, 1963. Pp. 265. $4.95.

state separation in education. He considers, instead, four intermediate compromise adjustments: (1) released time away from
public school buildings; (2) dismissed time; (3) shared time; and
(4) moral guidance without religious indoctrination. These might
result in some incidental status for religion in public schools, or
indirect financial help to church schools, but would not violate the
Supreme Court's interpretation of the First Amendment.

Mr. Blanshard allows that religion should "suffuse, inspire and
inform the whole body politic," but the isolation from government, which he requires, would impair the exercise of religious
freedom through which this might be achieved.

Federal Aid and Catholic Schools,[28] edited by Daniel Callahan,
treats the question of federal aid and the growing concern about
the quality of Catholic education along with the debate over the
wisdom of maintaining the system in its present form. The editor
feels that some type of aid to religious schools is feasible, legal, and
desirable, but counsels Catholics to self-restraint in the use of
political force to attain this end. This advice is not heeded by
groups like Citizens for Educational Freedom who base their
tactics on the thought of Father Virgil Blum, S.J., a contributor to
the book. His argument is logical and legally persuasive but posed
in terms that provoke opposition rather than enlist support.

Father Neil McCluskey, S.J., feels that the church is overcom-
mitted at the elementary level and should be willing to experiment
with co-operative ventures such as shared time and renovated released-time programs.

Father Robert Francoeur raises searching questions about the
place of parochial schools in the total mission of the church. Are
we concentrating too exclusively on children, and in too restricted
an area (Catholic schools), neglecting adults and the growing number of students on secular campuses? Can we continue to ignore
the fact that the sociological milieu and the need which brought
the system into existence are yielding to an adult-centered church
with the mission to teach all?

Philip Scharper invites Catholics to the twofold effort suggested
by their present diaspora situation: support of federal aid, whether
or not parochial schools are included; and attention to lifting the
cloud of religious illiteracy from public education, while respecting the delicate demands of religious pluralism.

Dean M. Kelley of the National Council of Churches of Christ

---

28 Baltimore: Helicon Press, 1964. Pp. 160. $3.95.

argues strongly against federal aid to parochial schools, on the ground that they are primarily *religious* institutions. Protestants, on principle, tend to oppose tax aid for church-related schools, while Catholics claim a share in public funds for equally valid motives of conscience. Recognizing this impasse, Dr. Kelley is quite willing to consider such compromise measures as federal income tax deduction for parochial school tuition and the shared-time proposal.

Milton Himmelfarb shows that Jewish objection to federal aid for parochial schools stems from a historical experience of anti-Semitism under a system of Christian dominance. Jewish commitment to a non-religious public school is understandably firm, since it has not only protected the Jew but enabled him to become a successful and respected part of American culture.

The essays in this volume can help us avoid the danger of fashioning public educational policies on "old myths" rather than on new realities. They suggest the folly of setting the sacred in opposition to the secular and identifying parochial schools with the former and public schools with the latter.

Religion in the Public Schools,[29] published by the American Association of School Administrators, is a well-modulated, forward-looking treatment of an old problem in its newly emerging aspects. A Commission on Religion in the Public Schools was mandated by the executive committee of AASA to examine the effect of recent Supreme Court decisions on religious practices in public schools. Focusing on the main thrust of the arguments in the cases from *Everson* to *Schempp,* the authors note that, in the Court's judgment, violation of the free exercise clause must be predicated on coercion, while the establishment clause need not be so accompanied. The neutrality required of public schools should not be antireligious or non-religious, but *constructive,* in the sense of providing an "environment in which practices and values that are rooted in the homes and churches can flourish" (p. 28). Indispensable to such a policy, the report says, are recognition in the curriculum of the impact of religion, individual and institutional, on the course of history; support for the acknowledged wisdom of personal commitment to something higher than self; and inculcation of an understanding of the great purposes of our Constitution. Accommodation to contemporary American pluralism is a challenging problem which admits of no perfect solution. But, says

29 Washington, D.C.: American Association of School Administrators, 1964. Pp. 67. $2.00.

the report, a false neutralism which ignores religion or substitutes a non-theist humanism fails in public responsibility. The commission is confident that the American public will find a way to preserve the institution of religion, which serves a diverse society so faithfully. Its report provides excellent suggestions for so doing.

In *Federal Aid to Private Schools*,[30] Father Leo Ward, C.S.C., brings the record up to date on the changing climate of opinion regarding the possibility of such aid. Cited as supporting evidence of a more open attitude are Robert M. Hutchins, Professor Francis W. Rogers of Harvard University, the prominent Protestant periodical *Christianity and Crisis*, and the liberal *New Republic*.

Father Ward's argument is five-pronged: (1) that the private, church-related school is an indigenous American institution which has always been state-aided; (2) that there is collaboration and interaction between church and state in many areas; (3) that a single, monolithic educational system would be un-American; (4) that to pressure church-related schools into mediocrity by withholding financial aid would be an infringement of religious liberty; and (5) that the United States ought to work out a unified pluralistic educational system which would give all children an opportunity to develop to their full potential. In order to develop national leaders who work with both public and private schools, he suggests more released-time and shared-time programs and a "creative inter-group peace corps" (p. 185). As a practical, pluralistic first step, he urges the formation of a representative advisory national school board to initiate studies and practices which would encourage excellence in education for *all* children and youth. Surely he is right in pointing to the quality of education which is available to all, as the "radical" issue to which Americans should address their best efforts.

Arthur Frommer has provided an extremely useful source book in *The Bible and the Public Schools*.[31] Included are documents dealing with the historical background of the First Amendment, and the entire text of the Supreme Court opinions in the *Murray*[32] and *Schempp*[33] cases of June, 1963. Editor Frommer frankly acknowledges a bias in favor of the decision in these cases which he calls "one of the great landmarks in the history of religious freedom" (p. 4).

30 Westminster, Md.: Newman Press, 1964. Pp. 222. $3.95.

31 New York: Liberal Press, 1963. Pp. 190. $1.25.

32 Murray v. Curlett, 374 U.S. 203 (1963).

33 School Dist. of Abington Township v. Schempp, 374 U.S. 203 (1963).

HISTORICAL ASPECTS

The history and evolving church-state structure of the unique American experience are the subject of Leo Pfeffer's revised and abridged edition of Anson Phelps Stokes's three-volume classic, *Church and State in the United States*.[34] The content of the topically arranged chapters is brought up to date and one entire section devoted to clear and cogent summaries of all Supreme Court decisions on church and state. Pfeffer cites, approvingly, the Supreme Court return, after the *Zorach*[35] retreat, to a broad interpretation of the establishment clause which imposes governmental neutrality between religion and non-religion, as well as among religions. Categorized as defending a narrow interpretation are those associated with Roman Catholicism and the Catholic Church, whose doctrine as late as 1964 characterized Church-State separation as "unfortunate' " (p. 101). Pfeffer does not mention the source of this "doctrine," nor does he indicate that separation" can be extreme or moderate and geared to the free exercise of religion. Only the extreme variety would be considered unfortunate by most Catholics.

Pfeffer acknowledges substantial agreement with the general conclusions of Stokes's study, although his own predilection is probably more strictly separationist. The updating and condensation make the book a valuable contribution to church-state literature.

For all those interested in separation of church and state, Donald L. Kinzer's *An Episode in Anti-Catholicism*,[36] a full-length history of the American Protective Association, provides a comprehensive study of one form of bigotry. The story serves as a reminder of the deep roots of this phenomenon in American life and of the persistence of the central issues: Catholic power—with its threat to American democracy; religion in the public schools; government aid to parochial schools. Catholics might ponder a fact brought out in this book, that the APA and anti-Catholicism were strongest in the states with the largest Catholic population.

Indicative of the heightened interest in a historical approach to American interfaith relations is the 1964 paperback edition of

---

[34] New York: Harper & Row, 1964. Pp. 660. $12.50.
[35] Zorach v. Clauson, 343 U.S. 306 (1952).
[36] Seattle: University of Washington Press, 1964. Pp. 342. $6.50.

Ray Allen Billington's *The Protestant Crusade, 1800–1860.*[37] First published in 1938, the book is a standard source for the study of American nativism. Understanding of, if not sympathy for, its present progeny should be facilitated by this handy volume.

A revised and enlarged edition of Joseph Blau's *Cornerstones of Religious Freedom in America*[38] traces through selected documents, and the comments of the editor outline, the struggle for religious freedom in this country. For Mr. Blau, religious freedom seems to be synonymous with absolute separation of government from religion. To maintain an unbreached wall of separation he calls all men of good will to the next major battleground in the perennial struggle—the effort to obtain public funds for religious schools. A defensive and polemic tone mar an otherwise valuable collection of documents which have gone into the building of religious freedom in America.

CONCLUSION

The impressive number of worthwhile books published in the past year indicates the laudable and growing concern of religious people to make a contribution to society's needs and desires. Recent studies of American life reveal the special characteristics of our structural pluralism and its changing trends. An activist Supreme Court has taken the lead in expanding the constitutionally protected area of personal freedom for believers and non-believers. Institutional rights of religiously organized groups are ambiguous, particularly in relation to government. Some writers think religion has failed in its social responsibilities and ought to be written off as a meaningful force in the future. Others, convinced that religion can stem the tide of social and moral decay, want to give it more prominence in public affairs. The most perceptive realize that society is increasingly secular and religion's influence must be channeled through this medium in ways that respect the authenticity of the natural. All agree that ghetto walls are doomed and the sooner they come down the better. While acknowledging the creative function of tension, intelligent efforts are increasingly directed to intergroup dialogue where personal experience can be most effective in promoting the co-operation necessary to build a genuinely *human* social order.

---

37 Chicago: Quadrangle Paperbacks, 1964. Pp. 514. $2.65.
38 New York: Harper Torchbooks, 1964. Pp. 344. $2.25.

THE YEAR IN REVIEW
SEPTEMBER, 1963—SEPTEMBER, 1964

JUDICIAL DEVELOPMENTS

RELIGION IN THE PUBLIC SCHOOLS

The Supreme Court decisions in the *Schempp*[1] and *Murray*[2] cases prohibiting prayers and devotional Bible reading in the public schools encountered considerable popular resistance, which was frequently encouraged or supported by state or local officials.[3] There was even resistance in some state and lower federal courts as efforts were made to restrict the two decisions closely to their facts and to view the facts narrowly.

The Florida Supreme Court indicated it would not extend the Court's decisions to somewhat similar cases unless clearly directed to do so. Soon after the *Schempp* and *Murray* cases the United States Supreme Court reversed and remanded for further consideration a Florida decision upholding a state statute requiring the Bible to be read in the public schools.[4] The Florida decision that was remanded had also permitted regular recitation of the Lord's Prayer and the presentation of baccalaureate services.

On remand the Florida high court decided that the state Bible-reading statute was intended to promote primarily secular goals[5]

---

[1] School Dist. of Abington Township v. Schempp, 374 U.S. 203 (1963).

[2] Murray v. Curlett, 374 U.S. 203 (1963).

[3] See *infra* pp. 243–51.

[4] Chamberlain v. Dade County Bd. of Pub. Instruction, 143 So.2d 21 (Fla. 1962), *judgment vacated and case remanded,* 374 U.S. 487 (1963).

[5] 160 So.2d 97 (Fla. 1964).

because, when it was first enacted, the purpose of the statute as stated in the preamble was to foster student morality. Because of this expressly secular statutory purpose, which the court apparently found applicable to the recitation of the Lord's Prayer as well, the state court concluded that the decisions dealing with the situations in Maryland and Pennsylvania were not in point. The court also said that it was confused by the several opinions in the *Schempp* and *Murray* cases and did not see a "clear course" to follow. It left to the United States Supreme Court any "enlargement" of its earlier decisions, particularly since the Florida court was convinced that the establishment clause of the Constitution was never intended to prohibit the practices of voluntary prayer and Bible reading.

At this point the Florida high court also reviewed three other issues that had been raised by plaintiffs concerning the propriety of baccalaureate services, a religious census of pupils attending public schools, and an alleged religious test for teachers in that applicants for teaching positions are asked if they believe in God and promotions depend in part on religious attitudes. It dismissed all these complaints because of lack of standing. Since the plaintiffs were parents of students not yet ready to graduate, it held that they would not be adversely affected by baccalaureate exercises. Also, since none of their children had been questioned in the religious census, which the court noted was taken only to determine attendance over religious holidays, and since no schoolteacher or applicant had brought suit, none of the plaintiffs could complain about the other two issues.

This decision was again appealed to the Supreme Court, which reversed the rulings allowing Bible reading and the recitation of prayers on the basis of the *Schempp* and *Murray* cases, without hearing any argument.[6] The other three questions raised were dismissed because they were not "properly presented" federal questions. The Court then cited some of its statements in *Asbury Hospital v. Cass County*[7] to the effect that the Supreme Court will not decide hypothetical questions regarding laws that have not yet been applied to persons challenging them.

Mr. Justice Douglas, joined by Mr. Justice Black, dissented. They believed that the appellants had standing as taxpayers to challenge the three practices. They would nonetheless have dis-

6 377 U.S. 402 (1964).
7 326 U.S. 207, 213–14 (1945).

missed the questions concerning baccalaureate services and the religious census for not presenting substantial federal problems and would have restricted argument to the religious test issue.

In contrast to the Florida high court other state and lower federal district courts were prompt to enjoin prescribed prayers and devotional Bible reading in the public schools. A three-judge federal court enjoined these practices in the Delaware public schools.[8] The State Board of Education had directed school administrators and teachers to continue the practices pursuant to a state statute, justifying them on the grounds that they were of a cultural, educational, and moral nature. The court, however, did "not entertain the slightest doubt" that the practices were of a religious nature in view of evidence concerning the reverential attitude of the pupils and teachers while participating in them. An Idaho federal district court enjoined such practices in that state,[9] as did the state courts in New Jersey[10] and Massachusetts[11] in suits brought by the Attorneys General of the respective states.

In cases involving practices in the public schools somewhat different from the prayers and Bible reading in *Schempp* and *Murray,* the lower courts were not at all ready to extend the reach of those decisions. A federal district judge for the Eastern District of New York ruled that the *Schempp* and *Murray* cases did not prohibit the offering of prayers during the school day[12] when this results from "a voluntary desire of the children without any coercion or pressure being brought" against them.[13] The court quoted extensively from the majority opinion in the *Zorach*[14] case, including the passage that implies that prayers in Congress and official references to the Almighty by public officers or in governmental proceedings and documents are proper. The court enjoined the principal of a public school from interfering with the common recitation of grace by kindergarten pupils and dismissed the case on a summary judgment without determining whether the children had originally learned the particular prayers from their teachers.

---

8 Johns v. Allen, 231 F.Supp. 852 (D. Del. 1964).

9 Adams v. Engelking, 232 F.Supp. 666 (D. Idaho 1964)

10 Sills v Board of Educ. of Hawthorne, 200 A.2d 615 (N.J. 1964).

11 Attorney General v. School Comm. of No. Brookfield, 199 N.E.2d 553 (Mass. 1964).

12 Stein v. Oshinsky, 224 F.Supp. 757 (E.D. N.Y. 1964).

13 *Id.* at 759.

14 Zorach v. Clauson, 343 U.S. 306 (1952).

In New York the Court of Appeals passed up an opportunity to explain why the *Schempp* and *Murray* decisions do not prohibit references to the Deity in official versions of the pledge of allegiance to the flag. It affirmed without opinion the dismissal of a petition seeking to compel the Commissioner of Education to eliminate the words "under God" in the form of the pledge of allegiance which he recommends for use in the public schools.[15] The petition had been dismissed in 1957 by the trial court,[16] which had then taken the position that the establishment clause forbids a "State Religion" but not a "Religious State." To support its views it cited the language of the *Zorach* released-time case: "We are a religious people whose institutions presuppose a Supreme Being."[17] It also relied on the many official references to the Deity in public life, such as the conclusion of the presidential oath of office: "So help me God."

This dismissal had been upheld by the Appellate Division of the Supreme Court in 1960,[18] prior to both the Regents' Prayer and the Bible-reading cases. The Appellate Division had also relied on the *Zorach* case, referring to the principle of governmental accommodation of religious interests in order to avoid state hostility to religion. Plaintiffs filed a petition for certiorari with the United States Supreme Court when the Court of Appeals in turn upheld the dismissal of the complaint, but the petition was denied.[19]

A new York lower court interpreted the Bible-reading cases as not prohibiting religious displays on public school premises.[20] In dismissing a complaint asking for a declaration that school boards have no authority to permit the erection or display on public school premises of any symbol of a deity or semi-deity belonging to any religion, a New York trial court said: "To grant the broad relief requested by the plaintiffs . . . would, in the opinion of the court, be tantamount to sanctioning judicially a policy of non-recognition of God in the public schools resulting in a denial that religion has played any part in the formulation of the moral standards of the community."[21] The court reasoned that the state and secular society require moral qualities, such as fortitude, loyalty,

15 Lewis v. Allen, 200 N.E.2d 767 (N.Y. 1964).

16 159 N.Y.S.2d 807 (Sup. Ct. 1957).

17 Zorach v. Clauson, 343 U.S. 306, 313 (1952).

18 207 N.Y.S.2d 862 (App. Div. 1960).

19 379 U.S. 923 (1964).

20 Lawrence v. Buchmueller, 243 N.Y.S.2d 87 (Sup. Ct. 1963).

21 *Id.* at 88.

honesty, decency, and compassion and that the majority of men
have found the moral law rooted in theistic beliefs. This being so
the court found that in order to fulfill the function of fostering
moral qualities in future citizens the schools must give some
"recognition of the possibility, at least, that God is the fountain-
head from which moral principles spring"; otherwise the schools
would become advocates of a "pragmatic morality."[22]

The immediate matter in controversy concerned the defendant
school board's action authorizing a group of taxpayers to erect a
Nativity scene at their own expense on the grounds of a public
school at a time when it was not in session. Since the plaintiffs did
not advert to any way in which their religious liberty had been infringed, the court treated the case as raising issues only under the
prohibition against establishment. Relying on the fact that the
board did no more than accede to a request to use school grounds,
the court distinguished the *Schempp* and *Murray* decisions on the
ground that those cases were concerned with "active involvement"
by the government with religious exercises whereas the instant case
involved only "passive accommodation of religion."[23]

RELIGIOUS RIGHTS OF INDIVIDUALS

Two very interesting cases involving religious rights resulted in decisions compelling adult Jehovah's Witnesses to submit
to court-ordered blood transfusions in spite of their religious objections.

In *Application of President & Directors of Georgetown College*[24]
the officials of a hospital sought a court order authorizing them to
administer blood transfusions to a patient, a Jehovah's Witness
who was bleeding to death from an ulcer. The patient, the mother
of a seven-month-old child, refused to consent to the transfusions
because of her religious convictions. Her husband also refused to
agree to them. When a district judge of the federal court for the
District of Columbia denied their request for an order, the hospital
officials immediately sought a reversal from Circuit Judge J. Skelly
Wright. Even though no suit had been formally brought by the
filing of a complaint, nor had any appeal been perfected, Judge

---

22 *Id.* at 89.

23 *Id.* at 90–91.

24 331 F.2d 1000 (D.C. Cir. 1964), *rehearing denied,* 331 F.2d 1010 (1964), *cert.
denied,* 377 U.S. 978 (1964).

Wright decided to hear the case and to act because of the emergency. He ordered the transfusions.

In an opinion subsequently delivered he was careful to state that his decision did not resolve the underlying issue of whether a person could be required to undergo life-saving medical treatment contrary to his religious scruples. He sought only to justify the action of granting a temporary order pending appeal. He viewed his decision as one essentially designed to preserve the status quo in an emergency, as he put it, so that the case would not be mooted without appeal because of the woman's death. But he did go on to say that even a temporary emergency order was not justified unless there was a likelihood of the action's being upheld on appeal.

Thereupon Judge Wright gave a number of reasons why he believed his order would be sustained on appeal. First, he emphasized that the patient was in critical condition at the time the transfusions were needed and was not legally competent to decide about them. Therefore, he concluded the court could in effect assume the responsibility of her guardianship and order transfusions contrary to her husband's wishes. To support this view the judge cited the generally recognized principle that a guardian can be appointed to consent to necessary blood transfusions in the case of a minor whose parents refuse to do so on religious grounds.

Second, he referred to the state's interest in seeing that parents do not voluntarily abandon their children, as, in his view, the patient was about to do in this case.

Third, he took the position that the case did not involve interference with religious beliefs concerning the value or necessity of self-destruction, since the patient wanted to live. He did pause to consider what principles would control if the case had in fact presented a conflict between society's demands and those of a religion that called for self-destruction. He pointed out that suicide was generally regarded as a crime and that religious liberty could not excuse criminal conduct. But he did go on to conclude that even if one viewed the instant case as presenting such a basic conflict, the answer was not clear, inasmuch as there was some doubt whether suicide was a crime in the District of Columbia.

Fourth, the judge pointed out that the hospital officials were not attempting to interfere with the freedom of just any citizen who they believed required medical treatment. They were trying to save the life of a patient, a person to whom they owed both moral and legal obligations. For failure to give proper care the hospital would be exposed to the risk of both civil and criminal liability. Judge Wright then seemed to imply that the interest of the hospital, and of society generally, in seeing that the patient obtained treatment necessary to save her life outweighed her religious objections, particularly because her beliefs merely prevented her from consenting to the transfusions. The judge reasoned that if the law undertook to order them without her consent, it would not involve sacrifice of her religious scruples.

Judge Wright concluded his opinion with these words:

> The final, and compelling, reason for granting the emergency writ was that a life hung in the balance. There was no time for research and reflection. Death could have mooted the cause in a matter of minutes, if action were not taken to preserve the *status quo*. To refuse to act, only to find later that the law required action, was a risk I was unwilling to accept. I determined to act on the side of life.[25]

After the patient had recovered, she filed a petition to have Judge Wright's order reconsidered and set aside by the court en banc. The petition was denied per curiam without any opinion. Judge Washington wrote a concurring opinion to point out that such a denial did not necessarily imply agreement with the action of the single judge. It simply meant that a majority of the judges did not believe the full court should consider the merits of the case, and this could be for a variety of reasons. The reason Judge Washington gave for his vote to deny rehearing was that the case had become moot when the patient had left the hospital because Judge Wright's order had expired at that time.

Four judges disagreed with the majority and would have dismissed rather than denied the petition for rehearing, on the ground that Judge Wright never had jurisdiction to grant the order in the first place. Judge Miller urged this course of rendering the order a nullity retrospectively so that no one could ever refer to it as a precedent in the future. None of the dissenting judges reached the constitutional issue of religious liberty in arriving at their conclusions. In his opinion Judge Miller emphasized procedural irregularities, particularly the lack of authority for a single judge to issue the kind of order under consideration.

Judge Burger, in an opinion in which Judges Miller and Bastian

---

[25] 331 F.2d at 1009–10.

joined, went further into the merits of the controversy. He suggested that federal courts were without authority to enter orders requiring persons to undergo medical treatment to save their lives. He saw this limitation of power as stemming from the constitutional provision that federal courts can take jurisdiction only over "cases or controversies." Since historically the English common-law courts had not established the precedent of issuing orders compelling people to perform or submit to acts designed to protect their health, applications seeking this relief could not be addressed to the inherent common-law powers of the courts. The order would have to rest upon statutory or similar authority, which was lacking in the instant case.

In the course of his analysis Judge Burger did have cause to touch upon the religious liberty issue obliquely. He did so in discussing the limits within which the common law should properly develop despite its dynamic quality and capacity for growth. In his view, assumption of jurisdiction over cases involving compulsory submission to medical treatment would raise problems that had puzzled and divided theologians and philosophers. He questioned whether courts had the common-law power to decide whether the life of the mother or the child should be sacrificed in a crisis at childbirth, or whether a patient should be forced to undergo generally approved surgical or medical procedures which he rejects for religious, medical, or other reasons. At one point Judge Burger's analysis implied that even the legislature might not be able to resolve such questions because to do so might interfere with an individual's liberty. He suggested that orders for compulsory medical treatment would violate the basic constitutional "right to be let alone" expounded by Mr. Justice Brandeis in his classic and seminal dissent in the *Olmstead* case.[26] Judge Burger's main point, however, was that courts should restrain themselves when operating on the periphery of legitimate governmental power.

The essence of Judge Burger's opinion was that the courts do not have the power to make "new law" in cases requiring resolution of questions that have divided society on basic philosophical issues and calling for serious interference with traditionally recognized individual freedoms.

A New Jersey trial court took a position opposed to that of Judge Wright and refused to order blood transfusions for a woman

---

26 Olmstead v. United States, 277 U.S. 438 (1928).

in her thirty-second week of pregnancy, although such treatment was considered necessary to save her life and that of her unborn child. As in the *Georgetown* case, the application for the order was made by a hospital and the woman was a Jehovah's Witness. The Supreme Court of New Jersey entertained an appeal even though the woman had left the hospital, contrary to the attending physician's advice. It did so because it believed that the matter would probably arise again.

In reversing the trial court[27] the New Jersey Supreme Court relied on *State v. Perricone*,[28] a New Jersey case appointing a guardian to consent to blood transfusions for a minor when required for his welfare, despite religious objections of the parents, and on *Smith v. Brennan*,[29] a New Jersey case holding that a child could sue for injuries negligently inflicted on him before birth. On the basis of these cases it found justification for ordering transfusions necessary for the welfare of the unborn child.

The court avoided the issue of whether an adult could be compelled to submit to blood transfusions over his religious objections. Since it found that "the welfare of the child and mother are so intertwined and inseparable that it would be impracticable to attempt to distinguish between them,"[30] it concluded that the welfare of the child required an order for blood transfusions whether to save the life of the mother *or* the child. It remanded the case to the trial court to have a guardian appointed to consent to the necessary transfusions.

Sherbert v. Verner,[31] the Supreme Court case which decided that the free exercise clause of the First Amendment prohibits a state from withholding unemployment compensation benefits from a Seventh-Day Adventist because she refused a job requiring Saturday work, has led several state courts to grant religious rights wide protection.

In Minnesota the state Supreme Court considered for a second time the conviction for contempt of a woman who had refused to serve as a juror on religious grounds. Originally that court had upheld the conviction on the ground that the fundamental obligation of a citizen to participate in the governmental processes of maintaining civil order outweighed his right to the free exercise

---

27 Raleigh Fitkin–Paul Morgan Memorial Hospital v. Anderson, 201 A.2d 537 (N.J. 1964), *cert. denied*, 377 U.S. 985 (1964).

28 181 A.2d 751 (N.J. 1962), *cert. denied*, 371 U.S. 890 (1962).

29 157 A.2d 497 (N.J. 1960).

30 201 A.2d at 538.

31 374 U.S. 398 (1963).

of religion.[32] On appeal the United States Supreme Court reversed and remanded the case to the Minnesota high court to reconsider in light of its recent decision in the *Sherbert* case. On remand, the Minnesota Supreme Court reversed.[33] It held that until further experience indicated that "indiscriminate invoking of the First Amendment" was interfering with the effective functioning of the jury system, the state's interests could not override the individual's interest in maintaining his religious convictions.

The court referred to several difficulties that might be encountered in future cases. It noted that the United States Supreme Court had yet to define "religion" for purposes of determining what beliefs are entitled to protection under the First Amendment. The court also anticipated difficulty in determining the sincerity of an individual's belief when the religious convictions put forward were unrelated to any "sectarian creed." In the instant case the court found no such difficulties, since the relator had convincingly demonstrated her sincerity by preferring jail to the compromising of her faith.

In *People v. Woody*,[34] the California Supreme Court applied the principle laid down in the *Sherbert* case and indicated that it had a significantly broad reach. The court reversed the narcotics convictions of several Indians, members of the American Native Church, who had admittedly used peyote, a hallucinogen, as part of their religious rites. The court used a balancing test that first required a measurement of the religious importance to the defendants of the practice which the state purported to prohibit. Against this it weighed the interest of the state in prohibiting the activity. The court interpreted the *Sherbert* case as requiring the state to assert a "compelling interest" where the religious interest interfered with is a substantial one. To determine whether the state's interest was "compelling" the court did not simply assess the importance of the social values behind the governmental regulation; it also required a demonstration of the need to interfere with the affected religious interests in order to protect those values. In effect, the court required more than a rational connection between the social end sought and a given regulation when religious liberty is impaired.

---

32 *In re* Jenison, 120 N.W.2d 515 (Minn. 1963), *judgment vacated and case remanded*, 375 U.S. 14 (1963).

33 125 N.W.2d 588 (Minn. 1964).

34 394 P.2d 813 (Cal. 1964).

Pursuing this line of analysis, the court concluded that the use of peyote was of central theological importance to the Native American Church. The drug, which produces a hallucinatory state, is used as a sacrament. It is considered a "teacher" because it induces a feeling of brotherhood with other men and enables the user to experience the Deity. The Indians also regard the non-religious use of peyote to be sacrilegious. The court found that in some ways peyote is more than a sacrament, since prayers are directed to it as prayers are directed to the Holy Spirit.

The state advanced several countervailing interests. One—brushed aside as being self-evidently spurious—was the contention of the California Attorney General that "peyote could be regarded as a symbol, one that obstructs enlightenment and shackles the Indian to primitive conditions."[35] Another was premised on the supposedly deleterious effects of peyote on the health of the Indian community. It was urged that peyote would be used in place of medical care and that there was a possible correlation between the use of peyote and the propensity to use more harmful drugs. This line of reasoning was rejected by the court because of generally recognized scientific opinion that peyote works no permanent harm on the Indian.[36] The third reason advanced by the state anticipated problems in enforcing the narcotics laws because of the difficulty of detecting fraudulent religious claims to justify the use of

---

[35] 394 P.2d at 818.

[36] It is interesting to contrast the California Supreme Court's opinion with the positions taken by the lower courts in the case. The trial court had relied on *Reynolds v. United States*, 98 U.S. 145 (1879), which held that freedom of religion protects only belief and opinion and does not exempt one from generally imposed social duties. Accordingly, it found that the use of peyote in violation of a criminal statute could not be exused on the ground of religious freedom.

The district court of appeal affirmed the trial court. 35 Cal. Rptr. 708 (1963). It considered the defendant's argument that religious practices are protected by the First Amendment as well as belief and opinion. It assumed that religious practices could be inhibited only for grave and immediate reasons, but found that the dangers arising from the use of peyote provided such reasons because large quantities of peyote could lead to the user's loss of self-control. This finding led the court to be concerned over the lack of clearly defined limitations set forth in the theology or liturgical practices of the American Native Church concerning who could use peyote during the religious ceremonies and how much could be used. It was also concerned over enforcing the law, since many Indians use peyote non-ritualistically as a "health restorer." Although the court spoke in terms of the "grave and immediate danger" test, it applied this standard primarily to assess the hazards resulting from the general use of peyote and not from just the religious use. After determining that the hazards of general use were grave and immediate, it decided that only a rational-basis test was to be used to determine whether legislation prohibiting general use could include religious use within its scope.

peyote. Here the court required more than "untested assertions." It pointed out that the Supreme Court in the *Sherbert* case had similarly rejected the argument that the possibility of spurious claims would undermine the unemployment compensation laws and had placed a similarly large burden on the sate to demonstrate the need for the religious interference. It also referred to the *Jenison*[37] case as an example of the application of the *Sherbert* rule. It pointed out that on remand the Minnesota Supreme Court had required excusal from jury duty upon claim of religious interference until *experience* had shown that such a course in fact interfered with the effective functioning of the jury system. The court then adverted to the fact that other states banning peyote made exceptions for religious reasons without impairment of the effectiveness of their narcotics laws.

The state had also argued that granting exemptions on religious grounds would require an inquiry into the defendant's good faith in asserting the religious claim and that this was not only difficult but also repugnant to our notions of religious freedom and separation of church and state. The court referred to *United States v. Ballard*[38] as holding that only examination of the truth of religious beliefs is foreclosed by the First Amendment, not inquiry into the sincerity of those beliefs. It pointed out that such examination is carried out in the other areas of the law, including the grant of exemption from the military draft to those who have religious objections to participation in war.

Shortly after the *Woody* decision the California Supreme Court granted a prisoner who had been convicted for illegal possession of peyote a writ of habeas corpus because he claimed the drug was to be used in the practice of his religious beliefs.[39] The court required that a trial be held on the factual issue of whether the petitioner's claim was made in good faith. The petitioner was a self-styled "peyote preacher" and "way shower" who had gathered a small group of followers. He taught them deep-breathing exercises, how to pray "and in general how to love the Christian Life." He also provided and prepared the peyote for the group.

The decisions in two state courts, following more or less unanimous precedents, held that the state's interest in protecting the

---

37 *In re* Jenison, 125 N.W.2d 588 (Minn. 1964).

38 322 U.S. 78 (1944). (This case involved the criminal prosecution of the founders and leaders of a religious sect for use of the mails allegedly to defraud their followers).

39 *In re* Grady, 39 Cal. Rptr. 912 (1964).

health of young children and achieving their secular education outweighed claims of free exercise of religion.

The Arkansas Supreme Court affirmed an order appointing a guardian for certain minor children with directions to take the children into custody and have them vaccinated.[40] Unless they were vaccinated, the children would not be permitted to attend school. Their parents had refused to have them vaccinated because of religious objections and had threatened not to accept them back if they were vaccinated under court order. The court regarded the principle that the state can compel vaccination over religious objections to protect the public as so firmly settled that it did not believe the point warranted extensive discussion.

The New York City Family Court found that parents who failed to send their child to school one day a week, from noon Wednesday to noon Thursday, violated the state compulsory education law, notwithstanding their claim that this was necessary for the proper observance of the Sabbath according to their religion, the Ancient Divine Order of Melchisadech.[41] The court consequently found them guilty of neglect in a proceeding that could lead to loss of the child's custody. In a brief opinion the court referred to the principle that whereas freedom of belief is absolute, freedom to act according to one's religious dictates is subject to public regulation for the "good order of society." It also cited New York cases and those from other jurisdictions holding that it is not a defense to the compulsory education laws that a child is withdrawn or kept from school for religious reasons.

A New Jersey appellate court recognized the power of the state to require medical treatment where there was danger to the public from possible spread of disease.[42] But it denied the state the power to exempt persons for religious reasons on a discriminatory basis. Rutgers, the State University of New Jersey, had refused to permit a student to begin his studies before he submitted to a smallpox vaccination. The student refused on the ground it would violate his religious belief that he should rely solely on the healing powers of God. The student's entire family held this same belief but did not assert as their basis for it the teachings of any organized church or denomination. For this reason Rutgers, which does exempt Christian Scientists from the vaccination requirement, would not excuse the plaintiff student. The school argued that the

---

40 Cude v. State, 377 S.W.2d 816 (Ark. 1964).

41 In the Matter of Currence, 248 N.Y.S.2d 251 (Fam. Ct. 1963).

42 Kolbeck v. Kramer, 202 A.2d 889 (N.J. Super. Ct. 1964).

controlling New Jersey statute provided that school authorities "may" excuse students from the vaccination requirement. It argued that it had properly exercised its discretion by requiring reliance on the established doctrine of some sect because in this way it could be sure that the student's belief was truly a religious one and that he in fact held it in good faith.

As for the nature of the belief, the court held that it was not within the power of the state to determine what was genuinely religious and what was not. If the state should attempt to judge among different beliefs to determine which ones were "truly" religious, it would violate the constitutional command of the First Amendment not to give preference to one religion over another. School authorities either have to require all students to be inoculated or exempt all those who object on religious grounds. On this basis the court ordered the state university to enroll the student and permit him to start classes without the inoculation.

The court did not deal directly with the question of whether the student's belief was held in good faith. It referred to some facts, however, that indicated it was ready to assume that his claim was sincerely made. It pointed out that neither he nor his family had ever sought treatment from a doctor and that his family had kept him from starting both elementary and secondary schools until such time as the local education authorities relented and waived the inoculation requirement.

During the 1964–65 Term the United States Supreme Court will be faced with the issue of the state's power to distinguish between religious and other strongly held beliefs and to take action on such distinction. Cases involving the exemption of conscientious objectors from military service have raised the issue of whether, and how far, the First Amendment protects claims of conscience not based on the demands of religion, as that term has been traditionally understood. A split among the circuit courts on the constitutionality of that provision of the Military Draft Act requiring belief in a Supreme Being as a condition of exemption has led the Supreme Court to review the issue by granting certiorari in several cases raising it.

The issue arises out of § 6 (j) of the Act, which exempts a person from military service if he is conscientiously opposed to war in any form by reason of "religious training and belief."[43] The Act goes on to define "religious training and belief" as "an individual's be-

---

43 50 U.S.C.A. App. § 456 (j) (1963 Supp.)

lief in a relation to a Supreme Being involving duties superior to those arising from any human relation, but does not include essentially political, sociological or philosophical views, or merely personal ones."

The Ninth Circuit has consistently held this section constitutional.[44] It has also required that the belief in a Supreme Being be of a more or less traditional kind. In *Peter v. United States*,[45] decided in the latter part of 1963, the court found that an inductee who claimed exemption for conscientious scruples based on a "belief in the mystery of the heart of . . . [living objects in the world]" and on "respecting and loving . . . livingness in other objects and human beings" did not meet the statutory requirements.[46] It upheld a denial of the exemption on the ground that his objection stemmed only from a "personal moral code."

Two decisions rendered by the Court of Appeals for the Second Circuit moved in a direction opposite to that of the Ninth Circuit. The first case, *United States v. Jakobson*[47] held that belief in "Godness" in the universe met the statutory requirement of belief in a Supreme Being. The second case, *United States v. Seeger*,[48] went on to hold that the requirement of belief in a Supreme Being is unconstitutional.

In the *Jakobson* case the defendant had claimed belief in a Supreme Being as the Ultimate Cause of all existence. He termed the Ultimate Cause "Godness" and claimed that man can know nothing of God but can approach Godness through psychic involvement with the reality of the three-dimensional world. The court found that the defendant's ideas concerning God and religion, which he defined as the sum and essence of one's attitudes to the basic problems of human existence, paralleled those of the eminent Protestant theologian Paul Tillich. In view of the large number of men in the modern world who believe in God but not in an anthropomorphic deity, the court concluded that the intent of Congress had not been to exclude these men from the benefits of the exemption.

The court decided to give the words "religious training and belief" the widest possible interpretation, on the ground this was

---

44 See Etcheverry v. United States, 320 F.2d 873 (9th Cir. 1963), *cert. denied,* 375 U.S. 930 (1963), and cases cited therein.
45 324 F.2d 173 (9th Cir. 1963), *cert. granted,* 377 U.S. 922 (1964).
46 324 F.2d at 177.
47 325 F.2d 409 (2d Cir. 1963), *cert. granted,* 377 U.S. 922 (1964).
48 326 F.2d 846 (2d Cir. 1964), *cert. granted,* 377 U.S. 922 (1964).

necessary to preserve the constitutionality of the statute. It pointed out that the Supreme Court in *Torcaso v. Watkins*[49] had said that the state could not aid those religions based on a belief in the existence of God as against those founded on different beliefs, and indeed it could not aid all religions against non-believers. The court recognized that this principle would appear to render an exemption based on "religious training and belief" necessarily unconstitutional. It found justification for the exemption nonetheless, on the basis of the privileged position accorded to religion under the free exercise clause, as long as all kinds of religious beliefs were given equal recognition.

The logical corollary of the court's view would appear to require Congress to grant an exemption to those who had religious objections to military service but did not believe in a Supreme Being at all. However, since the defendant did express belief in some kind of Supreme Being, the court did not have to decide to excise the statutory definition of "religious training and belief."

In the *Seeger* case the issue was presented squarely when a young man claimed he had conscientious objections to participation in a war and preparations for it based on religious training and belief but not on a belief in a Supreme Being. His objections were based on adherence to a "religious faith in a purely ethical creed" which called for belief in and devotion to goodness and virtue for their own sake. The government argued that the purpose of the exemption was to relieve the individual who felt impelled to follow what he believed was a divine command issued by a power higher than Congress. It was not meant to defer to those individuals who invoked their own fallible judgment in opposition to that of the legislature.

Although the court appreciated the force of the argument, it pointed out that for many modern men the internal demands of conscience are as compelling as the externally derived commandments of God have traditionally been. It also found it would be an impossible task for draft boards and courts alike to distinguish between the devotion to a mystical force of "Godness" involved in the *Jakobson* case and the ethical commitment to follow the paths of "goodness" involved in the case at bar.

It came to the conclusion that it would constitute unfair discrimination in violation of the due process clause of the Fifth

---

[49] 367 U.S. 488 (1961).

Amendment to restrict the exemption granted conscientious objectors to only those who profess a belief in a Supreme Being. In
coming to this conclusion, the court turned to modern definitions
of religion, particularly those that would achieve the broad purposes behind the free exercise clause. The court relied heavily on
a definition given by Judge Augustus Hand in *United States v.
Kauten.*[50] That case also involved defining "religious belief and
training" for purposes of exemption from the draft, but at a time
prior to the 1948 adoption by Congress of the definition referring
to belief in a Supreme Being. Judge Hand's definition referred
to "a belief finding expression in a conscience which categorically
requires the believer to disregard elementary self-interest and to
accept martyrdom in preference to transgressing its tenets."[51]

The two Second Circuit opinions began to make their influence
felt even before the Supreme Court had a chance to review the
question. The Ninth Circuit reversed the conviction of a defendant whose claim for exempt status had been rejected without a
hearing simply because he had indicated on his application for
exemption that he did not believe in a Supreme Being.[52] The
court did not arrive at this result by relying on the *Seeger* case. It
did so on the basis of the *Jakobson* case and the strict legislative
requirement that every applicant for exemption is entitled to a
hearing before the Justice Department unless his claim clearly
and incontrovertibly appears baseless on the record. The court
held that the defendant's denial of belief in a Supreme Being on
his application did not clearly destroy his case because he might
have misinterpreted the word to mean an anthropomorphic deity,
whereas the *Jakobson* case had held that Congress must have referred to a much wider meaning. There was some evidence of such
misunderstanding, since the defendant had requested a reopening
of his classification on the ground that he had misinterpreted the
phrase "Supreme Being" as referring to a "fundamentalist" anthropomorphic deity. The defendant did claim a belief in "a high
state of order and even disorder within the physical universe gov-
erned by laws which are presently above my ability or that of any
man to completely control or completely understand."[53] The court
did not rule on whether such a belief was sufficient for exemption

---

[50] 133 F.2d 703 (2d Cir. 1943).
[51] *Id.* at 708.
[52] MacMurray v. United States, 330 F.2d 928 (9th Cir. 1964).
[53] *Id.* at 930.

under the statute, leaving that question up to the defendant's draft
board in the first instance, if it chose to consider inducting him
again.

As in previous years there were some reported cases involving
the claims of Jehovah's Witnesses to exemption from both com-
batant and non-combatant service on the ground that they were
ordained ministers, and, as before, these Witnesses found it difficult
to establish their status on the basis of time spent on ministerial
functions.[54]

There were several cases brought under the Civil Rights Act involving the rights of prisoners to practice their religious beliefs. In
Cooper v. Pate,[55] a prisoner sought to compel the warden of Joliet
penitentiary to allow him to purchase the Koran and other religious publications and materials of the Black Muslim movement.
In his complaint he alleged that he had been discriminated against
because of his religious beliefs inasmuch as prisoners of other
faiths were allowed to possess comparable material. The district
court dismissed the complaint and the circuit court affirmed on the
ground that a person lawfully incarcerated cannot seek relief in
the federal courts against claimed interference with his constitutional rights by prison officials. It considered this a matter of internal prison discipline.

The court also relied to a large extent on social studies indicating that the Black Muslim movement was something of a terrorist
organization behind a religious façade. It seemed to make this
point for the purpose of establishing that adherents of the movement need not be accorded the privileges granted to other religious
groups, particularly in prisons, where they had "an impressive history of inciting riots and violence."[56] The court, interestingly enough, decided that it was quite proper to take judicial notice of social studies and not require proof of the movement's
nature at trial on the authority of *Brown v. Board of Education*,[57]
the case in which the Supreme Court found segregation in public
schools to be unconstitutional, relying in part on social studies
showing the harmful impact that separation of the races had on
Negro children.

---

54 Fitts v. United States, 334 F.2d 416 (5th Cir. 1964); Badger v. United States 322
F.2d 902 (9th Cir. 1963); United States v. Planas, 226 F.Supp. 803 (S.D. N.Y. 1964).

55 324 F.2d 165 (7th Cir. 1963).

56 *Id.* at 166.

57 347 U.S. 483 (1954).

The Supreme Court reversed the dismissal of the complaint in a brief per curiam opinion holding that the prisoner had stated a good cause of action by alleging discriminatory withholding of devotional literature and material because of his religious beliefs.[58]

In *Childs v. Pegelow*[59] several prisoners at the Lorton Reformatory sought to compel the warden to reschedule morning and evening meals for Muslim prisoners during the month of December, the Ramadan, at hours when it was so dark that one could not distinguish a white thread from a black one in the natural light. The warden did reschedule the meals of all prisoners before sunrise in the morning and after sunset in the evening, but the petitioners claimed this was not enough to meet the fasting requirements of their religion. The district court entered judgment for the warden after finding the prisoners' claim frivolous in light of the special accommodations made for them.

The Fourth Circuit affirmed, holding that the warden was not required to make any special accommodations at all. It recognized that prisoners could claim redress for deprivation of constitutional rights, particularly when they were treated discriminatorily. But it held that they could not claim preferred treatment, even for religious reasons, when this would disrupt internal prison routine, as in the present case.

Adhering to one of its recent decisions,[60] the Court of Appeals for the Second Circuit has recognized that the Black Muslims constitute a religion and that prison inmates who belong to it are entitled to some protection in the exercise of their beliefs, but only limited protection in view of the tenets of their faith.[61] Black Muslim inmates at a New York state prison brought suit to require prison authorities to permit them to hold communal services, to receive visits from their ministers, and to obtain literature of their religion. After observing that the practices of all religions must be restricted to some degree in prison to maintain discipline, the court went on to conclude that more serious restrictions might be required in the case of Black Muslims because of their advocacy of racial hatred, and it appreciated why prison authorities, to prevent possible violence, might even prohibit the circulation and display of Black Muslim literature.

---

58 378 U.S. 546 (1964).

59 321 F.2d 487 (4th Cir. 1963), *cert. denied*, 376 U.S. 932 (1964).

60 Pierce v. LaVallee, 319 F.2d 844 (2d Cir. 1963), *cert. denied*, 374 U.S. 850 (1963).

61 Sostre v. McGinnis, 334 F.2d 906 (2d Cir. 1964), *cert. denied*, 379 U.S. 892 (1964).

The court's final conclusion was that Black Muslim prisoners should be entitled to hold services, receive their ministers, and obtain their religious literature, but under special conditions conforming to prison discipline. It was decided, however, that this was a matter preferably to be determined by the state courts in the first instance. Instead of affirming a dismissal of the case, the court remanded it to the district court to retain jurisdiction should there be unreasonable delay in working out the necessary rules in the state courts. The court adverted to a section of the New York Correction Law which guarantees prisoners the right of free exercise of their religion and provides that religious services and spiritual advice be made available to the inmates under rules and regulations in harmony with prison discipline.[62] It also adverted to a 1962 New York case, *Brown v. McGinnis*,[63] which it regarded as requiring the Commissioner of Correction to promulgate rules and regulations concerning the conduct of religious services and exercise of religious rights in prisons. The court went on to observe that litigation involving such regulations was then pending in the state courts.[64]

In *United States ex rel. Cleggett v. Pate*[65] the interest in maintaining discipline in the prison was held to justify the warden's refusal to permit a prisoner held in solitary confinement to attend Sunday religious services with other inmates. The plaintiff had been allowed to have a minister visit him but had been denied the privilege of mingling with the other inmates during religious services because he had previously forced another prisoner to submit to sexual relations. The court, although agreeing that the religious interests of inmates should be given some constitutional protection, held that restrictions could be placed on actions when the well-being and safety of the prison community required them.

In *Dobkin v. District of Columbia*,[66] the court quickly found without merit the appellant's contention that his trial for violating the so-called "Baby Broker Act" should have been continued when it began to extend into the Jewish Sabbath. Even though the court

---

[62] N.Y. CORRECTION LAW § 610 (1944).

[63] 180 N.E.2d 791 (N.Y. 1962).

[64] During the period surveyed New York appellate courts reversed two lower court opinions denying requests by prisoners for opportunity to engage in religious activities. They remanded the cases with a direction that the trial courts determine what relief petitioners would be entitled to under reasonable rules and regulations. Shaw v. McGinnis 200 N.E.2d 636 (N.Y. 1964) Blazic v. Fay, 251 N.Y.S.2d 494 (App. Div. 1964).

[65] 229 F.Supp. 818 (N.D. Ill. 1964).

[66] 194 A.2d 657 (D.C. Ct. App. 1963).

"would agree at once that no man ought to be required to violate his conscientious scruples by submitting to trial on a day he actually observes as one of worship,"[67] it concluded that the principle did not apply in the instant case because the appellant went to his office and worked on Saturdays and had not objected when the time of trial was originally set.

The Connecticut Supreme Court of Errors upheld for the fourth time in twenty-four years the constitutionality of a criminal statute forbidding the use of contraceptive devices.[68] In a brief opinion the court declined to modify its prior decisions, a course defendants had urged "in light of . . . the current developments in medical, social and religious thought in this area, and the present conditions of American and Connecticut life."[69] The court held that these considerations were to be addressed to the legislature for determination of public policy and not to the courts for determination of constitutional law.

PUBLIC AID FOR RELIGIOUS INSTITUTIONS

During the period surveyed few cases were found involving public financial aid to religious institutions or in support of religious purposes.

In California an intermediate appellate court held that the state constitution forbade the use of public funds to achieve a secular purpose when the immediate necessary effect of the expenditure would be the promotion of religious ends.[70] Los Angeles County entered a contract to finance the taking of motion pictures of the annual parade of the Bethlehem Star Association. When the county auditor refused to pay the funds on the ground the contract was invalid, an action of mandamus to compel him to make the payments was brought. The primary purpose of the Association is to "restore the original significance of Christmas to the Holiday Season of the year through the presentation in Van Nuys, California, of a non-commercial religious parade made up of appropriate scenes from both the Old and the New Testament." The county agreed to finance the pictures for the purpose of publicizing the county and its attractions in states outside of California, and the Association agreed that the films would acknowledge they were

---

67 *Id.* at 659.

68 State v. Griswold, 200 A.2d 479 (Conn. 1964).

69 *Id.* at 480.

70 County of Los Angeles v. Hollinger, 34 Cal. Rptr. 387 (1963).

made possible by Los Angeles County and would contain sufficient
footage at regular intervals designed to give publicity to the county.

Aside from the guarantees of acknowledgment and minimum
footage, no limitation or regulations were specified concerning
what the association could produce. The court concluded that the
content of the film would naturally be devoted to advancing the
Association's purpose of restoring the religious significance of
Christmas. It considered such an end sectarian and decided that to
support financially an activity so directed would violate the California constitution's prohibition against the payment of public
funds "in aid of . . . [a] sectarian purpose." The court also quoted
the language of the *Everson*[71] case maintaining that aid to any one
or all religions, or the preference of one religion over another, is
unconstitutional under the First Amendment.

The court went on to say that even if the county had retained
control over the contents of the film with power to dictate the
script, this would still be improper. It found that such an arrangement would involve someone with public authority to decide what
the "official" attitude of the county would be toward such scenes
in the parade as "The Annunciation," "The Resurrection," and
"The Ascension."

Finally the court felt than an arrangement such as the one contemplated would be the cause of just the kind of controversy the
constitutional provisions against public aid to religion were designed to avoid. It noted that there were many groups sponsoring
religious spectacles and parades that might attract visitors to the
county and they would feel aggrieved if not given equal public
support.

Justice Ashburn dissented. He quoted language from the *Zorach*[72] decision approving accommodation of religion and disapproving hostility to it. He also quoted language which said that "ours is
a Christian Nation," found in a 1959 Oklahoma decision[73] permitting construction of a memorial chapel for a state orphanage.

In *Scales v. Board of Educ.*,[74] a New York lower court ruled that
a state law compelling local school boards to provide home teaching to physically handicapped children irrespective of the school
they attend does not violate the New York state constitution insofar as it requires that such teaching be given to a pupil regularly

71 Everson v. Board of Educ., 330 U.S. 1, 15 (1947).

72 Zorach v. Clauson, 343 U.S. 306 (1952).

73 State v. Williamson, 347 P.2d 204, 207 (Okla. 1959).

74 245 N.Y.S.2d 449 (Sup. Ct. 1963).

attending a parochial school when well. Petitioner brought a special proceeding in the nature of mandamus to order the local school board to provide home teaching to his daughter, a parochial school student who would be confined to her bed for months. Respondent board of education argued that such services to the child constituted indirect aid to the parochial school and therefore violated a provision of the New York constitution prohibiting both direct and indirect aid to any school under the direction of a religious denomination. It relied on earlier cases holding that the supply of free transportation[75] and free textbooks[76] to parochial school students constituted indirect aid in violation of this provision.

The court rejected this argument, relying heavily on the distinction that in the bus and the textbook cases the aid in question assisted the pupil *"in the very process of participating in the school activities at the time of that participation."*[77] It maintained that the benefits flowing from the teaching, which were that the petitioner's daughter would be able to progress in her studies while ill and return to the parochial school without serious academic loss or disadvantage, were of such slight and remote financial value to the school, if any, that they could not constitute indirect aid. The court reasoned that if every governmental service which had the effect of improving the pupil's scholastic performance were forbidden, then even presently available health services would be unconstitutional. The court said, "Obviously a line must be drawn somewhere and the Court has no hesitation in drawing it in a way which accords the fullest freedom of action to the State's statutory program of child welfare."[78]

The case also presented the issue of standing to raise a constitutional question. Although recognizing the existence of divergent authority on the point, the court ruled that an official could challenge the constitutionality of a statute that directed him to do an act that he considered unconstitutional.

SUNDAY CLOSING LAWS

Sunday closing laws continue their checkered career in the law courts, meeting with varying degrees of success the charges that they violate either due process standards because of vagueness

---

75 Judd v. Board of Educ., 15 N.E.2d 576 (N.Y. 1938).
76 Smith v. Donahue, 195 N.Y.S. 715 (App. Div. 1922).
77 245 N.Y.S.2d at 455.
78 *Ibid.*

or equal protection requirements because of unfair discrimination in their classifications or their enforcement. They have been generally successful in withstanding attacks charging them with violation of the religion clauses of the First Amendment, in large part because of the Supreme Court's rulings in the Sunday closing cases.[79] Nonetheless, on this point voices have been raised in vigorous dissent in some state decisions upholding these laws.

The New Hampshire Sunday closing law, which prohibits selling of all goods except "necessaries of life" and forbids all work, business, and labor "to the disturbance of others" on the "Lord's Day," was upheld even though the New Hampshire Supreme Court recognized that the original statute was designed to promote observance of religious duties on Sunday.[80] It found the existing legislation was primarily concerned with assuring a common day of rest and therefore essentially secular in character. To demonstrate the secular nature of the legislation the court referred to a provision enacted in 1931 which authorizes local towns to adopt ordinances permitting Sunday selling, plays, games, sports, and exhibitions. In its view such exceptions are inconsistent with a religious purpose. It found, however, that such exceptions are not similarly inconsistent with the secular purpose of insuring a day of rest because in 1933 the legislature enacted a "One-Day Rest in Seven" statute, which requires every employer who conducts business on Sunday to have employees who work on that day take one of the remaining six days off.

The court did not comment on a section of the statute prohibiting public dancing, horse racing, and prize fighting at any time on the "Lord's Day" and requiring sports events to begin after one o'clock on Sunday afternoon, and theatrical performances and motion pictures after two o'clock.

The Court of Appeals of New York affirmed the conviction, for Sunday selling, of an Orthodox Jewish storekeeper who observed Friday night and Saturday as the Sabbath and who claimed he could not make a living on the reduced net return that would result if he closed on Sunday.[81] A majority of the New York City

---

79 McGowan v. Maryland, 366 U.S. 420 (1961); Gallagher v. Crown Kosher Super Market, 366 U.S. 617 (1961); Braunfeld v. Brown, 366 U.S. 599 (1961). Two Guys from Harrison-Allentown, Inc. v. McGinley, 366 U.S. 582 (1961).

80 State v. Rogers, 200 A.2d 740 (N.H. 1964).

81 People v. Finkelstein, 239 N.Y.S.2d 835 (N.Y.C. Crim. Ct. 1963), aff'd, 244 N.Y.S.2d 727. (Sup. Ct. 1963) aff'd., 198 N.E.2d 265 (N.Y. 1964), cert denied, 377 U.S. 1006 (1964).

Criminal Court had found him guilty on the basis of the Supreme Court's decisions in the Sunday closing cases. Judge Shalleck dissented.[82] He urged that in view of Mr. Justice Frankfurter's statement in the *McGowan* case that each state statute and case arising thereunder should be examined separately,[83] in view of the change in the composition of the Supreme Court, and finally in view of the fact that the defendant had been unable to make a living in other occupations and was now threatened with failure as a storekeeper, the Sunday closing cases should not be regarded as precedents that would conclusively uphold the conviction of the defendant under the New York statute. Part of Judge Shalleck's opinion was addressed to the proposition that the free exercise clause of the First Amendment required that the defendant be exempted when it placed before him the choice of either violating "his religious belief" or going "into bankruptcy and on relief." In another part of his opinion he indicated that the nature of the New York Sunday closing law was such as to render it an enactment directed at religious ends. His opinion apparently indorses the views of Mr. Justice Douglas, who found traditional Sunday closing laws to be unconstitutional aids to religion.[84] At one point in the opinion Judge Shalleck suggested that "the junior members [of the Supreme Court] should be given an opportunity to explore the new frontiers of our current speedy, electronic living against the background of these ancient [Sunday] laws."[85] Both the appellate term of the New York Supreme Court and the Court of Appeals affirmed the defendant's conviction without opinions.

There are continued indications that some trial judges who have serious doubts about the constitutionality of Sunday closing laws are applying them in a restrictive fashion. In Ohio a trial judge refused to grant a private party an injunction requiring one of his competitors to observe the Sunday closing prohibition.[86] The suit had been brought because the city prosecutor announced he would prosecute only first offenses. The plaintiff claimed that this would not deter violators of the law because there was only a $25 fine for an initial violation whereas imprisonment was provided for second and subsequent offenses. The judge denied relief on the ground that he would not grant the extraordinary equitable

---

[82] 239 N.Y.S.2d at 838.

[83] McGowan v. Maryland, 366 U.S. 420, 459 (1961) (concurring opinion).

[84] *Id.* at 561 (dissenting opinion).

[85] 239 N.Y.S.2d at 840.

[86] Miles–Lee Auto Supply Co. v. Bellows, 197 N.E.2d 247 (Ohio C.P. 1964).

remedy of an injunction as long as the plaintiff had legal remedies he could resort to. He suggested either an action for mandamus to compel the city prosecutor to enforce the law or one against the plaintiff's competitor to recover damages for lost sales.

A significant portion of the judge's opinion dealt with the question of whether the Ohio Sunday closing law violates the free exercise and establishment clauses of the Federal Constitution or the due process requirement that criminal statutes be certain and uniform in application. Although he spoke approvingly of the reasoning in an Ohio trial court opinion delivered the previous year holding the law unconstitutional,[87] the judge believed it was not appropriate for a court of first impression to say that a statute previously upheld by the Ohio Supreme Court was unconstitutional.

Judicial hostility to Sunday closing laws is heightened when spotty enforcement leads the courts to become concerned about discrimination. For this reason an Ohio trial judge suspended a $50 fine and five-day sentence when a storekeeper was convicted of violating the law for the third time in fourteen months.[88] In all three cases the storekeeper had claimed his constitutional rights were being violated because he was the only businessman in town being prosecuted for Sunday violations even though many others did business on that day. This pattern of enforcement was the result of a policy adopted by the prosecutor of charging only those against whom a private complaint was filed. The judge sitting in the present case had convicted the defendant of his first violation and at that time had rejected his defense of unequal treatment on the ground that there had to be intentional and purposeful discrimination by the prosecutor to establish a constitutional violation. In an opinion referred to in our last survey, the judge did go on to criticize spotty enforcement of Sunday closing laws because of resulting unfairness.[89] In the opinion delivered at the time of the third conviction the judge criticized the prosecuting attorney for in effect placing the policy of criminal enforcement in private hands. He not only suspended the defendant's sentence for this reason but indicated that he might not even convict the

87 State v. Grimes, 190 N.E.2d 588 (Ohio, Lucas County Ct. 1963).

88 City of South Euclid v. Bondy, 200 N.E.2d 508 (Ohio, City of So. Euclid Mun. Ct. 1964).

89 City of South Euclid v. Bondy, 192 N.E.2d 139 (Ohio, City of So. Euclid Mun. Ct. 1963).

defendant a fourth time for Sunday selling if prosecutions were not initiated against others. His reasoning was that repeated enforcement against only one violator while many others are offending the law amounts to intentional and purposeful discrimination.

Although no Sunday closing law was declared unconstitutional for being vague and uncertain in application during the period surveyed, the Texas Supreme Court avoided this problem by interpreting the statute so restrictively as seriously to impair its effectiveness.[90] Under its interpretation a seller can make a sale on Sunday of any product if the buyer will sign a statement certifying to the necessity of the purchase to meet an emergency. An attempt to render the law effective to some degree by requiring the buyer to swear under oath to the emergency failed when the Texas Court of Civil Appeals held that such a requirement could not be read into the statute.[91]

The Kentucky decision upholding the state's Sunday closing law was appealed to the United States Supreme Court, where the appeal was dismissed for not raising a substantial federal question. The statute was attacked on the ground that it was so vague and uncertain in application, because it exempted a "work of necessity," that it violated due process.[92]

The New Jersey Sunday closing law was upheld by a federal district court despite the charge that one of its provisions permitting Sabbatarians to work on Sunday was vague and uncertain.[93] The exemption is limited and forbids Sabbatarians to "openly expose to sale" any merchandise on that day. The court found that the New Jersey Supreme Court's interpretation of the language in question was sufficiently clear. The language has been interpreted to mean that no store may be "open for the purpose of doing business indiscriminately with the public in the goods or wares usually sold therein."[94]

The Missouri Supreme Court has held that a statute outlawing the sale on Sunday of goods described by such generic categories as "housewares," "wearing apparel," and "toys" was not unconstitutionally vague.[95] The Louisiana Supreme Court took a similar position in reversing trial court decisions that had found certain

90 State v. Shoppers World, Inc., 380 S.W.2d 107 (Tex. 1964).
91 A. M. Servicing Corp. v. State, 380 S.W.2d 747 (Tex. Civ. App. 1964).
92 Arlan's Dept. Store v. Kentucky, 376 U.S. 186 (1964).
93 Fass v. Roos, 221 F. Supp. 448 (D.N.J. 1963).
94 State v. Fass, 175 A.2d 193, 201 (N.J. 1961).
95 State v. McQueen, 378 S.W.2d 449 (Mo. 1964).

statutory prohibitions against Sunday selling unconstitutionally vague for using the terms "building supply material"[96] and "wearing apparel."[97]

Sunday closing laws proved most vulnerable to the charge that they were unfairly discriminatory. The Delaware Supreme Court struck down a state law forbidding barbering on Sunday because the singling-out of that calling placed a discriminatory burden on it in violation both of the Fourteenth Amendment of the Federal Constitution and of the state constitution.[98] For the same reasons the Nebraska Supreme Court struck down a recently enacted Sunday closing statute that proscribed the selling of a wide variety of goods.[99] The court found it was unfairly discriminatory because it did not prohibit manufacturing, transportation, and a number of other activities on Sunday, permitted small stores with two or fewer employees to remain open, and expressly allowed the sale of some goods that were not necessaries. In the opinion of the court none of these was justified by reason of the common-day-of-rest purpose behind the statute. In a second case the same court predictably struck down a local ordinance because it prohibited only selling on Sunday and permitted manufacturing, personal services, and other laboring activities.[100]

New laws enacted in Kansas[101] and North Carolina[102] were struck down for a closely related reason. Both laws were found to violate state constitutional provisions prohibiting the passage of special laws, that is to say, laws which do not apply generally. The North Carolina statute excluded certain counties from coverage for the express reason that they were "resort or tourist" areas; but the state Supreme Court rejected this purported justification because other areas of the state not excluded could also be considered resort or tourist areas. The Kansas Supreme Court found that a Sunday closing law exempting stores below a certain size which employ three or fewer persons was an improper special law because the general purposes behind a closing statute would not be served by such exceptions.

96 State v. Deutch, 161 So.2d 730 (La. 1964).

97 State v. Wiener, 161 So.2d 755 (La. 1964).

98 Rogers v. State, 199 A.2d 895 (Del. 1964).

99 Terry Carpenter, Inc. v. Wood, 129 N.W.2d 475 (Neb. 1964).

100 Skag-Way Dep't. Stores, Inc. v. City of Grand Island, 125 N.W.2d 529 (Neb. 1964).

101 Boyer v. Ferguson, 389 P.2d 775 (Kan. 1964).

102 Treasure City of Fayetteville, Inc. v. Clark, 134 S.E.2d 97 (No. Car. 1964).

The Missouri Supreme Court arrived at a result somewhat opposite to that of the Nebraska court and upheld, over the charge
of arbitrary discrimination, the constitutionality of a new statute
that prohibited only Sunday selling.[103] It pointed out that, through
the efforts of labor unions and others, Sunday employment in
manufacturing and other fields had been significantly reduced
and that industries not following this trend for the most part involved necessary services or amusement and related activities, fields
which the legislature would want to exempt in order to achieve
its purpose of a common day of rest and recreation. It should be
noted, however, that the Missouri decision was placed on equal
protection and due process grounds rather than on the related
ground that it could not be a special law.

In Maryland[104] and North Carolina[105] Sunday closing laws treating market concessions and department stores differently from
small retail outlets were sustained over the objections of unfair
discrimination. The Maryland statute exempting small retail outlets from Sunday closing but not equally small concessions in a
large market was upheld on the ground that the operation of the
latter on Sunday would naturally interfere with the recreational
atmosphere of the day, whereas small retail operations would not.
The Supreme Court of North Carolina upheld a city ordinance
prohibiting department stores from making any Sunday sales, including sales of products that could be legally sold at certain stores
such as tobacco shops and drugstores on that day. The court held
that the guarantee of equal protection required equal treatment of
like classes, not equal treatment of competitors.

RELIGIOUS TAX EXEMPTIONS

In *Swallow v. United States,*[106] the defendant's conviction
for income tax evasion was upheld despite his contention that those
provisions of the Internal Revenue Code exempting religious organizations from the income tax and permitting donations to such
organizations to be taken as deductions violated the establishment
clause of the First Amendment. The court quickly disposed of this

---

[103] Gem Stores, Inc. v. O'Brien, 374 S.W.2d 109 (Mo. 1964).
[104] Richards Furniture Corp. v. Board of County Comm'rs, 196 A.2d 621 (Md. 1963).
[105] Clark's Charlotte, Inc. v. Hunter, 134 S.E.2d 364 (No. Car. 1964).
[106] 325 F.2d 97 (10th Cir. 1963), *cert. denied,* 377 U.S. 951 (1964).

objection by referring to *Abraham J. Muste v. Commissioner*,[107] which had held that a taxpayer could not refuse to pay income taxes because it would be contrary to the dictates of his religion to contribute funds for use in part for war purposes or preparations for war. The court also found the defendant had no standing to raise the constitutional objection, since he had "not shown how his rights could be affected if these activities were held to be unlawful."[108]

The Supreme Court of Alaska held that a broadcasting station owned by a church and used in large part for commercial purposes was subject to an ad valorem property tax and the sale of its radio time was subject to a consumer sales tax even though all the proceeds of the station's activities were used to pay costs of operation and to help support the missionary activities of the church.[109] In the same case, the court held that the residence furnished by the church to an assistant pastor was exempt from the property tax. The relevant Alaska statute exempted all "property used for nonprofit religious . . . purposes" and specifically included "the residence of the pastor, priest or minister of a religious organization and other property of the organization not used for business, rent, or profit." The court followed the majority view, which interprets exemptions in the case of "exclusive religious use" strictly and requires the immediate use to be a religious one. Of considerable significance to the court was the consideration that exemption would result in taxed commercial business being forced to compete at some disadvantage with the commercial activities of religious institutions. The court had little difficulty in finding the residence of the assistant pastor exempt by relying on the statutory language exempting "all other property . . . not used for business, rent or profit."

In *Young Women's Christian Ass'n v. City of Lincoln*,[110] the Nebraska Supreme Court held that a woman's residence hall run at a loss by the plaintiff and supported in part by gifts is tax exempt. The court found that the property was being used "exclusively" for religious, educational, and charitable purposes and therefore met the requirements for exemption. Only approved members of the plaintiff could reside in the building, and then for

---

107 35 T.C. 913 (1961).
108 325 F.2d at 98.
109 Evangelical Covenant Church v. City of Nome, 394 P.2d 882 (Alaska 1964).
110 128 N.W.2d 600 (Neb. 1964).

no more than three years. Every resident paid rent, but the plaintiff testified that no complaints had ever been registered by private houses or hotels concerning the operation of the residence hall. The purpose of the hall was to provide girls receiving a limited income with a safe, secure, and guided home, with religious overtones, where they would be cared for mentally and morally. The defendant urged that the plaintiff was not making such use of the building as would qualify for tax exemption. It argued that the building was being primarily used as a dormitory and that the plaintiff provided its tenants with nothing more than could be found in "an ordinary well-run Christian home." The court, however, found that the plaintiff's purpose of providing a home with a salutary mental, moral, and religious environment rendered the use of the property "exclusively charitable."

Two rulings[111] gave considerable support to the tax exempt status of the Fellowship of Reconciliation, an organization which seeks to apply the force of love to social relations, particularly on the international plane. A New York appellate court upheld, without opinion, the ruling of a trial court that the Fellowship's objectives were religious. In another proceeding the Internal Revenue Service reversed a prior ruling that had concluded the Fellowship was a political, rather than a religious, organization.

TORT IMMUNITY

A law suit involving the claim that statements made by two witnesses to a priest of the Catholic Church in the course of ecclesiastical proceedings were slanderous and part of a conspiracy to damage the plaintiff's person, reputation, and property has occasioned two rulings on the protection afforded confidential communications to clergymen.

During the pretrial discovery phases of the case the court ruled that neither the priest to whom the statements were made, nor another one to whom they were forwarded for examination at the office of the chancery, could be compelled to give testimony about them to a civil tribunal.[112] The basis for the ruling was an Iowa statute creating a testimonial privilege concerning confidential communications to a minister or priest. The plaintiff argued that

---

111 Religious News Service, June 16, 1964 p. 164, June 25, 1964 p. 1.

112 Cimijotti v. Paulsen, 219 F.Supp. 621 (N.D. Iowa 1963), *appeal dismissed*, 323 F.2d 716 (1963).

the statute was not applicable because the confidential character of the statements was destroyed by disclosure to the second priest. The court rejected this argument, pointing out that an Iowa case extended the privilege to any person whose duty and relationship under ecclesiastical discipline to the original recipient of the communication was such as to enable him to learn of the statement in due course. A second objection raised by the plaintiff turned on the established interpretation of the Iowa statute to the effect that privileged statements had to be made by a penitent and be of a penitential character. The ecclesiastical proceedings involved an application by the plaintiff's wife to obtain sanctions from ecclesiastical officials approving her efforts to receive a civil decree of divorce and separate maintenance. The court found that the statements by the plaintiff's wife to the priest were penitential in character simply because she claimed they were and there was no evidence to the contrary. As for the statements by the defendant witnesses, the court found they were made to corroborate the wife's testimony and that corroboration was necessary to obtain the desired sanctions. The court then quoted Wigmore[113] to the effect that sometimes it is necessary to have the penitential communications made known to others, in this case the defendant witnesses, before absolution can be obtained, and this should be permitted without loss of privilege. The court did note in passing that there was a common-law basis for the privilege and that there was a split of authority on the necessity of penitential character as a condition to such a privilege. The court saw as a policy reason for a wider privilege the removal of inhibitions from those seeking "religious or spiritual advice, aid or comfort."[114]

Subsequently, on a motion for summary judgment, the same trial court judge dismissed the case on the merits and ruled that "to allow slander actions to be based solely upon statements made to the Church before its recognized officials and under its disciplines and regulations would be a . . . restraint on free exercise of religion . . . [in] violation of the First Amendment."[115] The court reasoned that a person should be free to make any communication to his church's officials "in a required proceeding of the religion" without any fear of court action, civil or criminal, since it might inhibit him. The effect of this ruling is to make all state-

---

113 8 WIGMORE, EVIDENCE § 2396 (McNaughton rev. 1961).

114 219 F.Supp. at 625.

115 Cimijotti v. Paulsen, 230 F.Supp. 39, 41 (N.D. Iowa 1964).

ments to religious tribunals absolutely privileged. Accordingly, the court dismissed the complaint on the ground that a trial on the question of whether the defendants acted with malice was irrelevant because they could do so without liability. The court was careful, however, to consider the affidavits presented for summary judgment and to dismiss the case on other grounds as well. It found that since the statements made to the priests were privileged and could not be used in evidence, the plaintiff did not have any other proof to warrant the commencement of a trial, even if recovery were to be granted for malicious statements.

In *Murphy v. Harty*,[116] a libel action, the Oregon Supreme Court held that the defendant, a clergyman, had only a qualified privilege to comment on the character of the plaintiff, a foreign missionary at first endorsed by the defendant's congregation and then recalled because of allegedly improper conduct. Since the comments were made to a second clergyman, whose congregation had nominally supported the plaintiff and who was concerned over the recall, the court found that the common interest between the communicants justified a limited privilege. Such a privilege would protect untrue defamatory statements made in good faith, but not malicious ones. The court held that malice on the part of the defendant need not be shown by extrinsic evidence but could be demonstrated by the very statements made. It upheld a verdict for the plaintiff, permitting malice to be inferred from the fact that the defendant had attributed to the plaintiff the motive of dividing the churches of the American Baptist Association and had characterized the plaintiff's actions as Satan's plan of division and destruction. The court did not hold that such a statement was necessarily malicious. Instead it concluded that on the evidence the jury could find that the defendant did not have reasonable grounds for believing the defamatory statements he made.

RELIGIOUS INSTITUTIONS AND ZONING REQUIREMENTS

In *Sisters of Holy Cross v. Town of Brookline*[117] the Massachusetts Supreme Judicial Court viewed as constitutional a statutory provision rendering invalid any zoning regulation "which prohibits or limits the use of land for any church or other religious purpose." The plaintiffs were seeking to erect on their col-

---

[116] 393 P.2d 206 (Ore. 1964).
[117] 198 N.E.2d 624 (Mass. 1964).

lege campus a school building that did not conform to the dimensions required for one-family dwellings. A permit for construction of the building had been revoked after an ordinance was passed zoning the area for single-family dwellings only.

The appellate court reversed an order of the trial court declaring invalid the application of one-family dwelling requirements to the plaintiff's school building. It did so on the ground that the trial court lacked jurisdiction to make such a declaration, but it then went on to give its views on the issues presented because of their importance to the public. It agreed with the trial court that if the statutory exemption was to be meaningful it had to apply not only to restrictions on use but also to the related ones on size. It then went on to reject the argument that exempting buildings for religious purposes from zoning limitations violated the establishment clause of the Fourteenth Amendment. In its view the *McCollum*[118] and *Schempp*[119] decisions declaring religious instruction and devotional exercises in the public schools unconstitutional were not in point. Rather it turned to the *Zorach*[120] case, which permitted students to be released from school to attend religious classes elsewhere. It found in *Zorach* what it believed to be the controlling principle: that the state "may make exceptions to requirements generally imposed in order to benefit organized religion."[121] It found those state cases which have upheld the exemption of religious organizations from taxation as the ones most closely in point, and, following them, it regarded the zoning exemption as proper.

The court had a second reason for its conclusion that the plaintiff's school building could not be subjected to the single-family dwelling dimension requirements. The statute in question also specified that a building for an "educational purpose, which is religious, sectarian, denominational or public" was also exempt from the use limitations. The court went so far as to say that failure to exempt a denominational school building would be unconstitutional if a public school building were exempted because of its educational character.

In Georgia an appellate court ordered that a congregation of Jehovah's Witnesses be granted a special use permit to erect a

---

118 McCollum v. Board of Educ., 333 U.S. 203 (1948).
119 School Dist. of Abington Township v. Schempp, 374 U.S. 203 (1963).
120 Zorach v. Clauson, 343 U.S. 306 (1952).
121 198 N.E.2d at 633.

church in a residential zone.[122] The court rejected plaintiff's argument that a statute requiring a special-use permit for the erection of a church in a residential zone necessarily violated the free exercise clause of the First Amendment, as incorporated in the Fourteenth Amendment, or the equal protection clause. It found that only an absolute prohibition was unconstitutional. A restriction based on reasonable conditions—such as absence of traffic hazards and congestion and existence of adequate parking, the requirements involved in the instant case—was proper. The court nonetheless found for the church because of a showing that it met the necessary conditions.

INTRA-CHURCH DISPUTES

In several cases involving Baptist and other churches organized along congregational lines, the majority of the membership prevailed in property disputes related to schisms within the churches.[123] Although the courts applied the principle that the minority would retain control if the majority departed from basic doctrines, they never found this to have occurred in the cases before them. In two cases the majority changed the name of the church in a manner that could be interpreted as a change of affiliation with other congregations. In one of these cases, *Clemmons v. Smith*,[124] the majority changed the name of the church from "Congregation of Disciples of Christ at Higdon" to the "Independent Christian Church." The Missouri Supreme Court found that there was no evidence to support a claim of changed practices and that therefore the change of name was not important. Expert testimony on the record was more or less unanimous that for most purposes the titles "Christian Church" and "Disciples of Christ" could be used interchangeably. The main difference between the two groups, according to this testimony, is that the "Disciples of Christ" co-operate through district, state, and national organizations and also report to an international body, whereas the "Christian Churches Independent" do not.

[122] Rogers v. Mayor & Aldermen of City of Atlanta, 137 S.E.2d 668 (Ga. Ct. App. 1964).

[123] Barber v. Irving, 38 Cal. Rptr. 142 (D. Ct. App. 1964); Austin v. Mt. Zion Primitive Baptist Church, 165 So.2d 412 (Fla. 1964); Camp v. Durham, 134 S.E.2d 598 (Ga. 1964); Brown v. Mount Olive Baptist Church, 124 N.W.2d 445 (Iowa 1963); Whitely City Church of Christ v. Whitely City Christian Church, 373 S.W.2d 423 (Ky. 1963); Clemmons v. Smith, 379 S.W.2d 532 (Mo. 1964).

[124] 379 S.W.2d 532 (Mo. 1964).

In the second change-of-name case the majority of the Harvey Cedars Presbyterian Bible Conference caused it to drop the word "Presbyterian" from its title to indicate it was not affiliated with that branch of a denominational schism which retained the original title of the denomination, the Bible Presbyterian Church. Although this denomination is organized along presbyterial lines, its constitution provides that control of church property rests with the local congregations. Therefore, since the New Jersey court found that none of the other corporate changes made by the majority at the time of the change of name was fundamental enough to constitute a departure from basic doctrine, it decided in their favor.[125] In making this finding of continued adherence to basic doctrine, the court emphasized that the amended charter required the trustees to subscribe annually to the "System of Doctrine of the Westminister Confession of Faith, as Adopted by the First General Synod of the Bible Presbyterian Church in 1937."

Brown v. Mount Olive Baptist Church[126] raised the issue of whether the courts will impose procedural limits on the action of the majority in a congregational type of church when the rights of the minority will be affected adversely. Plaintiffs, former members of the church seeking reinstatement, argued that they had not received adequate notice of the move to expel them and that the courts should insure that the procedures of the church conformed to fundamental principles of equity and justice. They relied strongly on the following language in *Ragsdall v. Church of Christ:* "The majority's power is limited only by fundamental principles."[127] The Iowa court interpreted this reference to pertain to basic doctrines and beliefs of the church and not at all to principles of judicial procedure.

The Georgia Supreme Court was able to sidestep determining whether the minority of a congregational type of church was entitled to disputed property because the majority were violating a basic rule of the church.[128] The controversy involved use of materials other than the Bible in the Sunday school of the Mt. Zion Baptist Church. The plaintiffs alleged that the rules of the church prohibited use of other materials and that the defendants had been

---

125 Bible Presbyterian Church v. Harvey Cedars Bible Conference, Inc., 202 A.2d 455 (N.J. Super. Ct. 1964).

126 124 N.W.2d 445 (Iowa 1963).

127 55 N.W.2d 539, 545 (Iowa 1952).

128 Camp v. Durham, 134 S.E.2d 598 (Ga. 1964).

expelled from membership for advocating otherwise. The plaintiffs sought to obtain uninterrupted use and possession of the church property.

Hoping to resolve the controversy by agreement, the trial judge appointed a special master to hold a conference of reconciliation. The plaintiffs agreed that the expelled defendants could vote at the conference. A majority of the conference voted to permit use of materials other than the Bible in the Sunday school and also voted to reinstate the members who had been expelled for advocating such views. Thereupon the trial judge dismissed the case on the grounds the controversy was resolved.

The plaintiffs appealed, urging that the resolution was not valid since it was contrary to the faith and doctrine of the Mt. Zion Church. The appellate court recognized that there might be some "merit in the abstract" to their position, but held that the stipulation to hold a conference at which the defendants could vote was controlling in the case at bar.

A Texas case raised the question of whether a civil court was competent to act in a dispute concerning the duly authorized pastor of a church with an episcopal structure.[129] The Court of Civil Appeals sustained the action of the trial court in taking jurisdiction and deciding the controversy by enjoining the defendant from holding religious services, collecting tithes, and otherwise interfering with the duly constituted pastor. It quoted the following language from an earlier case to support its position: "Where rules and regulations are made by the church functionaries or by long and established custom and usage, they will be enforced by civil courts if not in conflict with some civil law bearing upon the subject of such rules and regulations."[130]

A New York trial court was faced with the problem of defining what is a "church."[131] The state Attorney General had brought an action to enjoin the respondent, Burden, from soliciting funds on behalf of a St. Mark's Church. Burden was rector of a church called by that name that had burned down and not been rebuilt. Most of the congregation had affiliated with other churches. No meetings or public services were held after the fire. Thereafter the respondent moved into some rooms behind a store and claimed this to be the church office. From here he solicited contributions

---

129 Darrett v. Church of God in Christ, 381 S.W.2d 720 (Tex. Civ. App. 1964).
130 Jones v. Johnson, 353 S.W.2d 82, 83 (Tex. Civ. App. 1962).
131 Lefkowitz v. Burden, 252 N.Y.S.2d 715 (Sup. Ct. 1964).

over the telephone with the aid of two paid assistants, also respondents in the case. Approximately $55,000 was collected in 1962 and over $54,000 disbursed in that year for items including the salaries of the assistants and necessaries for Burden. Over $20,000 in checks was paid to cash or unnamed payees. Burden did not explain how these funds were spent.

Despite Burden's claim that he performed marriages, baptisms, and confirmations in private homes and that he had frequently offered mass and communion and delivered sermons at two other churches in New York City, the court refused to consider these activities as justifying his solicitation for St. Mark's Church. It held that in the absence of trustees to hold the church's property and without a group of communicants to form a congregation for spiritual purposes, St. Mark's Church did not exist according to either a legal or an ecclesiastical standard. The court found it existed solely for Burden's purpose of soliciting funds from the public and creating the impression that donations received would go to a religious organization and its welfare activities.

Since Burden's activities "smack[ed] of gross misrepresentation and fraud," the court enjoined him and the other respondents from soliciting funds "directly or indirectly . . . for charitable, religious or eleemosynary purposes," not simply for St. Mark's Church or any other purported organization.[132]

CUSTODY OF MINOR CHILDREN

The few cases considering the religious factor with regard to the custody of minors have emphasized that the welfare of the child is of controlling importance.

The Supreme Court of Wisconsin has held that the religious attitudes of separated or divorced parents should be irrelevant in a custody proceeding unless the beliefs could "reasonably be considered dangerous to the child's health or morals."[133] It reversed a trial judge's award of custody to the father. The award had been made partly on the ground that the mother confessed to having doubts about the existence of God and to being an agnostic, even though she would send the child to Sunday school if awarded custody. The husband was a devout churchgoer. The trial judge had said, "[A] home in which a firm faith in deity is professed is considered . . . preferable to one in which doubt, skepticism or

---

132 *Id.* at 718.
133 Welker v. Welker, 129 N.W.2d 134, 138 (Wis. 1964).

agnosticism [*sic*] is professed."[134] The appellate court was of the view that since the state could not pass on the comparative merits of various attitudes regarding religion under the First Amendment, it could not take them into account in determining who would make a better guardian. It did recognize exceptions in cases where the parent's beliefs might endanger the child's health or morals, as would beliefs opposing blood transfusions and vaccinations.

Justice Hallows, concurring with the court's reversal for other reasons, dissented from its criticism of the trial judge's preference for a religious home atmosphere. He was of the opinion that the freedom to believe or disbelieve guaranteed by the First Amendment was irrelevant to the point in issue. He was of the view that:

> Morality, character and the dignity of human nature depends upon spiritual values and the recognition of a deity. While the court may not prefer one religion or religious faith over another, it might properly decide under what circumstances a child will best receive religious and moral training.[135]

A Florida appellate court credited the general welfare of the child with greater weight than religious considerations.[136] It upheld the modification of a final divorce decree requiring children in the custody of a non-Catholic parent to be "raised and educated" in the Roman Catholic faith and to attend Roman Catholic schools. It upheld modification because the trial judge had found that the welfare of the children would be served thereby. Interestingly, the same appellate court had reversed an earlier order for modification that would have permitted the children to attend non-Catholic schools because of difficulty and inconvenience in complying with the original decree.

Legislative, Administrative, and Other Developments
RELIGION IN THE PUBLIC SCHOOLS

Throughout the 1963–64 school year the initial resistance of state and local officials to the Supreme Court decisions in the *Schempp*[137] and *Murray*[138] cases prohibiting prayers and Bible reading in the public schools continued to a considerable degree.

---

134 *Id.* at 136.
135 *Id.* at 140.
136 In the Interest of W. S. B., 157 So.2d 548 (Fla. Dist. Ct. App. 1963).
137 School Dist. of Abington Township v. Schempp, 374 U.S. 203 (1963).
138 Murray v. Curlett, 374 U.S. 203 (1963).

Prior to these decisions thirteen states required prayers or Bible reading by statute or constitutional provision.[139] In four of these—Maine,[140] Massachusetts,[141] New Jersey,[142] and Pennsylvania[143]—the Attorneys General rendered opinions concluding that in light of the Supreme Court's rulings there could be no devotional exercises during any part of the scheduled school day. Despite these opinions some local school districts persisted in continuing these practices. In some communities in Pennsylvania,[144] New Jersey,[145] and Massachusetts,[146] only the vigorous prosecution or successful termination of litigation directed against these exercises led to their abandonment.

Six of the remaining nine states that required prayer or Bible reading by statute or constitutional provision—Alabama, Arkansas, Delaware, Florida, Idaho, and Mississippi—decided to continue these practices notwithstanding the *Schempp* and *Murray* decisions. A common justification for this position was that the Supreme Court had ruled only on the laws and practices of Pennsylvania and Maryland and it was not certain that the laws and practices of other states were unconstitutional. The Florida high court continued to hold this position even after the United States

---

139 BLANSHARD, RELIGION AND THE SCHOOLS 97 (1963).

140 Letter from the Attorney General of Maine to the Commissioner of Education, June 21, 1963.

141 Letter from the Attorney General of Massachusetts to the Commissioner of Education, Aug. 20, 1963.

142 Formal Opinion No. 2, 1963, letter from the Attorney General of New Jersey to the Commissioner of Education, June 26, 1963.

143 Official Opinion No. 260, letter from the Attorney General of Pennsylvania to the Superintendent of Public Instruction, Aug. 26, 1963.

144 In Cumberland, Pennsylvania, the local school board scheduled daily Bible-reading until suit was threatened by parents supported by the local chapter of the American Civil Liberties Union. Religious News Service, Sept. 12, 1963. The Cornwall-Lebanon school district continued to require daily Bible reading even after suit was commenced in the federal district court. While the suit was pending the school board altered the practice and substituted a required course in Bible study. Plaintiffs characterized the change as a subterfuge to continue devotional Bible study and reading. The court continued the case to permit the plan to be implemented and to provide for an opportunity to study it in practice.

145 In New Jersey the Hawthorne Board of Education was finally restrained from authorizing the continuation of daily Bible-reading by court order. Sills v. Hawthorne Board of Education, 200 A.2d 817 (Super. Ct. 1963), aff'd, 200 A.2d 615 (1964).

146 The Massachusetts Attorney General brought suit against local officials of North Brookfield after advising them that continued recitation of prayers and reading of the Bible of the Bible as daily opening exercises violated their oath to uphold the Constitution. He was successful in obtaining an injunction. Attorney General v. School Comm. of No. Brookfield, 199 N.E.2d 553 (Mass. 1964).

Supreme Court remanded to it for reconsideration in light of the *Schempp* and *Murray* cases its decision holding that the state statute requiring Bible reading was constitutional. In this way the Supreme Court on a second appeal, rather than the state court, was compelled to enter an order declaring that the Florida statute and practices were unconstitutional.[147] Lower level federal courts did not follow such a temporizing course with regard to practices continued under statutes prescribing prayers or Bible reading in the public schools. Three-judge federal district courts in Idaho and Delaware declared the continuation of Bible reading in those states unconstitutional.[148] After the Delaware decision, the state Attorney General advised that the court decree applied to all public schools in the state and that he would make every effort to ensure compliance with it.[149] He did go on to conclude that student-conducted prayer and Bible reading sessions were proper during "free time," which included the period before the beginning of classes, recesses, and the lunch hour. He also concluded that teachers could attend these sessions, but not organize or conduct them for the students.

In many states attempts were made to find limiting interpretations to the Supreme Court's opinion in the *Schempp* and *Murray* cases. As reported in our last survey one area of disagreement concerned whether teachers or students could engage in prayer or other devotional exercises on their own initiative.[150] The apparent uncertainty over the proper resolution of this issue was revealed by the reactions in two remaining states that had statutes requiring Bible reading, Georgia and Kentucky.

In Georgia the Attorney General did not directly take up the question of spontaneous prayers by teachers or pupils during the school day. He did render an opinion that the Georgia statute would be found unconstitutional on authority of the *Schempp* and *Murray* cases if tested in the courts.[151] He advised Georgia officials that they were bound by these Supreme Court decisions even though he personally believed the Court had been mistaken. With regard to the legality of "specific exercises," he stated that this

---

[147] See discussion in text *supra* at notes 4–7.

[148] See discussion in text *supra* at notes 8–9.

[149] Letter from the Attorney General of Delaware to the State Superintendent of Public Instruction, Sept. 4, 1964.

[150] 1963 RELIGION AND THE PUBLIC ORDER 289.

[151] Letter from the Attorney General of Georgia to the State Superintendent of Schools, Sept. 18, 1963.

depended on the "specific facts involved." But he did elaborate on what he thought would be unquestionably lawful practices. He saw as permissible the conducting of devotional exercises during unscheduled portions of the day "on a voluntary basis" without any official direction or supervision and "under arrangements made entirely by students." This position was very similar to the views of both the Pennsylvania[152] and Massachusetts[153] Attorneys General. The Georgia opinion, however, may have gone further in two respects. First it would expressly permit teachers as well as students to participate in the exercises as long as they did not direct or supervise them. Second, it would permit the exercises "before [the] classroom period." This language could be interpreted as permitting the exercises to take place between classes, whereas the Massachusetts opinion only expressly approved of them before the beginning of the school day. The Pennsylvania opinion was somewhat ambiguous on this point, permitting "unorganized, private or personal prayer or Bible reading during free moments of the day" as long as it did not "interfere with the school schedule."

Unlike either the Pennsylvania or the Massachusetts opinion, the Georgia opinion did not flatly state that any prayer during scheduled school hours was unconstitutional. Shortly after this opinion the Georgia Superintendent of Schools urged local boards to work out procedures that would permit Bible reading and religious exercises on a "voluntary basis."

In Kentucky, Attorney General Breckinridge initially issued an opinion concluding that Bible reading or praying by "volunteer pupils" was unlawful in regular classroom situations.[154] But Attorney General Matthews, successor to Breckinridge, subsequently qualified this opinion to the extent of permitting a student "voluntarily or spontaneously" to say prayers "silent or vocal" during periods set aside for silent meditation.[155] He would also permit prayers at PTA meetings and the saying of grace before lunch. Regarding lunch-time grace, he did not distinguish between periods used to meet the state six-hour school work requirement

---

152 See *supra* note 143.

153 See *supra* note 141.

154 OAG 63–790, letter from the Attorney General of Kentucky to the Superintendent of Public Instruction, Sept. 3, 1963.

155 OAG 64–111, letter from Attorney General of Kentucky to the Superintendent of Public Instruction, Feb. 7, 1964.

and those of "complete freedom," a distinction he made elsewhere in the opinion. A survey by the Kentucky Department of Education revealed that 116 school districts still prescribed Bible reading and organized prayers after the *Murray* and *Schempp* decisions.[156]

Among the many states having laws that neither required nor prohibited Bible reading or prayers in the public schools the reaction to the Supreme Court decisions was mixed. State officials in several jurisdictions, including North Dakota, Indiana, Iowa, Minnesota, and Ohio, did not take any position on the issue, in effect leaving the matter to be determined by local authorities. In such states local practices varied widely. In Iowa, for instance, a survey by the local chapter of the American Civil Liberties Union revealed that about 15 per cent of the public schools in the state reporting had some sort of organized prayer during the school day, even though in most cases this was "in a few classes."[157] The survey also showed that about 10 per cent of the schools permitted Bible reading during school hours. Questionnaires were sent to 453 superintendents, and 329 answered. Many of the school superintendents admitting to such readings in their schools described the exercises as part of the study of literature. In Indiana a survey of 227 school corporations revealed that prayers, led either by a teacher or a student, are said in about 60 per cent of the school districts, and Bible reading at the start of the school day is practiced in about one-third of the districts.[158]

State officials in other jurisdictions that had no laws either prohibiting or requiring Bible reading and prayers did issue statements or rulings. As reported in last year's survey, the New York Department of Education promptly ruled that any prayer said during the school day would receive the implicit sanction of the teacher and be unlawful.[159] Similar opinions were delivered by the Attorneys General of Colorado,[160] West Virginia,[161] and Vermont.[162] On the other hand, the Superintendent of Public Instruc-

---

[156] Religious News Service, Aug. 17, 1964, p. 4.

[157] *Id.,* July 15, 1964, p. 3.

[158] *Id.,* Apr. ˙0, 1964, p. 12.

[159] 1963 RELIGION AND THE PUBLIC ORDER 289.

[160] Letter from the Attorney General of Colorado to the Commissioner of Education, Oct. 1, 1963.

[161] Letter from the Attorney General of West Virginia to the State Superintendent of Schools, Sept. 12, 1963.

[162] 1963 AGO No. 66, letter from the Attorney General of Vermont to the Commissioner of Education, Sept. 9, 1963.

tion of Oklahoma announced that the state's existing practice of leaving to the individual teacher the decision whether to say prayers or read the Bible could continue unaffected by the Supreme Court's decisions.

Some states, such as Connecticut, took a stand somewhere between these two positions, although in practical effect they tended to come closer to Oklahoma. Shortly after the Supreme Court's opinion the Connecticut Department of Education issued a brief and simple statement disapproving prayers officially prescribed by school boards. It is said nothing about prayers initiated by teachers individually. Most districts thereupon decided to leave prayers and Bible reading up to the discretion of the individual teacher, even though the state Attorney General subsequently delivered an opinion concluding that all devotional exercises during the school day were proscribed by the Supreme Court's decisions.[163] It appears, however, that when a parent protests about the exercises, it is common practice for the local school board to request the teacher to terminate the practice.[164] A similar pattern has emerged in some localities of North Carolina, where the state superintendent decided that a formal announcement or ruling following the Supreme Court's decisions was unnecessary because there were no prescribed religious exercises in the public schools, only "voluntary" ones.

On one point limiting the Court's decisions—the use of public school classrooms by students before the beginning of the school day to recite prayers or engage in Bible reading—there appeared to be no dissenting voices among state officials. The Attorneys General of Massachusetts, Georgia, Pennsylvania, and Kentucky all concluded such practices were proper,[165] as did their counterparts in Connecticut,[166] Colorado,[167] West Virginia,[168] New Hampshire,[169] and Maryland.[170] The New Hampshire opinion went further than the others and maintained that students could gather

---

[163] Letter from the Attorney General of Connecticut to the Commissioner of Education, Nov. 13, 1963.

[164] Religious News Service, Sept. 27, 1963, p. 1.

[165] See text *supra* at notes 150-55.

[166] See *supra* note 163.

[167] See *supra* note 160.

[168] See *supra* note 161.

[169] Letter from the Attorney General of New Hampshire to the Governor, Nov. 6, 1963.

[170] Letter from the Attorney General to the State Superintendent of Education, Dec. 16, 1963.

voluntarily to recite prayers in school buildings after as well as before the start of the official session and that school officials could encourage such prayer gatherings. Soon after this opinion, the Manchester school board voted to permit voluntary recitation of prayers before the school day began in the morning. To facilitate this it rescheduled the beginning of classes at a time five minutes later than the previously established hour.

Recitation of historic documents and singing of patriotic songs making religious references were generally viewed as permissible with some qualification. The Attorney General of West Virginia approved of historical documents and songs that make "casual reference to the Deity,"[171] and the New York Commissioner of Education ruled that such items could not be selected for the purpose, or presented in the manner, of a religious devotion.[172]

Another practice that was widely regarded as proper was the period of silent meditation. There was, however, some disagreement over what the school authorities could do in relation to such periods. Whereas the New York Commissioner of Education believed that neither the school board nor the teacher could in any way influence the content of the period,[173] the Attorney General of New Hampshire concluded that school boards could schedule regular periods for silent readings of prayers and tracts, which the students could bring with them, as long as this was done on a voluntary basis and the teachers did not predesignate a particular prayer or reading.[174] The New Hampshire opinion admitted that the rationale of the *Schempp* case requiring state neutrality toward religion could be interpreted as an "ironclad" prohibition of any religious exercise in the public schools; but the Attorney General went on to express the belief that the Supreme Court did not mean to ban all prayers, silent as well as vocal. Therefore, he decided to read the *Schempp* case restrictively in light of its facts and to limit its prohibition to vocal prayers. In Kentucky, although Attorney General Matthews did not indicate the extent to which school authorities could influence the content of periods of silent meditation, he was of the opinion that students could spontaneously recite their prayers aloud.[175] The Attorney General of Mary-

---

171 See *supra* note 161.
172 See 1963 RELIGION AND THE PUBLIC ORDER 290.
173 *Ibid.*
174 See *supra* note 169.
175 See text *supra* at note 155.

land took a rather firm stand that teachers could in no way influence the periods of silent meditation.[176] Therefore, although he concluded that a proposed law requiring a period of daily meditation in the public schools was constitutional, he found that one of its sections permitting students or teachers to read the Bible during it unconstitutional. He was of the opinion that silent reading of the Bible by the teacher while in charge of the class would give official recognition to a religious activity.

The courts of a number of states, including those in Louisiana, Nebraska, South Dakota, Washington, and Wisconsin, had already declared that Bible reading in the public schools was unconstitutional,[177] and the Attorneys General of several states, such as Arizona, California, Nevada, and Oregon, had expressed opinions that such religious exercises were unlawful.[178] The Supreme Court decisions in the *Schempp* and *Murray* cases however, did have implications for these states, as well as others, with regard to such matters as baccalaureate services, the presentation of pageants and symbols with a religious theme, hymn-singing, and the celebration of religious holidays in the public schools.

As for the legality of baccalaureate services, there were differing opinions, with the majority maintaining they were permissible if voluntary. The Superintendent of Public Instruction of Pennsylvania suggested that such services were unconstitutional, and at least one state teacher's college in that state announced it would have none at the 1964 graduation exercises. But the Attorneys General of Massachusetts,[179] Kentucky,[180] and Oregon[181] all concluded they were permissible under public school sponsorship as long as participation was voluntary. The Oregon opinion rested this conclusion on the ground that the services were not part of the "regular curriculum activities of the school district," nor "a necessary or integral part of the educational process."

As for the celebration of religious holidays and presentation of pageants and symbols, there was general agreement that if the purpose and dominant tone of the activities was to promote historical, cultural, or intergroup understanding, then they would be

---

176 Letter from the Attorney General of Maryland to the Governor, Mar. 20, 1964.

177 BLANSHARD, *op. cit. supra* note 139, at 97.

178 *Ibid.*

179 See *supra* note 141.

180 See *supra* note 155.

181 Opinion No. 5783, letter from the Attorney General of Oregon to the Superintendent of Public Instruction, March 12, 1964.

permissible. But if there were religious overtones of a sort to give
the appearance of a "service" or to result in the "endorsement,"
"promotion," or "advancement" of any "particular religious
dogma," then the activity would be illegal in the view of the West
Virginia Attorney General.[182] In the opinion of the Massachusetts
Attorney General such activities could be used to promote understanding between children but not the advancement of religious
belief.[183]

Referring to Nativity scenes on school grounds, the Attorney
General of Kentucky concluded they were lawful "so long as no
religious significance is attached thereto."[184] The legal counsel for
the state of New York found "that school plays or even . . . sets
which depict the historical traditions which relate to the Birth
of Christ" were proper.[185] Recognizing the difficulty of drawing a
line between the historical features of Christmas and its religious
meaning, he believed the factual material relating to the birth of
Christ could be presented as long as "no religious connotations are
drawn therefrom by school teachers and school officials." Equating
Christmas verses and carol-singing to patriotic exercises that contain religious references, he found them permissible in the schools.
As did most of the other state officials who concluded that Nativity
scenes, plays, and similar exercises were permissible, he emphasized that the facts of each case must be examined to determine
whether religion is being improperly advanced.

In an opinion upholding the legality of a Nativity scene, which
was part of the decoration in a city park rather than in a public
school, the city attorney of Kalamazoo, Michigan, took a different
tack.[186] After pointing out that public places are traditionally
open to religious meetings, addresses, and other group activities—
if indeed not constitutionally compelled to be—and that the public
funds being expended to support the scene were trivial and could
not be accurately segregated, the opinion concluded that the display was a "passive accommodation of religion" involving no element of compulsion and not establishing or officially approving
any religion. The city council avoided a possible court challenge

---

182 See *supra* note 161.
183 See *supra* note 141.
184 See *supra* note 155.
185 Opinion No. 130, letter from the Legal Counsel of the New York State Education Department to Mrs. Sue Fruchtbaum Berger, Nov. 29, 1963.
186 Letter from City Attorney to the City Commission, Kalamazoo, Michigan
(undated).

by the local chapter of the American Civil Liberties Union by accepting an offer of the local Council of Churches to pay for the costs of erecting, removing, and storing the scene.

As reported in our last survey, efforts—begun after the New York Regents' Prayer had been held unconstitutional—to amend the Federal Constitution to permit prayers and Bible reading in public schools were renewed and increased after the *Schempp* and *Murray* decisions. Over one hundred congressmen introduced resolutions in the House calling for a constitutional amendment. The most prominent of these was one sponsored by Congressman Frank Becker of New York. It would have permitted prayers and Bible reading in the public schools notwithstanding any existing constitutional provision against the establishment of religion.

Because of the failure of the House Judiciary Committee to report out his bill, Representative Becker circulated a discharge petition among his colleagues and obtained slightly over 160 of the 218 signatures needed to have the bill discharged from the committee. When Republican House leaders indicated they would support a move to force discharge, Representative Celler, chairman of the Judiciary Committee and an opponent of amendment, scheduled committee hearings.

Religious leaders testifying on the desirability of an amendment to permit prayer in public schools were sharply divided, with the majority opposing. The fundamentalist and more conservative Protestant groups, such as the National Association of Evangelicals, supported an amendment. So did some individual clergymen from the other Protestant denominations, such as Episcopal Bishop James Pike. The majority of Protestant spokesmen from the larger denominations, including Episcopal, Presbyterian, Methodist, and Baptist representatives, opposed an amendment, along with officials from the National Council of Churches. Jewish leaders almost unanimously were opposed.

Although a number of leaders in the Catholic hierarchy had spoken critically of the Supreme Court decisions prohibiting prayer and Bible reading at the time they were delivered in June, 1963, very few actively supported a prayer amendment. Bishop Fulton J. Sheen spoke in favor of an amendment before the Judiciary Committee, as did several Catholic clergymen. But there were Catholics, both lay and clerical, who spoke against such an amendment, and the Catholic Press Association went on record opposing one.

The critics of an amendment generally agreed that official sanction of religious exercises by constitutional amendment would engender governmental involvement with religion contrary to the tradition of separation of church and state in the United States. Some of the opposing religious spokesmen were also critical on the ground that official prescription of piety would be a disservice to the vitality of genuine religious commitment and expression. Those in favor of an amendment, on the other hand, argued that the religious liberty of the majority was being restrained if they could not pray when they wanted to and that banishment of all expressions of religious commitment from public education would result in a godless and secularistic state and society.

One avenue of criticism, developed by Chairman Celler, the legal staff of the Committee, and some of the lawyers testifying before it, referred to a number of anticipated difficulties in formulating and implementing a prayer amendment, difficulties that could lead to the kind of strife and dissension the First Amendment was designed to avoid. In particular, questions were raised concerning how the content of the prayers and scriptural readings would be determined and whether any restrictions would be placed on their selection in order to avoid offending the religious sensibilities of some groups.

The National Catholic Welfare Committee's legal department issued a statement soon after the hearings were concluded advising caution in adopting any proposal that would modify the First Amendment. It found that the free exercise and establishment clauses of the Constitution were of "incalculable benefit" and were "too vital to be tampered with lightly." In addition the legal department found that the "hearings by the House Judiciary Committee [had] contributed to the confusion presented by the proposals themselves and provided added reason for caution."

Viewing this statement as in effect a criticism of his amendment, Representative Becker challenged it as not representative of the collective views of the American Catholic bishops. To remove any implications that it was, he sent a letter to all the bishops in the United States asking them two questions: whether they supported "the premise that children in public schools be permitted to pray on a voluntary basis," and whether they opposed an amendment permitting such prayer. He received relatively few replies to the letter and consequently decided to send a second one. Most of the replies that were received supported an amendment. Some of them, however, expressed caution about a constitutional change.

For instance, Bishop Hodges of Wheeling, West Virginia, replied that he subscribed to prayers in the public schools on a voluntary basis but questioned whether a constitutional amendment was advisable at the time.

There was considerable popular support for some amendment that would permit prayer in the public schools. The legislatures of a number of states, including those of Michigan, South Carolina, and Rhode Island, passed resolutions calling for congressional approval of a prayer amendment. The International Christian Youth in the U.S.A. presented the House Judiciary Committee with a petition, allegedly containing one million signatures, favorable to an amendment. Ranged in opposition, however, were not only a large number of religious leaders but also 223 constitutional lawyers, including a number of deans and faculty members of law schools with religious affiliations. They filed a statement with the Committee which recognized strong popular disapproval of the Supreme Court decisions prohibiting state-sponsored prayers and devotional Bible reading in the public schools; but they nonetheless opposed a prayer amendment on the ground that it would be the first time the Bill of Rights would have been amended and this would be a dangerous precedent. The statement said, "Whatever disagreements some may have with the Bible–Prayer decisions we strongly believe they do not justify this experiment."

By revealing the criticism of and opposition to a prayer amendment by responsible church leaders and legal scholars, the House Judiciary Committee's hearings appeared to slow down the increasing momentum behind the proposed amendment. In August, 1964, after the hearings had been concluded, Representative Becker made what he termed was his last call for the remaining signatures required on his discharge petition. The legislative session ended without his bill reaching the floor of the House.

A proposed constitutional amendment was also introduced in the Senate. It was of a more radical nature than the Becker amendment. It would have modified the establishment clause of the First Amendment to limit its prohibition to the "establishing [of] any organized church or religious association of any faith, denomination, or sect as a preferred or favored church or religious association." Although a large number of senators joined in sponsoring the joint resolution, no action was taken on it because popular attention focused on the House Judiciary Committee's hearings.

The *Schempp* and *Murray* decisions stimulated increased interest in finding legitimate avenues to enlarge the opportunities of children to obtain religious instruction. Shared-time experiments were viewed with growing interest (*infra* p. 265). There were also some developments leading to more favorable treatment of released-time programs. In Michigan legislation was passed authorizing public school students to be released during the prescribed school day for up to two hours to permit attendance at religious instruction classes held off the school property.[187] The Arizona Attorney General overruled an earlier opinion and concurred in the opinion of a county attorney that local school boards had authority to establish released-time programs even in the absence of a statute expressly providing therefor.[188] The opinion quoted extensively from the *Zorach*[189] case to support the conclusion that such programs would not violate constitutional prohibitions against government support of religion.

Also relying on the *Zorach* case, the North Carolina Attorney General concluded that it would be constitutional to set up a mobile chapel for religious training of young people in connection with their school attendance.[190] He went on to take the position that the program could be carried out with the co-operation of school administrators if it was voluntary and was conducted at the request of the parents off the school premises and without conflict with the normal operations of the public school and its classes.

Despite a consensus of legal opinion that the conduct of religious classes on public school premises during periods of released time is unconstitutional, this practice continues in some localities, as reported in last year's survey.[191] There is some difference of legal opinion, however, on whether it is constitutional to use public school facilities for religious classes and meetings outside of periods scheduled for school activities. The city attorney of Dracutt, Massachusetts, has ruled that public schools cannot be used for weekend religious classes.[192] But the Attorney General of Kentucky has ruled that pursuant to a state statute authorizing

---

187 Mich. Pub. Acts, 1964, No. 270.

188 Letter from the Attorney General of Arizona to Vincent Mulvaney, Jan. 30, 1964, concurring in School Opinion No. 63–57 of the Maricopa County Attorney, Oct. 30, 1963.

189 Zorach v. Clauson, 343 U.S. 306 (1952).

190 Letter from the Attorney General of North Carolina to the State Superintendent of Public Education, Oct. 10, 1963.

191 1963 RELIGION AND THE PUBLIC ORDER 295–96.

192 Church and State, Vol. 17, Jan. 1964, p. 13.

school property to be used for public meetings of an educational, religious, political, civic, or social nature, voluntary Bible classes not part of the school curriculum could be held on school property outside scheduled school hours.[193]

The division of opinion on this point may be due in part to the different wording of the state constitutional provisions prohibiting aid to sectarian schools. In California, where the state constitution prohibits "granting anything . . . in aid" of or "in support" of religious purposes or schools, the Attorney General has taken the position that public schools could be leased to groups conducting religious instruction or services only if certain conditions were met.[194] A fair rental had to be charged, the lease had to be of very limited duration, the school must not need the property during the time for which it was let, and the periods leased must not precede, coincide with, or immediately follow periods of formal class instruction. On this basis he concluded that a statute authorizing lease of school buildings to religious organizations upon payment of the direct costs incurred because of such use was unconstitutional. There were two reasons for this conclusion. First, since other organizations had to pay full rental value under certain circumstances, the Attorney General viewed the preferred treatment given to religious organizations as violating the prohibition against public "support" of religious activities and organizations in the state constitution as well as the establishment clause of the Federal Constitution. Second, even though many other organizations were charged no more than religious organizations were, the Attorney General still found that the leasing statute involved unconstitutional support because the rental value of the premises ordinarily would be in excess of the direct costs incurred.

The Attorney General of New Mexico, interpreting a constitutional provision prohibiting the use of "funds . . . collected for educational purposes . . . for the support" of private as well as sectarian schools, concluded that non-discriminatory leasing of schools to religious groups was proper as long as reimbursement was made for "actual expenses" incurred by the use.[195] In Oklahoma, on the other hand, where the state constitution forbids the "use" of public funds or property by any "sectarian institution as

193 See *supra* note 155.

194 Opinion No. 63/248 of the Attorney General of California, Feb. 7, 1964.

195 Opinion No. 63–106, letter from the Attorney General of New Mexico to the Assistant District Attorney of Rio Arriba County, Aug. 20, 1963.

such," the Attorney General concluded that any lease of school property for religious activities would be unconstitutional.[196]

The issue of using public school property for religious purposes was not discussed at any length in those attorney general opinions maintaining that students could voluntarily say prayers or read the scriptures on school premises before the scheduled sessions began. Most of those opinions did emphasize, however, that at the time the prayers were said the school premises had to be open for other orderly, although non-supervised, activities of students.[197] In ruling that students could engage in voluntary prayers before the beginning of the school day the chairman of the Board of Education of New Hampshire took the approach that since a New Hampshire statute permitted use of school buildings for religious meetings, students could gather there to recite voluntary prayers.

Protests against teaching about evolution in the public schools continue to come from parents who reject that theory on religious grounds. In California the Board of Education rejected a suggestion that texts be edited to make it clear that evolution was only a theory. The most vigorous and sustained protests came in Arizona. There the Reverend Aubrey L. Moore, a Southern Baptist minister, began to collect signatures for a petition demanding a referendum on banning the teaching of evolution in the public schools. His campaign met opposition from Protestant, Catholic, and Jewish clergymen and spokesmen. The deadline for filing the petition passed without his doing so.

Student refusal to salute the flag as part of the required public school activities continued to create some controversy in a few communities. In Elizabeth, New Jersey, children of Black Muslims who refused to pledge allegiance to the flag were barred from school. The children refused to salute for the reason that the Islamic religion called for their sole allegiance to Almighty God —Allah. This contention was rejected by local authorities on the ground that their beliefs were motivated as much by political considerations as by religious ones. The parents appealed to the Commissioner of Education for reinstatement and were successful.[198] After noting that it was often difficult to separate political and re-

---

[196] Letter from the Attorney General of Oklahoma to Representative McCarty, May 27, 1964.

[197] *E.g.*, Pennsylvania, *supra* note 143; West Virginia, *supra* note 161.

[198] Holden v. Board of Educ., Decision of the Com. of Educ., M–7374, Dec. 18, 1963.

ligious ideologies, the Commissioner concluded that he did not have to decide whether the petitioner's objections were based on religious grounds, since the New Jersey statute exempts students who have "conscientious scruples" against the pledge. He ruled that these words should be interpreted broadly to go beyond religious objections to include those emanating from the much broader sphere of "intellect and spirit."

In his opinion the New Jersey Commissioner referred to the language of the majority Supreme Court opinion in the second flag-salute case that reads "no official . . . can prescribe what shall be orthodox in politics, nationalism, religion, or other matter of opinion or force citizens to confer by word or act their faith therein."[199] He regarded this passage as an indication that the Supreme Court views the First Amendment as protecting more than just those beliefs that can be denominated religious. Sometime after the Commissioner's ruling, the New Jersey legislature passed a bill that would have repealed the statutory exemption for those with conscientious scruples. The bill was vetoed by Governor Hughes who agreed with the Commissioner of Education's reading of the second flag-salute case and concluded that the proposed amendment would be unconstitutional.[200]

On the other hand, the legal counsel for the New York State Board of Education reads the second flag-salute case as protecting only religious beliefs. Therefore, he has taken the position that the New York statute requiring students to salute the flag must, in the absence of an express exemption for those having conscientious objections, be enforced against those who object on other than religious grounds until a court of competent jurisdiction declares otherwise.[201] In the course of this opinion, he made reference to the havoc that would ensue if students could refuse to take particular courses or refuse to go to school at all on the ground that to do so would go contrary to conscience.

PUBLIC AID TO RELIGIOUS INSTITUTIONS

Church-state issues continued to create problems for various federal welfare and education programs. As reported in our last annual survey, church-state controversies created such serious

199 West Virginia Board of Educ. v. Barnette, 319 U.S. 624, 642 (1943).

200 Veto letter of Governor Hughes *re* Senate Bill No. 344, June 22, 1964.

201 Opinion of Counsel No. 135, letter from the Legal Counsel of the New York State Education Department to Mrs. Leonard Salitan, Apr. 8, 1964.

obstacles to the passage of an omnibus aid-to-education bill introduced in Congress by the Administration in the early part of 1963
that efforts to pass it in its entirety yielded to a strategy calling for
several bills to deal with specific areas of aid.[202] In December, 1963,
the Higher Education Facilities Bill was passed.[203] It provides
grants for construction of facilities to be used for mathematics,
modern languages, science, engineering, and libraries, all on the
level of higher education. Under the law private, church-related
colleges and graduate schools are eligible for the grants. This fea-
ture of the law had caused considerable debate over its constitutionality. Because of the constitutional issue the Senate had insisted on restricting the aid to facilities used for express purposes
instead of taking an across-the-board approach, as the original
House version of the bill had done. The Senate approach prevailed
in conference, but there was compromise to the extent of adding
mathematics and modern foreign languages to the categories
originally proposed by the Senate.

The version originally passed by the Senate had also contained a
provision for judicial review of the constitutionality of the bill.
This provision had been strongly supported by the National Education Association, which had previously opposed federal aid for
church-related schools on all levels without any qualification. It
was, however, eliminated in conference. But about this time Senators Wayne Morse and Joseph Clark introduced a separate bill that
would permit any institution or taxpayer to challenge in court the
constitutionality of federal aid extended to a religious institution.
The right to sue would also be granted to any institution or agency
whose application for aid was denied on the ground that the First
Amendment forbids such assistance. No action had been taken on
this bill by the end of the congressional session.

Efforts to extend federal aid to education on the lower levels
were not so successful. Because of the impasse over aid to parochial
schools the part of the Administration's original program that
would have provided grants for improvement of teachers' salaries
and emergency classroom construction was in effect abandoned.

Under the 1958 National Defense Education Act college students who obtained tuition loans provided by the law would be
entitled to cancellation of up to one-half of their loans if they

202 1963 RELIGION AND THE PUBLIC ORDER 298.
203 20 U.S.C.A. §§ 701–757 (1963 Supp.).

went on to teach in public schools. In 1963, when the NDEA was renewed for an additional year, Congress failed to adopt a proposal contained in the Administration's omnibus bill to extend the loan-forgiveness program to teachers in private schools as well. When the Act was extended for two more years in 1964, teachers in private schools were given the same benefits as those in public schools.[204] The 1964 amendments also grant private school teachers who attend summer training institutions established by the Act a weekly cost-of-living and dependents allowance.[205] Previously, only public school teachers attending summer institutes obtained such benefits. The 1964 amendments further provide for an extension of federal financial assistance into new course areas to help purchase special equipment. Whereas such aid was restricted to the sciences, mathematics, and foreign languages before 1964, now it will also go to support instruction in history, civics, geography, English, and reading.[206] As did the original Act, the amendments limit assistance to loans in the case of private schools in contrast to provision for outright grants to public institutions.

Senator Ribicoff attempted to provide indirect financial relief to parents sending their children to private colleges by means of a sliding income tax credit inversely proportional to the taxpayer's income. A maximum credit of $325 would have been provided. The bill was narrowly defeated in the Senate after the Treasury Department opposed the credit as too costly and suggested that direct assistance to college students would be more effective and economical. There were also several efforts to provide direct assistance to parents whose children attend private school. Among these were a bill introduced by Senator Hartke that would have established scholarships, loan insurance, and work-study programs designed to extend financial assistance to college students. Representative Delaney continued his efforts to obtain passage of his "Junior G.I. Bill," which would provide for government payments of a specified sum to each parent paying tuition of that amount or more to a private non-profit school.

The church-state issue also became involved in President Johnson's antipoverty program. When introduced, the Administration bill provided for federal assistance to "community action" programs undertaken to reduce poverty and unemployment in eco-

204 National Defense Education Act Amendments, 1964, § 205 (b), 78 Stat. 1101.
205 *Id.* § 505 (b), 78 Stat. 1106.
206 *Id.* § 304, 78 Stat. 1103.

nomically depressed areas. Such assistance was to be extended to programs in the "field of education," among other areas. Only public schools could be recipients of the aid, although the proposed act expressly provided that no child was to be "denied benefit" of any educational program because he was not regularly enrolled in the public schools.

During the course of hearings on the bill, some of the members of the House subcommittee as well as some of the witnesses called for participation by parochial schools in the community action programs. Because members of the subcommittee could not reach a satisfactory compromise on the issue, general programs in the field of education were eliminated from the bill. As finally passed, the bill did provide for assistance to programs extending "special remedial and other noncurricular educational assistance for the benefit of low-income individuals and families."[207] Unlike the original version, it did not specify that such programs had to be under the control of public agencies. This omission led some critics to oppose the bill on the ground it would provide federal aid to private, church-related elementary and secondary schools. The American Civil Liberties Union, for example, proposed an amendment that would have rendered any school or school system affiliated with a religious institution ineligible for a grant under the Act.

The church-state issue was raised by some with regard to community action programs generally. These programs are not detailed in the Act and it is expected that they will be formulated at the local level and presented to the federal government for consideration. Critics, including Representative Goodell of New York pointed out that there was no limitation preventing a church from receiving direct assistance as part of a community action program involving job training, welfare, or any of the other fields specified in the Act. He also pointed out that there was no prohibition preventing community action programs from benefiting facilities used for sectarian instruction or worship. Other sections of the Act establishing work programs for unemployed youth or part-time job programs for needy college students do contain such a prohibition.

In answer to such criticism Representative Carey of New York argued that fears about use of federal aid to build, maintain, or repair religious facilities, or to promote religious instruction, were

---

[207] Economic Opportunity Act of 1964, § 205 (a), 78 Stat. 517.

unfounded because community action programs were limited to certain specified fields, such as health, welfare, employment, and, to a very limited extent, education—areas which by their nature could not be considered religious.

Despite the fact that many state legislatures do not meet in even numbered years, the issue of state aid to private education was kept very much alive in a significant number of states, including some that do not have legislative sessions. Citizens for Educational Freedom (CEF), a growing national organization representing parents of children attending private elementary and secondary schools, was very active in keeping these issues in the public eye. There were two reasons for activity in those states not having legislative sessions. In some, such as Iowa and Minnesota, plans were being made to bring about enactment of laws extending aid to parochial school students in the next legislative session. In some there were efforts to obtain aid from local governments. This was particularly true in Ohio, largely because of the efforts of the state federation of CEF.

In several Ohio communities members of CEF urged the creation of an educational fund against which would be charged vouchers of a specified amount. These vouchers would be given to all public, private, and parochial students for application against the cost of their tuition. A referendum was held in the community of Wickcliffe on a proposed $50 annual tuition voucher grant. The proposal was rejected by a three to one majority.

There were also demands for public transportation of parochial students in a number of Ohio localities. As reported in our last survey, the Attorney General of Ohio delivered an opinion that under existing statutes local school boards were not authorized to use public buses to transport private school students.[208] This conclusion was not welcomed by local officials in a number of communities that wanted to provide bus service. The Northwest District School Board of Hamilton County decided to get a second opinion on the matter from the county prosecutor, only to find that he agreed with the Attorney General. A survey by a Roman Catholic diocesan newspaper in Ohio revealed that at least ten school districts were in disagreement with the Attorney General's opinion and intended to continue carrying parochial school students.

In Ohio also, the claim that new sources of financial assistance are needed for parochial schools was dramatized by the Archiocese of Cincinnati, which decided to eliminate the first grade in all its schools. Archdiocesan officials announced that the step was taken to reduce class size, cut down the staff, and raise salaries. Ten thousand children who ordinarily would have entered the parochial schools were affected. Three thousand were from the Cincinnati public school system, where it was estimated that their absorption would cost over $600,000 during the 1964–65 school year. Congressmen Adam Clayton Powell and Hugh Carey, both from New York and both strong supporters of federal aid to private as well as public schools, commented that the Cincinnati experience pointed out the choice before the nation very clearly: some federal aid to parochial schools or sharply rising public education costs at the local level.

Attempts to obtain financial aid for students attending parochial schools were not restricted to the Midwest. In New York, where the legislature was in session, two proposals were introduced. One would have provided scholarship aid to the extent of $100 per year for "students attending private high schools." The other would have authorized the lending of science, mathematics, and foreign language textbooks purchased with state funds to students in private schools. Opponents of both measures, which included the New York Council of Churches and the American Civil Liberties Union, claimed these proposals would violate article XI of the New York constitution, which prohibits the use of public funds "directly or indirectly" to aid religiously affiliated schools. The local federation of the CEF took the position that if the existing law providing regents' scholarships for attendance at colleges and universities chosen by the recipients themselves was constitutional, so also would be a similar scholarship program for the lower educational levels. Neither piece of legislation was enacted in 1964.

In Michigan a bill was passed extending financial assistance to students who attend college, whether public or private.[209] It establishes a program for payment of tuition and fees incurred by qualified Michigan residents at any Michigan college or university up to a maximum of $800.

In several states where legislative proposals to finance the transportation of private school children failed to pass in 1963, such as

---

[209] Mich. Pub. Acts, 1964, No. 239.

Pennsylvania, Missouri, Nebraska, Minnesota, and Iowa, plans were being made for renewed efforts in the 1965 sessions. The bus-ride issue also arose in a number of communities where state law permits but does not require public financing. In Maine, for instance, the town of Auburn ratified by referendum the long-standing practice of carrying parochial school students in public buses, but in Farmington a proposal to provide public bus transportation to parochial school students was rejected.

In New Hampshire, where there is no state statute covering bus rides for private school children, the school committee of Dover authorized a plan to provide such service to some students attending a regional diocesan high school. The city attorney delivered an opinion that there were no legal restrictions preventing adoption of the plan.[210] The opinion conceded that the First Amendment precluded use of public funds to support a church school, but it went on to conclude that it was proper for the state to transport all children to their place of education and to protect them from "the ever-increasing hazards of modern day traffic." Reference was made to the long-standing and generally accepted practice by the city of providing police to protect children in the immediate areas of parochial schools. Reference was also made to the United States Supreme Court's decision in the *Everson* case[211] upholding the constitutionality of publicly financed transportation of private school children.

In New Jersey a local dispute arose over the interpretation of a statute that authorizes local school boards to transport children to private, non-profit schools in one paragraph and in the next one requires them to do so between any two points on "established" public school routes.[212] Parents whose children had been carried along established routes protested the loss of service when the routes were rearranged after the opening of a new public school. These parents claimed that the local school board was required to establish new routes accommodating the parochial school students even if this were to mean redesigning the routes so that they would extend beyond the public school terminus or would deviate from a straight line to pass by the parochial schools and then backtrack to resume a direct line of movement. When the board refused, the

---

210 Letter from the City Attorney of Dover, New Hampshire, to the Superintendent of Schools, July 24, 1964.
211 Everson v. Board of Educ., 330 U.S. 1 (1947).
212 N.J.S.A. § 18:14-8 (1963 Supp.).

parents appealed to the state Commissioner of Education. He upheld the board, ruling that local school boards may design routes
to meet the public school needs and that private school students
had to be carried only as an incident to this established service.[213]

After this ruling the parents dropped their demand that new
school routes be required by law and requested the board to adopt
such routes in the public interest. They maintained that the board
had the power to do so if it chose. Expressing uncertainty on the
extent of its powers, the board agreed to establish new routes if it
could obtain an authoritative ruling declaring it could legally do
so. It sought to obtain such a ruling by filing a suit for a declara-
tory judgment in the Superior Court in August, 1964.

Shared-time programs were examined with increasing interest
as a possible way out of the church-state impasse concerning
whether federal aid to education must include parochial elementary and secondary schools. A survey of the National Education
Association indicated that adoption of shared-time programs was
increasing. Responses by 183 school superintendents who had taken
part in such programs revealed that 63 per cent of them favored
shared-time arrangements, 9 per cent were opposed, and the rest
were non-committal.

In Congress a bill was introduced to extend $15 million of fed-
eral assistance to a three-year program of pilot projects and a
"study of shared time." Protestant denominations, including some
that strongly oppose public educational grants to church-related
schools because of their strict views on separation of church and
state, have approved of such programs. The 176th General Assembly of the United Presbyterian Church accepted a report advocating federal aid to shared-time programs, although there was
opposition expressed by some delegates on grounds of church-state
separation. The General Board of the National Council of
Churches approved of "dual enrollment" as an appropriate technique to help relieve the financial burdens of public schools. The
militant separationist group, Protestants and Other Americans
United for Separation of Church and State (POAU), expressed
willingness to study various experiments in shared time. One of its
spokesmen characterized the POAU attitude as one of "watchful
waiting."

Although a number of Catholic parochial schools were taking

---

[213] St. Joseph's Church v. Board of Educ., Decision C–1 of the New Jersey Commissioner of Educ., April 22, 1964.

part in shared-time programs, the Education Department of the National Catholic Welfare Conference did not take an official position on the proposed bill to extend federal aid to an experimental study. Its attitude also appeared to be one of watchful interest.

Considerable opposition to the shared-time idea was expressed by spokesmen for Jewish agencies. Professor Leo Pfeffer of the American Jewish Congress was concerned lest shared-time arrangements create havoc in the public school system and water down its effectiveness in developing democratic attitudes. Also opposing programs of shared time, but for opposite reasons, was the CEF. It regarded federal aid to shared-time programs as an unacceptable substitute for aid to church-related schools. Spokesmen for the organization rejected any compromise plan providing for a system of education that is not wholly God-centered. In his article on shared time in this volume (*supra* p. 62) Dr. Powell gives the details concerning current controversies and experiments relating to shared-time programs.

Some have questioned the constitutionality of shared-time arrangements under the establishment clause of the First Amendment by charging that their main purpose is to promote religion and religious institutions. Questions about the constitutionality of shared time have also been raised under state constitutions that have provisions prohibiting expenditure of public funds in support of religion. In his article on shared time in this volume (*supra* p. 85) Professor Katz discusses both of these issues and points out that there is very little auhority on either point. He presents a handful of opinions by state officials—most of them delivered within the past year. They are about evenly divided on the state constitutional issue (see *supra* pp. 91–94).

The opinions of three attorneys general with regard to the constitutionality of the direct payment of funds or grant of services to sectarian schools illustrates a variety of approaches. At one extreme the Attorney General of Maryland concluded that for parochial schools at their own expense to tie into the public school system's closed circuit for educational television and to receive the programs would violate neither the establishment clause of the First Amendment nor the prohibition in the Maryland constitution of the maintenance of "any ministry."[214] The opinion relied

---

[214] Letter from the Attorney General of Maryland to the State Superintendent of Education, Mar. 23, 1964.

on the principle of neutrality and the proposition that "mere accommodations to religious and religious institutions are not forbidden, especially where the object is to further the secular education of school children." At the other extreme the Attorney General of Iowa concluded that it would be an unlawful appropriation to a religious institution for a local school board to rent a classroom from a parochial school.[215] He relied not only on the state constitution's prohibition of "an establishment of religion" or the "maintenance of any . . . ministry . . . ," but also on a state statute prohibiting the appropriation or giving of public money to or in favor of any sectarian institution.[216]

When asked whether the state department of education could appraise parochial schools and provide them with consultative services at their request and prepare, approve, and implement plans prerequisite to the receipt of federal moneys for the use of such schools along with public and other private schools,[217] the Attorney General of Colorado took a position somewhere in the middle. He concluded that appraisal and consultation were proper if conducted for the purpose of accrediting parochial schools for purposes of the state compulsory education laws. He declined to give an opinion relating to services connected with the receipt of federal funds until advised concerning the details of the federal program and the requirements it would impose on the state Department of Education.

CHAPLAINS IN GOVERNMENT SERVICE

The role of chaplains in government service, particularly those attached to the military branches, came under fire from several sources for various reasons during the past year. Two local chapters of the American Civil Liberties Union questioned two different practices, one at the Army installation at McGuire Air Force Base in New Jersey, the other one on the naval carrier, U.S.S. "Midway."

A member of the New Jersey chapter questioned the propriety of having army chaplains teach religion to the children of servicemen. He was particularly concerned because public schools built

---

[215] Letter from the Attorney General of Iowa to the Carroll County Attorney, Aug. 23, 1963.

[216] I.C.A. § 343.8 (1949).

[217] Opinion No. 64–3769, letter from the Attorney General of Colorado to the Hon. Ruth B. Clark, Jan. 29, 1964.

and maintained by the Army and administered by the local public school board were being used. He questioned whether agents of the United States government, the chaplains, could teach religion in the public school classrooms when agents of the state government, teachers, had been prohibited from doing so by the United States Supreme Court.

The executive director of the northern California chapter wrote a letter to the Secretary of the Navy complaining that evening prayers were recited daily over the public address system of the carrier U.S.S. "Midway" during which time all personnel were required to stay at attention. The letter also objected to the opening of wardroom meals with a prayer. The executive director of the national ACLU followed up this complaint with a letter taking the position that the practices on the "Midway" violated the establishment clause as interpreted in the recent Bible-reading cases. The Department of the Navy took the stand, however, that in the absence of coercion directed at enlisted personnel the public recitation of prayers on a naval carrier was proper in light of the reasoning of the Supreme Court's opinion in *Zorach v. Clauson*.[218] In a letter to the executive director of the ACLU, the Chief of Naval Personnel took the position that "it was never intended that the First or Fourteenth Amendment to the Constitution should isolate a person from exposure to positions other than his own."[219]

At its annual convention the Military Chaplaincy Association passed a resolution criticizing the ACLU chapters in Camden and southern California for challenging the constitutionality of the military chaplaincy. One of the speakers at the convention singled out the Camden chapter particularly for challenging "the constitutional right of the federal government to pay chaplains to teach religion to servicemen and their dependents." The convention also resolved to place "all its resources" in the impending legal battle.

The national office of the ACLU subsequently issued a statement indicating that the resolution adopted by the chaplains' association "wholly misrepresents the facts." Its executive director, Mr. John deJ. Pemberton pointed out that the southern California chapter never brought or considered bringing a suit involving the chaplaincy. He also observed that the Camden chapter had only

---

218 343 U.S. 306 (1962).

219 Letter from Vice Admiral W. R. Smedberg III to Mr. John deJ. Pemberton, Jr., Oct. 29, 1963.

protested the use of chaplains for religious classes held in public school buildings for military dependents. Even then he claimed no legal action had been taken or contemplated.

Mr. Pemberton went on to state flatly that the ACLU "has never attacked the concept of the chaplaincy programs." He said the organization agreed wholeheartedly with the distinction made by the United States Supreme Court in the Bible-reading cases between the military chaplaincy and religious practices in the public schools. The Court had pointed out that if the government did not provide men with the facilities for voluntary religious services, it would interfere with the practice of their religion because of the large degree of regulation it exercised over the daily activities of military personnel.

In a recent opinion the Attorney General of Nevada also relied on the proposition that the government may provide religious services for those individuals whose general freedom has been restricted by the state.[220] On this basis he justified payments to a prison chaplain despite a state constitutional provision forbidding expenditure of public funds for sectarian purposes.

There were complaints from religious quarters to the effect that various aspects of military programs involving religion interfered with religious liberty. The National Association of Evangelicals (NAE) criticized the "Unified Curriculum" for military chaplains because it advised teachers to differentiate between "legendary" and "historical" parts of the Bible. The NAE regarded this as a heretical position and protested against its official adoption. In response the Chief of Chaplains justified the Curriculum on the ground that no chaplain is compelled to follow it. In answer to this contention a spokesman for the NAE referred to an Air Force directive stating that its chaplains are "expected to give . . . their support and leadership" to the Curriculum. He also pointed out that the Army and Navy "strongly recommend" the Curriculum, while observing that in the armed services a recommendation from a superior is tantamount to a command to a junior.

The National Lutheran Council protested the practice of compulsory chapel attendance at the various service academies. The Air Force Academy at first took the view that no students complained of this requirement. However, when protests from students came to public notice, some grounded on interference with the

---

[220] Opinion No. 67, letter from the Attorney General of Nevada to the Director of Administration, Sept. 5, 1963.

ability of students to attend denominational services of their choice in town because of conflict with the mandatory service, and when five local ministers also protested, the Academy issued a statement emphasizing that religious and spiritual education was a necessary part of a commander's training.

SUNDAY CLOSING

There was relatively little activity concerning Sunday closing legislation in comparison to the previous year.[221] Two of the three state Sunday closing laws enacted in 1963 to replace previous ones that had been declared unconstitutional suffered the same fate as their predecessors. Laws passed in Kansas[222] and North Carolina[223] were struck down, whereas the new Missouri statute was upheld.[224]

As for new legislation, changes were made in the Louisiana and Massachusetts Sunday laws. In Louisiana the sale of new or used cars or trucks and the sale of parts for and servicing of motor vehicles by car dealers were activities added to the proscribed Sunday list.[225] An exception was made for the sale of motor vehicle parts or servicing "in the case of an emergency." In Massachusetts an effective exemption from the Sunday closing laws was created for the benefit of merchants who observed the seventh day of the week, or from sundown Friday to sundown Saturday, as the Sabbath.[226]

In New York attempts to liberalize exemptions from the Sunday closing laws made very limited headway. As noted in our last survey, a bill was passed in the 1963 session of the state legislature authorizing the New York City Council to exempt from the Sunday closing laws owners of small stores who observe some day other than Sunday as the Sabbath,[227] with the result that in September, 1963, the Council exempted such owners and their immediate families from the Sunday prohibition. A bill that would have ex-

---

221 *Cf.* 1963 RELIGION AND THE PUBLIC ORDER 311–14.

222 See discussion in text, *supra* at note 101.

223 See discussion in text, *supra* at note 102.

224 See discussion in text, *supra* at note 103.

225 Acts of La., 1964, No. 458 § 1.

226 Mass. Acts, 1964, ch. 216. This bill removed a condition requiring Sunday selling by Sabbatarians not to create a nuisance. The nuisance condition was substituted in 1962 for a previous one requiring that the Sunday selling not disturb others. This earlier condition had been interpreted to prohibit the opening of a store.

227 1963 RELIGION AND THE PUBLIC ORDER 314.

tended throughout the state the local option to exempt family-owned and -operated stores that were closed on another day for religious reasons was introduced in the 1964 session but not enacted.

In South Dakota and Kentucky proposed changes in current Sunday legislation were introduced but also failed of enactment. The South Dakota bill, which was tabled by the House State Affairs Committee, would have banned the sale of certain items, including dry goods, housewares, furniture, and jewelry. In Kentucky a number of bills were proposed in the wake of the tentative decision by the Court of Appeals that the only goods that could be sold on Sunday under the "work of necessity" exemption were items required in "emergency" situations or one of "vital interest." Even after the court modified its opinion by eliminating its definition of the phrase, there was considerable sentiment to clarify the situation by legislation. The proposed bills ranged from a general prohibition of Sunday work and selling with specified exceptions, including cultural, educational and recreational activities, to a bill that would prohibit only the sale of specific items. Both these bills provided for local option. The State Council of Churches opposed any change on the ground a new bill would be subjected to court test, as was the current bill, and in the interim it would not be vigorously enforced.

TAX EXEMPTIONS

A few relatively minor changes were made in the tax exempt status of churches under state laws. Alaska modified its laws in a direction that tended to restrict the scope of the exemption. It deleted from the statute exempting "property used for religious purposes" a clause that specified "property . . . not used for business, rent or profit" as being within the exemption. Prior to this deletion the Alaska court relied in part on this clause to find that the church-owned house of an assistant pastor was exempt from the real property taxes.

In two other states legislative enactments expanded the scope of tax exemptions relating to church-owned property. In Massachusetts the total exemption granted each parsonage owned by a religious organization was raised from $10,000 to $15,000, and in New Jersey limitations restricting the exemption to two parsonages and a total of $25,000 were removed entirely.

Proposed legislation designed to exempt the Old Order Amish from coverage under the Social Security Act because of their religious beliefs raised the question whether such exemption would constitute aid to religion in violation of the establishment clause of the First Amendment. The General Counsel of the Treasury delivered an opinion concluding that the proposed exemption would probably be held a valid accommodation of government regulation to religious liberty.[228]

He relied on *Zorach v. Clauson*,[229] and particularly on *Sherbert v. Verner*,[230] to support this conclusion. He pointed out that in the latter case the Supreme Court was unanimous in its opinion that the state could grant a special exemption from conditions placed on the receipt of unemployment compensation benefits so that Seventh-day Adventists would be able to observe Saturday as the Sabbath. The justices who dissented in the case did so on the ground that although the state was permitted to grant such an exemption despite the establishment clause it was not required to do so under the free exercise clause. In referring to the *Sherbert* case, the General Counsel remarked that in some respects the justification for exemption of the Amish was clearer. Whereas the plaintiff in *Sherbert* was subjected to the indirect burden of losing a welfare benefit if she followed the dictates of her religion, the Amish were subject to the direct burdens of civil and criminal penalties, including imprisonment and forfeiture. As examples of traditionally recognized accommodation to religious liberty, the General Counsel adverted to the exemption from the military draft of conscientious objectors with religious scruples and the exemption from taxation of property used for religious purposes.

Legislation granting the Old Order Amish exemption from the Social Security tax has been introduced in Congress in the last several years. One of the difficulties encountered has been the challenge of drafting legislation that on the one hand would not extend the exemption to religious sects established for the reason of avoiding the tax and on the other hand would not unconstitutionally discriminate between various religions.

The need for action on the proposed legislation in 1964 or soon thereafter appeared particularly urgent. In 1961 the Internal

---

228 Opinion letter dated Aug. 6, 1964.
229 343 U.S. 306 (1952).
230 374 U.S. 398 (1963).

Revenue Service agreed to suspend forceful collection of the tax from the Amish until the question of exemption was finally resolved. It is estimated that as of 1964 fifteen hundred Amish accounts remained unpaid, involving nearly $250,000 in tax liabilities. Since the period of limitations on collection of the tax began to expire in 1964 in some cases and since some Old Order Amish indicated they would not sign waivers to extend the period of limitations, the government would be compelled to lift the moratorium or lose its collection rights.

RELIGIOUS PRESSURES AND TENSIONS OVER PUBLIC ISSUES

Religiously generated tensions were marked in two areas of public affairs involving questions of morality. Governmental policies with regard to birth control and gambling raised moral issues involving religious controversy.

The more acute controversies in the birth control area involved Catholic opposition to the use of public monies to promote contraceptive practices. Owing in large part to such objections, an amendment to the foreign aid bill providing assistance to birth control programs in overpopulated countries was eliminated in conference. In a number of states, including Pennsylvania, Oregon, New York, Delaware, and the District of Columbia proposals to initiate or expand programs making birth control information or services available as part of public welfare assistance met Catholic protests. Proposals to extend such information and services to unmarried women were found particularly objectionable by opponents.

The adoption of a state lottery as a revenue source by New Hampshire has led other states to consider such a course. Lotteries were proposed in a number of states, including New Jersey, Maine, Massachusetts, Rhode Island, and Vermont. The proposals were generally opposed by the various state councils of churches and made little headway. Other proposals, such as legalization of off-track betting in New York City and New Jersey and parimutuel betting in Texas, North Dakota, and Montana, also met Protestant opposition. North Dakota voters rejected, by a margin of about two to one, a proposal to permit parimutuel betting on horse and dog races. In Montana enough signatures were obtained to place an initiative legalizing gambling on the ballot. However, the state Supreme Court enjoined the initiative, holding that only an amendment to the constitution could legalize gambling.

The National Council of Churches, concerned by the growing interest in legalized gambling as a potential source of state revenue, proposed a concerted effort to resist the nationwide movement to legalize gambling.

DONALD A. GIANNELLA

COMMENTS BY THE EDITORS

POLICY AND DOGMA IN
CHURCH-STATE LAW

Confusion regarding the nature of religious liberty still continues. This is perhaps to be expected in a period when according to a recent survey 87 per cent of the population still favors religious observances in the public schools. The courts are, in the main, caught between the legitimate desire to give some sensible standing to customs which have prevailed for generations and the judicial necessity of protecting the rights of minorities and individuals in a society now pluralistic rather than religiously monochromatic.

There are several factors which contribute markedly to the confusion. One of the most important is surely the appalling disregard for law and due process sometimes displayed by lower courts, particularly at state level. Even after the highest court has made its rulings, state authorities have in some cases continued to resist. It can be predicted with reasonable assurance that when the political capital has been exhausted in such resistance, it will disappear. A more fateful consequence, in the long run, is that many cases must be brought to the level of a national settlement which were far better settled closer to home. Furthermore, the circuit courts of appeals and the Supreme Court, in seeking to handle such cases in terms suitable for the country at large, are pressed to take generalized and theoretical positions marked by dry logic rather than by reference to history and real life.

Second, it is evident that judicial officers are sometimes so enamored of abstract doctrine that they ignore the tradition and lessons of the common law. Such, for example, is revealed in Mr. Justice Douglas' conviction that Sunday closing laws are unconstitutional because they are in aid of religion. Such is also revealed in the attenuated logic of the court's decision in the forcible blood transfusion case. Certainly a doctor and a hospital are to be protected in making a conscientious professional decision. But why must a matter of high constitutional theory be elaborated where no actual legal controversy exists? How vastly preferable is the common-sense approach taken in handling the appeal of the woman who had conscientious scruples against jury duty, or the case of the peyote cult's religious rites. Certainly the government should be required to prove a "compelling interest" before the "right to be let alone" is invaded or abridged. In the sometime addiction to abstract dogma, with the elaborate speculations which grow out of it, the courts are assisted in the church-state field by the doctrinaire politics of pressure groups. Of this a suitable example is the amendment to the Anti-Poverty Bill proposed by the American Civil Liberties Union, to render any school or school system affiliated with a religious institution ineligible.

There are reasons against various types of governmental aid to religious or other private institutions, just as there are arguments *pro,* but they lie in the area of public discussion and public policy —not dogma. The courts would do well, as in the conscientious objector cases, to give some consideration to the question of what the legislature intended. And, although injustice is regrettable, there is no common-law tradition that the courts must actively intervene to prevent every injustice or to manufacture a theoretical equity. The truly religious person is not protected, nor does he expect to be insulated, from all suffering for his beliefs—although he has of course the right to be protected from abuse, persecution, unequal treatment, and so on.

Furthermore, the courts' sometime devotion to abstract doctrine tends to obscure the question of standing. Who is being hurt if Nativity scenes still are erected in some communities? Such practices are probably in bad taste in cities of mixed religious populations, but are the courts to be the arbiters of custom? Some years ago, in New Haven, Connecticut, a group of insensitive logicians attacked Christmas exercises in the public schools as an unconstitutional breach of the immutable wall of separation. The old settlers, who had been keeping such customs since long before there was a Federal Constitution, were understandably incensed.

Yet *both* parties were *wrong*. Those protesting were wrong in trying to make a court case, and the defenders of the old order were wrong in assuming that customs which had been appropriate to an era of Protestant hegemony were right for a pluralistic society. What is wrong with the judicious principle that some old customs and culture lags are no longer appropriate or equitable for the simple reason that America has changed and her citizens now have a variety of religious commitments?

If the judges sometimes make bad philosophers and theologians, the spokesmen for old customs usually seem far worse. Cultic practices which once expressed the highest religious concern then known have now become political weapons of disloyalists, American nativists, and bad citizens ready to use any weapon to discredit the Supreme Court and the Constitution. From the point of view of high religion, the most atrocious arguments to be advanced for school prayers, Nativity scenes, Christmas songs, etc., is that they are all right "so long as no religious significance is attached thereto," when they involve only "casual reference to the Deity," when they consist merely of "passive accommodation of religion," when they have "primarily secular goals," etc. The prayer amendments were of course primarily political in intent, but it should also be said loudly and often that they represented *low-grade religion*. The God of believing Jews, Catholics, and Protestants is not served by the outward display of casual courtesies! And what does the present flurry of display of "under God" flags represent but the manipulation of bad religion to bolster up bad politics? If our tradition had been Shinto, such exercises might be authentic; but among those whose culture and language were shaped by the Bible, the thought might arise that God requires justice and mercy and righteousness and despises false façades.

A continuing area of dispute, and one of fatal consequence, is whether tax exemption of church properties used solely for church purposes consists of a "subvention" or "grant of state assistance." This argument is now being advanced by many church leaders, as well as anti-clericals, and it seems to be expressed in the decision of the Supreme Court of Alaska to subject a church broadcasting station to an ad valorem tax, even though all the proceeds of the station's activities were used for operational costs and to help support the missionary activities of the church. The argument that tax exemption of church properties is a governmental grant is both historically and constitutionally false, and it conceals a faulty understanding of the origin and intent of religious liberty. Toleration may be a grant of government, but religious liberty is a "natural right": *i.e.,* it existed "before" a frame of government itself. This truth, which our fathers often asserted, is not chronological but a matter of principle. The five fundamental liberties, which have a special status in the American constitutional tradition, were all "prior" to the frame of government. That is, they exist not by grant or sufferance or intervention but by right. They were true and sound long before there was any government prepared to acknowledge them.

This is particularly true of religious liberty, for the end of such liberty is the service of Truth. The best government is that which recognizes its own incompetence to manipulate or even define, except in cases of dire necessity, such liberties. A society is blessed not when religious institutions shore up its power structures, not when religion and religious exercises are used to serve it, but when churches and synagogues truly serve the ends for which they were called into being. This is the real beginning of a sound case against the low-grade religion which seeks political preference and establishment, and it is also the beginning of the case against governmental patronage or intervention where the churches and synagogues exercise their God-given (not government-granted!) liberty. Since "the power to tax is the power to destroy," we should be very chary of conceding to any government at any time the asserted or usurped power to tax or regulate church properties used for church purposes. The crippling of church integrity and discipline by the *apartheid* legislation of the Union of South Africa is certainly contrary to the traditions of the common law. So is the use of police force to abrogate freedom of worship in Jackson, Mississippi. We cannot allow to amiable and well-meaning, if confused, courts or legislatures an authority which is not theirs by right and which may, tomorrow, be the weapon to destroy our fundamental liberties.

FRANKLIN H. LITTELL